Please remember that this is a library book,
and that it belongs only temporarily to each
person who uses it. Be considerate. Do
not write in this, or any, library book.

THE AGE OF REASON
The Culture of the Seventeenth Century

The Cultures of Mankind

GREEK CULTURE: The Adventure of the Human Spirit
Edited by Alice von Hildebrand

ROMAN CULTURE: Weapons and the Man
Edited by Garry Wills

MEDIEVAL CULTURE: The Image and the City
Edited by Ruth Brantl

RENAISSANCE CULTURE: A New Sense of Order
Edited by Julian Mates and Eugene Cantelupe

THE AGE OF REASON: The Culture of the Seventeenth Century
Edited by Leo Weinstein

THE ENLIGHTENMENT: The Culture of the Eighteenth Century
Edited by Isidor Schneider

ROMANTICISM: The Culture of the Nineteenth Century
Edited by Morse Peckham

TWENTIETH-CENTURY CULTURE: The Breaking Up
Edited by Robert Phelps

The Age of Reason

The Culture of the Seventeenth Century

Edited by Leo Weinstein

George Braziller · New York

ACKNOWLEDGMENTS

The editor and publisher have made every effort to determine and credit the holders of copyright of the selections in this book. Any errors or omissions may be rectified in future volumes. The editor and publisher wish to thank the following for permission to reprint the material included in this anthology:

Lionel Abel—for selections from his translation of *Andromache* by Racine; published in *The Genius of the French Theater,* ed. by A. Bermel, published by New American Library.

Eric Bentley—for selections from "Life Is a Dream" by Pedro Calderón de la Barca, tr. by Roy Campbell and "The Trickster of Seville" by Tirso de Molina, from *The Classic Theatre, Vol. 3, Six Spanish Plays,* ed. by Eric Bentley. Both selections reprinted by permission of Mr. Bentley.

The Bobbs-Merrill Co., Inc.—for selections from René Descartes: *Discourse on Method,* tr. by Laurence J. Lafleur, copyright ©, 1950, 1956 by The Liberal Arts Press, Inc., reprinted by permission of the Liberal Arts Press Division of The Bobbs-Merrill Co., Inc.

Cambridge University Press—for selections from René Descartes: *The Passions of the Soul,* 1649, tr. by Elizabeth S. Haldane and G. R. T. Ross, in *The Philosophical Works of Descartes,* Cambridge University Press, 1911. Reprinted by permission of the publisher.

The Clarendon Press, Oxford—for selections from Hugo Grotius: *De Jure Belli ac Pacis,* 1625, tr. by F. W. Kelsey. Oxford: at the Clarendon Press; London: Humphrey Milford, 1925. Reprinted by permission of the publisher.

Angel Flores—for two poems from his book *An Anthology of Spanish Poetry From Garcilaso to García Lorca:* "O Noble and Most High in Beauty,

4

Thou . . ." by Luis de Góngora, tr. by Iain Fletcher and "On the Triumph
of Judith" by Lope de Vega, tr. by Brian Soper. Reprinted by permission of
Professor Flores.

Harcourt, Brace & World, Inc.—for selections from *The Misanthrope,* © copyright, 1954, 1955, by Richard Wilbur. Reprinted by permission of the publisher. *Caution:* Professionals and amateurs are hereby warned that this
translation, being fully protected under the copyright laws of the United
States of America, the British Empire, including the Dominion of Canada,
and all other countries which are signatories to the Universal Copyright Con-
vention and the International Copyright Union, is subject to royalty. All
rights, including professional, amateur, motion picture, recitation, lecturing,
public reading, radio broadcasting, and television, are strictly reserved. Particular emphasis is laid on the question of readings, permission for which
must be secured from the author's agent in writing. Inquiries on professional rights (except for amateur rights) should be addressed to Mr. Gilbert
Parker, Savan-Parker, Inc., 59 East 54th Street, New York, New York;
inquiries on translation rights should be addressed to Harcourt, Brace &
World, Inc., 757 Third Avenue, New York, New York. The amateur acting
rights are controlled exclusively by the Dramatists Play Service, Inc., 440
Park Avenue South, New York, New York. No amateur performance of the
play may be given without obtaining in advance the written permission of
the Dramatists Play Service, Inc., and paying the requisite fee.

Routledge & Kegan Paul Ltd.—for selections from *The Princess of Cleves* by
Mme de Lafayette, tr. by H. Ashton. Reprinted by permission of the
publisher.

The Viking Press, Inc.—for a selection from "Letters of Madame de Sévigné"
from *The Portable Age of Reason Reader,* ed. and tr. by Crane Brinton.
Copyright 1956 by The Viking Press, Inc. Reprinted by permission of the
publisher.

PREFACE

The fact that the present volume deals with the principal themes of the seventeenth century explains to a great extent the choice of material and the omission of works that would normally be included in any anthology of masterworks.

There are definite advantages in this method, for it permits the inclusion of authors who have been neglected in previous anthologies of the seventeenth century. Among these are Grimmelshausen, Tommaso Campanella, Madeleine de Scudéry, Tirso de Molina, and John Lyly, each of whom presents an important aspect of the century. As for the standard authors, the works selected are at times off the beaten path, such as Descartes' *The Passions of the Soul.*

On the other hand, a few omissions require an explanation. It should be noted, right from the outset, that, while the interest of the reader has always been a primary consideration, aesthetic judgments were not the exclusive guide in determining the selection of the material. Hence an omission is not to be viewed as a sign of disapproval.

The fact is that I have regretfully omitted plays by two of my favorite authors: Pierre Corneille and Lope de Vega. Corneille's *Le Cid,* a standard masterpiece, illustrates very well the period of heroism, but I decided on Tirso de Molina's *The Trickster of Seville* not only because it has been much neglected but also because the Don Juan legend has been far more fertile in modern times than that of the Cid.

Lope de Vega presents a different problem, for in his case a woeful lack of adequate translations presents a serious obstacle in obtaining for this great dramatist the recognition he deserves. *Fuente Ovejuna* is usually included in anthologies for its social implications and could have been used for this volume, but Calderón's *Life Is a Dream* seemed to me a more typical example of the Spanish atmosphere.

In the text it will be noted that French works predominate. The reason is very simple: French culture reigned almost unchallenged in the seven-

7

teenth century. This does not mean, of course, that other countries did not produce great works, but the French writers usually set the pattern of the intellectual movements and their clearness of presentation makes them ideal vehicles for illustrating themes and cultural trends.

I am particularly dealing with the criteria for selection of material in order to incite the reader to read more widely in this period. For this purpose a suggested reading list will be found at the end of the book.

Omissions within works are indicated by three dots centered on the page.

Finally, I wish to express my gratitude to those who have helped me in my work. First of all, to three of my former professors, all of Stanford University: Professor F. W. Strothmann, who aided and encouraged me in teaching world literature and the history of ideas; Professor Georges E. Lemaître, who made me appreciate the period of French classicism; and Professor Aurelio M. Espinosa, Jr., who introduced me to the Spanish theater of the Golden Age.

I am also much indebted to Professor Ruby Cohn of San Francisco State College for advice on English literature; to Marianne Clouzot for books on art and a drawing; to the Bibliothèque Nationale in Paris for help in my research; and especially to my wife Claire for taking care of the illustrations with unfailing good taste.

L. W.

Contents

Part I   Kings, Nobles and Commoners

Part II   Heroism and Affectation

Part III　The Rational Revolution

Part IV　The Ways of Reason

Part V　The Countercurrents

Part VI   The Triumph of Reason and Science

List of Illustrations

INTRODUCTION

In retrospect, the seventeenth century presents us with an image that is both uniform and instructive. Uniform, because during two-thirds of the century all major concerns revolve around the proper use of reason and the enormous progress accomplished in science; instructive, because, if one of the principal purposes of the study of history and ideas is to teach us how to avoid the mistakes of the past and to judge our own age fairly, we have a great deal to learn from the seventeenth century, a period that not only had to deal with issues in many ways similar to those of our own times but that set the Western world on a new course from which it has hardly deviated since.

It would be unwise to praise the seventeenth century at the expense of the Renaissance or the Middle Ages, or to claim that reason was invented at that time. Yet it is safe to state that the seventeenth century was a revolutionary one, not politically or socially, but in philosophy and science; for it was then that new physical phenomena were discovered, that new methods of inquiry were being devised, and that new criteria of judgment were being proposed.

Reason, truth, nature, fact, proof — these terms underwent changes such that they seemed no longer the same as in previous periods. And the impulse came from the progress of science. It took Galileo's discoveries to destroy not merely the old universe but to shake off the stultifying influence of ancient authority and of scholasticism. It took the impressive advances made in mathematics and geometry to provide Descartes with the overwhelming vision that mathematical procedures could perhaps be applied to the solution of all problems. As a consequence, old reputations were overturned and Aristotle, the great authority during the four preceding centuries, turned out to have been a bad physicist, and Galen a poor physician.

It is illustrative of the century that the two greatest representatives of opposing views were both highly respectable scientists: Descartes, the advocate of the rational method, invented the Cartesian co-ordinates; Pascal, the opponent of unlimited application of reason, had a calculating machine named after him. Typical too is the fact that the adversaries in these disputes had accepted certain ground rules, so to speak. Both sides agreed that past authority may not be appealed to, that reason is not to be abandoned in favor of uncertain instincts, that arguments are to be presented in clear language, and that subjects be viewed from a universal rather than an individual point of view. Even when Henry More wants to prove that spirits are material, he uses a geometrical figure to illustrate his point. Even when the mystics proclaim the impotence of reason to make us see ultimate reality, they, by the very vehemence of their attack, pay an indirect homage to the powerful role reason had assumed in the century.

But the dispute does not concern reason and its limits alone. It deals with issues that seem indeed very modern. What influence should the discoveries of science have on our intellectual and religious beliefs? Only the most closed-minded partisans of Aristotle would deny their importance in physiology, in astronomy, in architecture. But was the monk who refused to look through Galileo's telescope really so ridiculous as he may appear on first view? Must we necessarily re-examine or change all our fundamental beliefs or turn to different systems of art because it turns out that the earth is round or square or elliptical, and that it revolves around the sun and not vice versa? The answer would depend on the extent to which these beliefs are tied to the functioning of the physical universe; the systems of Aristotle and St. Thomas Aquinas were dependent on their respective natural scientific outlooks. But need our moral values, our artistic ideas, or our emotional life undergo changes corresponding to the new, or the latest universe?

On the negative side, one might well point out the haste with which Descartes and Hobbes applied the new findings of physiology and mechanics to psychology and the errors into which this precipitation led them, so that, however brilliant their theories may be, they are based on false assumptions and thus to a great extent out-of-date. (A similar shortcoming can be observed in the *Rougon-Macquart* novels by Emile Zola, which are based on an outdated theory of heredity. Their continued popularity is due to literary and social factors.)

A related question is represented by the quarrel of the Ancients and the Moderns. Viewed from a larger perspective, the issue was not merely whether the seventeenth century could compare itself with (and perhaps even surpass) the age of Pericles or Augustus; it was equally, and especially for us, whether scientific attitudes could be applied to all fields of human endeavor. The debate was won by the Moderns, but many of their arguments may seem to us naïve today. Of course, today's automobile is superior to that of twenty years ago and techniques have been improved in the arts and sciences; but does this mean that today's theater is superior to Euripides', that today's musicians are preferable to Bach, or our present painters to Rembrandt? The seventeenth century has bequeathed to us an awareness of the action-paralyzing awe that can be caused by an excessive admiration of former masters, but we, in turn, are, or ought to be, far more wary of applying scientific measurements to the humanities.

It is not my intention here to berate the seventeenth century; far from it. But, due to the dominant themes of the period, so much space is devoted to the champions of rationalism in the pages below that it seemed advisable to insert a few words of caution and to point out some of the flaws and excesses in this brilliant age that prided itself in its sense of moderation.

That it was a great and exciting century no one will deny, not even the romantic critics of the nineteenth century who shook their fists at the gigantic shade cast by it which threatened to deprive new artists of their rightful place in the sun. Rarely before had an age so thoroughly re-evaluated all the past in terms of new criteria; rarely before or after have so many great thinkers and artists lived in one century. In the sciences, Galileo, Boyle, Huygens, Leibnitz, and Newton; Grotius and Pufendorf in international law; in painting the list is inexhaustible: Poussin, Claude Lorrain, Mignard, Velásquez, Ribera, Murillo, Rubens, Rembrandt, Hals; Bernini in sculpture; Borromini, Mansart, and Wren in architecture; Boileau and Dryden in criticism and satire; Frescobaldi, Monteverdi, Lully, M. A. Charpentier, Schütz and Purcell in music; Corneille, Racine, Molière, Lope de Vega, Tirso de Molina, Calderón, Ben Jonson, Congreve and Wycherley in the theater; Milton, Donne and Góngora in poetry. The list could be continued indefinitely. Yet, even if the accomplishments of the seventeenth century had been limited to the philosophical works of Descartes, Pascal, Hobbes, Spinoza and Locke, it could have laid claim to a uniqueness rivaled only by the golden age of Greek philosophy.

Just as the Moderns, in speaking of antiquity, raised the problem of how genius is produced and why it should flourish at one time rather than another, so we might today ask ourselves the same question about the seventeenth century. True enough, tools had been forged to permit the production of masterpieces: language had been polished, rules for the arts had been set up. But it does not suffice to see the principal cause for this explosion of genius in improved techniques, for this would make us fall into the error of equating artistic and philosophical success with technical progress. True likewise, the other explanation advanced that governments and patrons were encouraging the arts, subsidizing them, and incorporating them into courtly festivities; but experience has shown that governmental patronage does not necessarily provide the kind of panacea that creates a flourishing of the arts (although it may advance the sciences). Finally, there is the public to consider. One can point to an aristocratic elite and an upper middle class that were well educated, that had the leisure to read and discuss new works, to see and judge new plays. While the taste of this public was not infallible, it scored relatively well compared to other periods: it celebrated Corneille's *Cid* despite criticism from the French Academy, it flocked to see Molière's *School for Wives* over the howls of protest from jealous authors.

This brings us to the much-maligned critics and the rules of art. Boileau and Dryden may have erred occasionally, but on the whole their judgments were based on good sense and good taste. The restrictions imposed by the rules of art had likewise a benevolent effect, provided, of course, that they were not set up as commands to be followed unswervingly, as pedantic critics demanded. So long as the rules served as a general guide, they fulfilled at least two very useful functions: first, they imposed restraints that forced the artist to learn his craft thoroughly and probably tended to eliminate those who were unable to master the fundamentals of their art (even though they may have discouraged some whose talent required complete liberty in order to develop fully); and second, they provided the artist with standards against and by which he could measure his work, and deviation from which he had to justify. Even if authors protested against the mechanical application of the rules as the exclusive basis for judgment, they were nonetheless obliged to be conscious of the problems involved in artistic creation. And the best plays produced during the seventeenth century are not those that contain involved and unlikely plots (the late plays of Corneille) or that fail to observe the three unities (Molière's *Dom Juan*).

All these factors certainly contributed to the flowering of the arts, but none of them can claim the exclusive credit for this development, for, contrary to a school of thought in the seventeenth century, we no longer believe that genius is produced by formula; so that we might even be tempted to consider the unlikely theory that perhaps at that time the trees were larger and more beautiful and brains "formed of stronger and more delicate fibers, and filled with more animal spirits," as Fontenelle proposed in jest.

It should be added that, except for the sciences, of course, genius in the seventeenth century was not necessarily equated with originality. An author was not expected to invent his own subject matter; in fact, it was not subject matter that mattered but the treatment given it by the author: his choice of scenes, his interpretation, his style; in short, the refinements he applied to his material and the new meanings he was able to draw from it. Nor was success achieved by expressing one's own personality or one's private life in a work. The belief in the universality of reason led to an interest in universal problems, in universal man rather than in the private experiences of an individual, in plots stripped of all exterior or surprising elements, in the elevation of individual insights to the level of instructions for humanity in general.

Let us hasten to add that there existed many exceptions to this general attitude, that original plots were used by some, and that the application of the rational method to all fields was neither unopposed nor uniformly beneficial.

There is no need to indulge here in the type of criticism often leveled by romantic writers against the seventeenth century: that it was cold, formal, and arid in its appeal to good sense and moderation. These very critics, who were defending their own works by attacking those of their predecessors, failed or refused to see that their favorite bête noire, Racine, had presented characters that were at least as passionate as their own, that each age has its particular way of conveying emotions, and that an exterior display of passions and an immediate appeal to the senses are not the only legitimate means of capturing one's audience, especially when it is a sophisticated one.

Nevertheless, it must be admitted that rationalism, when made the exclusive standard of judgment, tended to discourage lyrical poetry whose characteristic expression often fails to obey the rules of clear and universally comprehensible expression; and that the insistence that reason must strive to dominate passion threatened to eliminate from the deeper emotions and the most intimate experiences everything that enriches our personal lives.

However, this impoverishment of the emotions became a serious problem only in the next century, when, moreover, a strong reaction against this attitude began to develop. During the seventeenth century, in varying degrees and at different times, this conflict between emotions, on the one hand, and reason and restraints, on the other, resulted in a tension that constitutes one of the principal traits of baroque art.

Unfortunately, this term has led to much confusion. "Baroque" has at least two distinct meanings. One is pejorative and describes a type of syllogism used to support far-fetched arguments; one can possibly speak in this sense of baroque poetry when referring to the extremely involved con ceits found in mannerism. The other meaning of the term is derived from the Portuguese *barroco* or the Spanish *barrueco* (also *berrueco*) which signifies a large irregular pearl. It is a sphere straining outward at one point, bulging and almost breaking but not yet bursting into fragments.

This latter description applies to a great portion of the works of art produced during the seventeenth century, particularly in painting, sculpture, and architecture. (In their treatment of religious subjects these arts often identify themselves with the Catholic Counter Reformation.) For there we discover an interplay of strong emotions tempered by social, intellectual, aesthetic, moral and religious restraints. This results in a contrast between content and form: the subject may be passion, violence or death; the expression is likely to be formal. We find female saints and mystics flying almost up to heaven, but conventionally draped and elegantly posed. Symmetrical churches and cathedrals of austere design are provided with soft decorations and rich colors and fabrics.

One must be cautious in attempting to establish parallels among the different arts; in fact, the French refer to their literature of the seventeenth century as "classical," and would probably unload all their Gallic gall on anyone who would call it baroque. Similarly, the works by Dutch painters presenting scenes from everyday life express a realism that bears little relation to baroque art. Nevertheless, certain tendencies should be noted. One of these is movement. Just as the scientists had turned their attention to motion, so the artists endowed their creations with a nervous mobility. Furthermore, in many of its subjects baroque art expresses an emotional attitude that found relatively little representation in literature but which nevertheless was widespread: the religious sentimentality of pietism found in the bittersweet aspects of the sufferings and the gentleness of Jesus.

Chronologically, the plastic arts, on the one hand, and literature and philosophy, on the other, undergo opposite developments. In the former, the baroque appears as a decomposition of the perfection of Renaissance art, while literary baroque served rather as an intermediate movement out of which neoclassicism eventually developed.

However, during the first third of the century, one can notice baroque features in literature, expressed in the excessive fantasy and horrifying depictions by poets such as Théophile de Viau, in the overrefinements of mannerism or in the emphasis on low-life aspects in the novels of Paul

Scarron and Antoine Furetière. All of these, even though in different ways, represented a distorted view of life by pushing one of its aspects to the breaking point.

In music the term "baroque" leads to even greater confusion than in the other arts, for it has been used vaguely to describe a period covering some one hundred and fifty years (1600–1750); at any rate, of the great "baroque" composers, only Corelli belongs partly to the seventeenth century. Nevertheless, important developments took place that gave birth to new forms (the trio sonata, the suite, and the concerto grosso, among others) and especially to the opera.

Although theoretical discussions concerning opera can be traced back to the Florentine Camerata that met at Giovanni Bardi's home between 1576 and 1582, the first opera, called "favola per musica," was *Dafne* (1594) with words by Ottavio Rinuccini and music by Jacopo Peri. While in this and in the later *Euridice* (1600) by the same authors the music is subordinated to the text, Claudio Monteverdi achieved a balance between words and music and established the modern opera in *Orfeo* (1607), *Arianna* (1608), and *L'Incoronazione di Poppea* (1642).

Jean Baptiste Lully, in his collaboration with Molière (*Love's the Best Doctor, George Dandin, The Would-Be Gentleman*), may actually be credited with having forecast the modern musical; he also introduced the recitative in his operas. Finally, at the end of the century, the opera attains a new perfection, being completely sung, in the works of Henry Purcell: *Dido and Aeneas* (1689); *King Arthur* (1691), on a libretto by Dryden; and *The Fairy Queen* (1692).

Among the various countries, France dominates in almost all cultural and political aspects, symbolized by the splendor of Louis XIV's court to which all of Europe looked for a model of good taste and good manners. Descartes and Pascal are among the most significant philosophers of the century; the plays of Corneille, Molière, and Racine are universally admired; La Fontaine is the master of the fable as La Rochefoucauld of the maxim and Bossuet of oratory; and Mme de La Fayette stands at the origin of the modern novel.

England's contribution is rich and varied, including the philosophical works of Bacon, Hobbes, and Locke; the poetry of Donne, Crashaw, Vaughan, and Marvell; and the Restoration plays by Wycherley and Congreve. The greatest triumph, however, was achieved in Milton's *Paradise Lost,* which proved that a modern author was capable of writing a heroic poem which could rival those of antiquity.

Justice has not always been done to the importance of Spain, especially for the first half of the seventeenth century. Spain provided the rest of Europe with a multitude of dramatic and comic subjects that were exploited by authors elsewhere. It is noteworthy that the first French classical play, Pierre Corneille's *Le Cid* (1637), was based on a Spanish model, that the Italian commedia dell'arte, the comedy of masks and improvisation, utilized numerous Spanish plots, and that Molière drew on Spanish sources, either via the Italian comedy or directly, for a number of his plays.

It is difficult to understand why the Spanish theater of the Golden Age, which can boast of the enormous and brilliant production by dramatists such as Lope de Vega, Tirso de Molina, and Calderón (among many others), does not enjoy the same universal appreciation as that extended to the French playwrights of the century. When we add to this wealth of theater the fact that Cervantes wrote his *Don Quixote* between 1604 and 1614, that Luis de Góngora was one of the most important poets of mannerism, and that the subject of Don Juan finds its first artistic expression in Tirso de Molina's *The Trickster of Seville,* we have at least some idea of the role Spain played in injecting vitality into the cultural life of the seventeenth century.

Italy and Germany were both handicapped by an unfavorable political situation, the former by foreign occupation, the latter by the disastrous effects of the Thirty Years' War and a lack of political unity. As a result we find in Italy primarily satire and *marinismo,* the mannerism inspired by the poems of Marino; while in Germany translations and the imitation of foreign models predominate.

Holland and Flanders, for their part, have left us paintings that are among the great treasures of all times.

Artistic excellence was usually paralleled by political power. The first third of the century was dominated by the Thirty Years' War, which devastated Germany, reducing its population by more than one half. In this struggle for power France emerged triumphant, thus taking over the position until then occupied by Spain. But the latter, England, and Holland, thanks to their naval strength, controlled maritime trade and accumulated great economic power.

After a period of political instability, marked in France by the disorders of the Fronde and in England by the civil wars, the new trend was dominated by strong royal governments, the weakening of the aristocracy, the gradual rise of the capitalist middle class, and the continued impoverishment of the peasants and the workers.

Reason, order, stability, avoidance of excess — these watchwords of rationalist attitudes were reflected in the political and social structure of Europe between 1660 and 1685. And it is not by mere chance that Louis XIV was the most important man of the century. We shall have occasion to read various estimates and criticisms of this great monarch; yet it cannot be denied that he had perfectly understood the spirit of his age and of his nation which saw in him a savior who would finally establish order out of chaos.

While the divine right of kings was not questioned in France, royal authority fared less well in England where Parliament rebelled against the king and Charles II was beheaded. But this was a political and not a philosophical development, for the rationalist thinkers did not, as a rule, extend their revolt against philosophical authority to the political field; in fact, most of them were political conservatives, and Hobbes even devoted his efforts to an apology of autocratic government. For reason was at first not employed to question religious and political institutions. Being in part a reaction to religious wars and political upheavals, rationalism strove to substitute order and a methodical approach for emotional arguments and unexamined procedures. During this transitional stage, when all accepted beliefs were temporarily dismissed while being tested by new standards, Descartes chose to follow for the time being the most moderate opinions. While superstition was being attacked, religious dogma was treated with utmost respect and care was taken that rational and scientific views were not interpreted as invalidating faith when the two were in disagreement.

In summary, we can distinguish four major periods in the seventeenth century.

The first, until about 1637, is dominated by political unrest due to the struggle for internal power between king and nobles or Parliament, and for external power during the Thirty Years' War. The times call for heroism and individual excellence, but efforts are made to improve social manners, which results in literary coteries and affectation in style. The excesses of this movement, in turn, call forth satire or the completely opposite trend of low-life realism.

The second period, from 1637 to 1660, sees the formation of the rational method. Former philosophical and scientific authorities are being criticized or entirely rejected, while, under the impulse of scientific advances, new ways are devised to establish knowledge on a rational and more factual basis. These are years of transition during which political unrest continues. But people are growing tired of the situation and desire settlements that will provide them with stability and security.

The third period, from 1660 to 1685, represents the high point of rationalism which invades and dominates all fields of endeavor. At the same time the internal situation of the major powers stabilizes. In general, this is a period of equilibrium during which the greatest works of the century are produced.

The last period, from 1685 to the end of the century, witnesses the complete triumph of reason and science which are now being applied to matters that had formerly been carefully excluded from rational scrutiny: social conditions, religious dogma and authority, governmental policies. At the same time, religious intolerance becomes a problem again and royal excesses cause individual and popular reactions.

A great and unique century is coming to a close. It had nearly exhausted the artistic possibilities that reason, science, and vastly improved techniques had provided. In the theater, in heroic poetry, in philosophy, only imitation or refinement was left at the disposal of the next century. But in satire, in the novel, and in social and political philosophy, the eighteenth century carried the rational method to its ultimate implications with results that had not even been dreamed of in the Age of Reason.

PART

I

Kings, Nobles
and Commoners

What were people like in the seventeenth century and how did they live? Our information on this subject is less complete than we would wish. Our most helpful sources are memoirs, but since they were written by aristocrats or well-to-do bourgeois, the impression we are likely to receive of the century is at best partial, for we learn a great deal about a closely knit minority but almost nothing about the majority of the people.

The gulf that separated the upper and lower classes was enormous. On the summit all was splendor, elegance, bravery, wit. Very fittingly, Louis XIV was called the Sun King, and it is appropriate that we open this study of the seventeenth century with the man who dominated his time so completely that, later on, Voltaire was to refer to it as the age of Louis XIV. We shall hear witnesses speak of his education, of his great years (1661–1685) when France became the model and the envy of all Europe, and of his decline (1685–1715), marked by his marriage with Mme de Maintenon and an increasing religious intolerance that caused him to revoke the Edict of Nantes, which had granted religious freedom to Protestants, and to persecute the Huguenots. Pomp and splendor reigned likewise during festive occasions, such as the coronation of Charles II of England; banquets seemed to be made for Gargantuan appetites.

And the people? To be sure, there were well-educated middle-class men such as Colbert in France or Samuel Pepys in England, who could rise to high and responsible positions. But the workers and the peasants had no rights, were heavily taxed, and lived difficult and miserable lives. When reading the brilliant works of this period, we must not forget that it was a century of wars, most notable among which was the Thirty Years' War (1618–1648), which almost depopulated Germany; that those who escaped the ravages of war still had to face the repeated plagues that swept through Europe; that fires were a constant threat; and that the treatment of criminals was inhuman.

The high and the low. For the time being there is no tension between them, for kings rule by divine right and everybody knows his place in a stable society. But kings are being deposed in England, and the task of supporting an idle nobility in France is becoming more and more of a burden. Grandeur is expensive. And while dazzling royal festivities succeed each other at Versailles, the seeds of the French Revolution are being sown.

1
Kings and Nobles

A. LOUIS XIV

1. THE EDUCATION OF A KING.

In 1645, Louis XIV was seven years old. Pierre La Porte, his First Valet, probably exaggerates his own importance in the upbringing of the royal child, but he gives us a realistic description of the atmosphere in which the future King grew up.

In 1645, after the King was taken away from the women, . . . I was the first to sleep in the bedroom of His Majesty. This astonished him at first, but what bothered him most was that I could not supply him with the fairy tales which the women used to read to him in order to put him to sleep.

One day I spoke of this to the Queen and added that, if she agreed, I could read him some good books: if he would fall asleep, fine and good; if not, he might retain something of it. She asked me which book. I told her I thought the best book for him would be the history of France. I could call his attention to the evil kings in order to make him detest vice, and to the virtuous ones in order to show him good models and create in him the desire to imitate them. The Queen thought this was a good idea.

Consequently, I read to him the History of France by Mézeray every night as if it were a tale, so that the King, who took pleasure in it, promised to emulate the noblest of his ancestors. He would get very angry when he was told he would be another Louis-Do-Nothing, for, on orders from the Queen, I frequently criticized him for his shortcomings.

One day, at Rueil, having noticed that in all the games he played the role of the valet, I sat down in the armchair and put on my hat. He was so scandalized by my behavior that he went straightaway to complain to the Queen. That was exactly what I had wanted him to do. She sent for me at once and asked me smilingly why I was sitting down in the King's room and covered myself in his presence. I replied that, inasmuch as the King was doing my job, it was only reasonable for me to assume his, which was certainly to my advantage; that, in his amusements, he always played the valet, and that this was a bad attitude. The Queen, who was unaware of this, reprimanded him severely. . . .

M. de Beaumont, the King's tutor, did his utmost to educate him, and I can say that, during the lessons I witnessed, he did complete justice to his subject. But those around the King, instead of making him practice the precepts he had been taught, looked only to his amusement or solicited on their own behalf.

When M. de Beaumont pointed out to His Eminence, Cardinal Mazarin, that the King did not apply himself to his studies and requested that he use his authority to reprimand him, since the King might do no better when charged with serious matters, the Cardinal replied: "Don't worry about it, leave it to me. He will soon know too much; for, when he attends council meetings, he asks me a hundred questions about the discussions."

Another factor which hampered the King's education was his anger at being scolded by his true servants who did not let him get away with anything. All children react this way. Hence he stayed as little as possible in his own quarters and spent most of his time at the Queen's where everybody applauded him and nobody contradicted him. . . .

I observed several times that, while alone with his governor, M. de Villeroy, the King was misbehaving. After waiting for the governor to intervene and seeing that he did not say a word, I said all I could to the Child-King to make him think of what he was and what he ought to do. When I had told him off sufficiently, the governor would say: "La Porte is telling you the truth, Sire; La Porte is telling you the truth." That was the sum total of his teaching and he never said anything that might displease the King; in fact, he was so obliging that the King himself became aware of it and made fun of it. When His Majesty called him, saying: "Monsieur le Maréchal," he would reply: "Yes, Sire," even before knowing what it was all about, so afraid was he to refuse him anything.

The Queen's attitude was not much better. One day the King had set up a fort in the Palais-Royal and got so excited in attacking it that he was covered with perspiration. Someone came and told him that the Queen was about to take her bath. He ran at once to share her bath and ordered me to undress him for that purpose. I refused. So he went to the Queen to tell her. She did not dare refuse. I told Her Majesty that letting

1. Anonymous, French, *Louis XIV as a Child.*

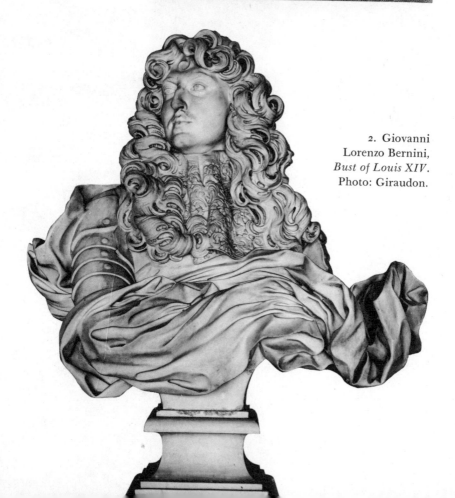

2. Giovanni Lorenzo Bernini, *Bust of Louis XIV.* Photo: Giraudon.

3. Gerard Edelinck,
*Louis XIV in
Old Age.*

4. Nicolas Mignard,
Madame de Maintenon.
Photo: Giraudon.

him take a bath in the state he was in would kill him. As I saw that she only replied that it was his wish, I repeated that I was warning her and that, if an accident should happen, I was washing my hands of it. When she saw that I was placing the responsibility on her, she said we would have to consult Vautier, his First Physician. I promptly had him sent for and he arrived just in time to tell the Queen that he could not vow for the King's life if he took a bath in the state he was in.

(Pierre La Porte: *Memoirs*, published in 1755)

2. *THE GREAT YEARS (1661–1685).*

Mme Françoise de Motteville (1621–1689), who was close to the Queen Mother, Anne of Austria, presents a glowing portrait of the Sun King in all his splendor.

The King acceded to the French throne the day his father, Louis XIII, died. He was then only four years old, and it may be said that only upon the death of Cardinal Mazarin did he truly wear the crown, begin to be King and to show himself worthy of his title. It was then that he decided to take charge himself of all his tasks and that the favors to be bestowed upon great and small would entirely be received from his hands. To that end he began to arrange his schedule as follows:

He resolved to rise at eight or nine o'clock, even though he used to go to bed very late. On getting out of bed, he would pray to God and get dressed. Then he had the doors locked to devote himself to matters of state and to keep people out. . . . About ten o'clock, the King went to the Council Chamber where he stayed until noon. Next he went to mass and, before dining, spent his time with the public or, privately, with the Queens. After the meal he remained often, and for a long time, with the royal family; afterwards he would leave to work with some of his ministers. He granted audience to anybody desiring one and listened patiently to those who came to speak to him. He accepted petitions from all who presented them and gave his reply on specified days. . . .

As his heart was filled with the ambition to carry out the duties of a great king, he applied himself to his work and began to take pleasure in it; and the desire to learn all he needed to know soon turned him into an expert. His great intelligence and his good intentions revealed the seeds of a universal knowledge that had been hidden from those who did not know him intimately. For suddenly he turned out to be a statesman in matters of state, a theologian in matters concerning the Church, and precise in those of finance. He spoke well and always defended the right cause in council meetings, watchful of the interests of individuals but hostile to intrigues and flattery, and severe towards the nobles of his kingdom whom he suspected of a desire to take over the reins of government. As a person he was amiable, honorable, and easily accessible to everybody. But he had a great and serious air about him that impressed respect and fear on the public and prevented even those he esteemed most from being at ease, even in private, although he was unceremonious and jovial with the ladies.

(Mme de Motteville: *Memoirs*, published in 1723)

3. THE DECLINE (*1685–1715*).

Louis de Rouvroy, Duc de Saint-Simon (1675–1755), lived at the court of Louis XIV during the decline of the great monarch. He could not forgive the King's efforts to keep the nobility in check and this resentment colors much of his description of court life; however, his account of the King's last days is quite accurate.

This same Monday, 26th of August, after the two Cardinals had left the room, the King dined in his bed in the presence of those who were privileged to enter. As the things were being cleared away, he made them approach and addressed to them these words, which were stored up in their memory: "Gentlemen, I ask your pardon for the bad example I have given you. I have much to thank you for the manner in which you have served me, and for the attachment and fidelity you have always shown for me. I am very sorry I have not done for you all I should have wished to do; bad times have been the cause. I ask for my grandson the same application and the same fidelity you have had for me. He is a child who may experience many reverses. Let your example be one for all my other subjects. Follow the orders my nephew will give you; he is to govern the realm; I hope he will govern it well; I hope also that you will all contribute to keep up union, and that if anyone falls away you will aid in bringing him back. I feel that I am moved, and that I move you also. I ask your pardon. Adieu, gentlemen, I hope you will sometimes remember me."

A short time after, he called the Maréchal de Villeroy to him, and said he had made him governor of the Dauphin. He then called to him M. le Duc and M. le Prince de Conti, and recommended to them the advantages of union among princes. Then, hearing women in the cabinet, questioned who were there, and immediately sent word they might enter. Madame la Duchesse de Barry, Madame la Duchesse d'Orleans, and the Princesses of the blood forthwith appeared, crying. The King told them they must not cry thus, said a few friendly words to them, and dismissed them. They retired by the cabinet, weeping and crying very loudly, which caused people to believe outside that the King was dead; and, indeed, the rumour spread to Paris, and even to the provinces.

Sometime after, the King requested the Duchesse de Ventadour to bring the little Dauphin to him. He made the child approach, and then said to him, before Madame de Maintenon and the few privileged people present, "My child, you are going to be a great king; do not imitate me in the taste I have had for building, or in that I have had for war; try, on the contrary, to be at peace with your neighbours. Render to God what you owe him; recognize the obligations you are under to him; make him honoured by your subjects. Always follow good counsels; try to comfort your people, which I unhappily have not done. Never forget the obligation you owe to Madame de Ventadour. Madame (*addressing her*), let me embrace him (*and while embracing him*), my dear child, I give you my benediction with my whole heart."

As the little Prince was about to be taken off the bed, the King redemanded him, embraced him again, and raising hands and eyes to Heaven, blessed him once more. This spectacle was extremely touching.

On Tuesday the 27th of August, the King said to Madame de Maintenon, that he had always heard, it was hard to resolve to die; but that as for him, seeing himself upon the point of death, he did not find this resolution so difficult to form. She replied that it was very hard when we had attachments to creatures, hatred in our hearts, or restitutions to make. "Ah," rejoined the King, "as for restitutions, to nobody in particular do I owe any; but as for those I owe to the realm, I hope in the mercy of God."

The night which followed was very agitated. The King was seen at all moments joining his hands, striking his breast, and was heard repeating the prayers he ordinarily employed.

On Wednesday morning, the 28th of August, he paid a compliment to Madame de Maintenon, which pleased her but little, and to which she replied not one word. He said that what consoled him in quitting her was that, considering the age she had reached, they must soon meet again!

About seven o'clock in the morning, he saw in the mirror two of his valets at the foot of the bed weeping, and said to them, "Why do you weep? Is it because you thought me immortal? As for me, I have not thought myself so, and you ought, considering my age, to have been prepared to lose me."

A very clownish Provençal rustic heard of the extremity of the King, while on his way from Marseille to Paris, and came this morning to Versailles with a remedy which, he said, would cure the gangrene. The King was so ill, and the doctors so at their wits' ends, that they consented to receive him. Fagon tried to say something, but this rustic, who was named Le Brun, abused him very coarsely, and Fagon, accustomed to abuse others, was confounded. Ten drops of Le Brun's mixture in Alicante wine were therefore given to the King about eleven o'clock in the morning. Sometime after he became stronger, but the pulse falling again and becoming bad, another dose was given to him about four o'clock, to recall him to life, they told him. He replied, taking the mixture, "To life or to death as it shall please God."

Le Brun's remedy was continued. Someone proposed that the King should take some broth. The King replied that it was not broth he wanted, but a confessor, and he sent for him. One day, recovering from loss of consciousness, he asked Père Tellier to give him absolution for all his sins. Père Tellier asked him if he suffered much? "No," replied the King, "that's what troubles me: I should like to suffer more for the expiation of my sins."

On Thursday, the 29th of August, he grew a little better; he even ate two little biscuits steeped in wine, with a certain appetite. The news immediately spread abroad that the King was recovering. I went that day to the apartments of M. le Duc d'Orléans, where, during the previous eight days, there had been such a crowd that, speaking exactly, a pin would not have fallen to the ground. Not a soul was there! As soon as the Duc saw me he burst out laughing, and said I was the first person who had been to see him all the day! And until the evening he was entirely deserted. Such is the world!

In the evening it was known that the King had only recovered for the moment. In giving orders during the day, he called the young Dauphin "the young King." He saw a movement amongst those around him. "Why not?" said he, "that does not trouble me." Towards eight o'clock he took the elixir of the rustic. His brain appeared confused; he himself said he felt very ill. Towards eleven o'clock his leg was examined. The gangrene was found to be in the foot and the knee; the thigh much inflamed. He swooned during this examination. He had perceived with much pain that Madame de Maintenon was no longer near him. She had in fact gone off on the previous day with very dry eyes to St. Cyr, not intending to return. He asked for her several times during the day. Her departure could not be hidden. He sent for her to St. Cyr, and she came back in the evening.

Friday, August the 30th, was a bad day preceded by a bad night. The King continually lost his reason. About five o'clock in the evening Madame de Maintenon left him, gave away her furniture to the domestics, and went to St. Cyr never to leave it.

On Saturday, the 31st of August, everything went from bad to worse. The gangrene had reached the knee and all the thigh. Towards eleven o'clock at night the King was found to be so ill that the prayers for the dying were said. This restored him to himself. He repeated the prayers in a voice so strong that it rose above all the other voices. At the end he recognized Cardinal de Rohan, and said to him, "These are the last favours of the church." This was the last man to whom he spoke. He repeated several times, *Nunc et in hora mortis,* then said,"Oh my God, come to my aid: hasten to succour me."

These were his last words. All the night he was without consciousness and in a long agony, which finished on Sunday, the 1st Sept., 1715, at a quarter past eight in the morning, three days before he had accomplished his seventy-seventh year, and in the seventy-second of his reign. He had survived all his sons and his grandsons, except the King of Spain. Europe never saw so long a reign or France a King so old.

(Duc de Saint-Simon: *Memoirs,* after 1721)

B. THE CORONATION OF CHARLES II
OF ENGLAND (1661)

The solemn festivities of this great event are evoked by two eyewitnesses: the parade by Samuel Pepys and the ceremony by John Evelyn, both authors of diaries that are precious documents on life and manners in seventeenth-century England.

Up early and made myself as fine as I could, and put on my velvet coat, the first day that I put it on, though made half a year ago. And being ready . . . went to Mr. Young's, the flagmaker, and there we had good rooms to ourselves, with wine and good cake, and saw the show very well. In which it is impossible to relate the glory of this day, expressed in clothes of them that rode, and their horses and horses-clothes, among others, my Lord Sandwich's. Embroidery and diamonds were ordinary among them. The Knights of the Bath was a brave sight of itself. Remarkable were the two men that represent the two Dukes of Normandy and Aquitaine.[1] The Bishops come next after Barons. My Lord Monk rode bare after the King, and led in his hand a spare horse, as being Master of the Horse. The King in a most rich embroidered suit and cloak looked most noble. Wadlow, the vintner, at the Devil in Fleet street, did lead a fine company of soldiers, all young comely men, in white doublets. There followed the Vice-Chamberlain, Sir G. Carteret, a company of men all like Turks; but I know not yet what they are for. The street all gravelled, and the houses being with carpets before them, made brave show, and the ladies out of the windows. . . . So glorious was the show with gold and silver, that we were not able to look at it, our eyes at last being so much overcome with it.

(Samuel Pepys: *Diary*, April 22–23, 1661)

The next day, being St. George's, he went by water to Westminster Abbey. When his Majesty was entered, the Dean and Prebendaries brought all the regalia, and delivered them to several noblemen to bear before the King, who met them at the west door of the church, singing an anthem, to the choir. Then, came the peers, in their robes, and coronets in their hands, till his Majesty was placed on a throne elevated before the altar. Afterwards, the Bishop of London (the Archbishop of Canterbury being sick) went to every side of the throne to present the King to the People, asking if they would have him for their King, and do him homage; at this, they shouted four times "God save King Charles the Second!" Then, an anthem was sung. His Majesty, attended by three Bishops, went up to the altar, and he offered a pall and a pound of gold. Afterwards, he sate down in another chair during the sermon, which was preached by Dr. Morley, Bishop of Worcester.

After sermon, the King took his oath before the altar to maintain the religion, Magna Charta, and laws of the land. The hymn *Véni S. Sp.* followed, and then the Litany by two Bishops. Then the Archbishop of Canterbury, present but much indisposed and weak, said "Lift up your hearts"; at which, the King rose up, and put off his robes and upper garments, and was in a waistcoat so opened in divers places, that the Archbishop might commodiously anoint him, first in the palms of his hands, when an anthem was sung, and a prayer read; then, his breast and betwixt the shoulders, bending of both arms; and, lastly, on the crown of the head, with apposite hymns and prayers at each anointing; this done, the Dean closed and buttoned up the waistcoat. After which, was a coif put on, and the cobbium, sindon or dalmatic, and over this a super-tunic of cloth of gold, with buskins and sandals of the same, spurs, and the sword; a prayer being first said over it by the Archbishop on the altar, before it was girt on by the Lord Chamberlain. Then, the armill, mantle, &c. Then, the Archbishop placed the crown-imperial on the altar, prayed over it, and set it

5. W. Sherwin, *A perspective of Westminster Abbey Shewing his Majesties Crowning*.

6. Pierre Philippe, *Banquet*.

on his Majesty's head, at which all the Peers put on their coronets. An-
thems, and rare music, with lutes, viols, trumpets, organs, and voices, were
then heard, and the Archbishop put a ring on his Majesty's finger. The
King next offered his sword on the altar, which being redeemed, was
drawn, and borne before him. Then, the Archbishop delivered him the
sceptre, with the dove in one hand, and, in the other, the sceptre with the
globe. The King kneeling, the Archbishop pronounced the blessing. His
Majesty then ascending again his royal throne, whilst *Te Deum* was singing, all the Peers did their homage, by every one touching his crown. The
Archbishop, and the rest of the Bishops, first kissing the King; who received the Holy Sacrament, and so disrobed, yet with the crown-imperial
on his head, and accompanied with all the nobility in the former order,
he went on foot upon blue cloth, which was spread and reached from the
west door of the Abbey to Westminster stairs, when he took water in a
triumphal barge to Whitehall, where was extraordinary feasting.

(John Evelyn: *Diary*, April 23, 1661)

C. A ROYAL BANQUET

At the Banquet, came in the Queen, and stood by the King's left hand but
did not sit. There was the banqueting-stuff flung about the room profusely.
In truth, the crowd was so great, that though I stayed all the supper the
day before, I now stayed no longer than this sport began, for fear of disorder. The cheer was extraordinary, each Knight having forty dishes to
his mess, piled up five or six high; the room hung with the richest tapestry.

(John Evelyn: *Diary*, April 23, 1667)

2
The Preoccupations of Everyday Life

A. MR. AND MRS. SAMUEL PEPYS

*Samuel Pepys (1633–1703), of rather humble origin, received a
good education at Cambridge. In 1655, he married a 15-year-old
Huguenot refugee girl and soon identified himself with the
cause of Charles II. The Restoration provided him with a bril-*

*liant career as secretary to the Admiralty. Accused of being a
papist and a traitor, he fell out of favor in 1669 but was rein-
stated in 1684; however, the Revolution of 1688 put a definite
end to his career. His* Diary *(1660–1669) is one of the most spon-
taneously human documents of the century.*

To my office (being come to some angry words with my wife about neglecting the keeping of the house clean), I calling her beggar, and she
me pricklouse,[2] which vexed me. (May 2, 1661)

I was very angry and began to find fault with my wife for not command-
ing her servants as she ought. Thereupon she giving me some cross answer
I did strike her over her left eye such a blow as the poor wretch did cry
out and was in great pain, but yet her spirit was such as to endeavour to
bite and scratch me. But I coying with her made her leave crying and sent
for butter and parsley, and friends presently one with another, and I up,
vexed at my heart to think what I had done, for she was forced to lay a
poultice or something to her eye all day, and it is black, and the people of
the house observe it. (December 19, 1664)

Home in the evening, and there to sing and pipe with my wife, and that
having done she fell all of a sudden to discourse about her clothes and my
humours in not suffering her to wear them as she pleases, and grew to high
words between us, but I fell to read a book (Boyle's Hydrostatics) aloud
in my chamber and let her talk, till she was tired and vexed that I would
not hear her, and so became friends. (June 4, 1667)

My wife being busy in going with her woman to a hot-house to bathe
herself, after her long being within doors in the dirt, so that she now pretends to a resolution of being hereafter very clean. How long it will hold
I can guess. (February 21, 1665)

At night late home, and to clean myself with warm water; my wife will
have me, because she do herself, and so to bed. (February 25, 1665)

B. CLOTHES MAKE THE MAN . . .
AND THE WOMAN

Bought my cloth, coloured, for a suit and cloak, to line with plush the
cloak, which will cost me money, but I find that I must go handsomely,
whatever it costs me, and the charge will be made up in the fruit it brings.
(October 21, 1664)

This day I first began to go forth in my coat and sword, as the manner
now among gentlemen is. (February 3, 1661)

By and by comes Chapman, the periwig-maker, and upon my liking it,

7. I. Clark, *Bull Baiting.*

without more ado I went up, and there he cut off my hair, which went a
little to my heart at present to part with it; but, it being over, and my
periwig on, I paid him £3 for it; and away went he with my own hair to
make up another of, and I by and by, after I had caused all my maids to
look upon it; and they concluded it do become me. (November 3, 1663)

I found that my coming in a periwig did not prove so strange to the
world as I was afraid it would, for I thought that all the church would
presently have cast their eyes all upon me, but I found no such thing.
(November 8, 1663)

Home to dinner where my wife having dressed herself in a silly dress of
a blue petticoat uppermost, and a white satin waistcoat and white hood,
though I think she did it because her gown is gone to the tailor's, did, together with my being hungry, which always makes me peevish, make me
angry, but when my belly was full were friends again. (March 29, 1667)

About five o'clock I took my wife (who is mighty fine, and with a new
pair of locks, which vex me, though like a fool I helped her the other night
to buy them) and to Mrs. Pierce's. (October 29, 1666)

When the House began to fill she put on her vizard, and so kept it on all
the play; which of late is become a great fashion among the ladies, which

8. I. Clark, *Cock Fighting.*

hides their whole face. So to the Exchange, to buy things with my wife; among others, a vizard for herself. (June 12, 1663)

C. POPULAR ENTERTAINMENT

After dinner, with my wife and Mercer to the Bear-garden, where I have not been, I think, of many years, and saw some good sport of the bull's tossing of the dogs: one into the very boxes. But it is a rude and nasty pleasure. (June 14, 1666)

Being directed by sight of bills upon the walls, I did go to Shoe Lane to see a cock-fighting at a new pit there, a sport I was never at in my life: but Lord! to see the strange variety of people, from Parliament-man to the poorest 'prentices, bakers, brewers, butchers, and what not; and all these fellows one with another in swearing, cursing, and betting. I soon had enough of it, and yet I would not but have seen it once, it being strange to observe the nature of these poor creatures, how they will fight till they drop down dead upon the table, and strike after they are ready to give up the ghost, not offering to run away when they are weary or wounded past doing further, whereas where a dunghill brood comes he will, after a sharp stroke that pricks him, run off the stage, and they wring off his neck without more ado, whereas the other they preserve, though their eyes be both out, for breed only of a true cock of the game. . . . One thing it is strange to see how people of this poor rank, that look as if they had not bread to put in their mouths, shall bet three or four pounds at one bet, and lose it, and yet bet as much the next battle (so they call every match of two cocks), so that one of them will lose £10 or £20 at a meeting. (December 21, 1663)

(Samuel Pepys: *Diary*, 1660–1669)

D. SOCIAL ETIQUETTE

Just as the ordinary people, the nobles have their preoccupations and their games, except that the stakes are not so obvious. They are concerned with matters of prestige and protocol. Handing the King his nightshirt is a great honor; or else, among ladies, presenting a napkin to Mademoiselle, a member of the royal family. Mme de Sévigné (1626–1696), the famous French letter-writer, demonstrates how to embarrass an enemy in society.

A circumstance took place yesterday at Mademoiselle's, which gave me no small pleasure. Who should come in but Madame de Gêvres, in all her airs and graces! I fancy she expected I should have offered her my place; but, to say the truth, I have owed her a little grudge for her conduct the other day, and now I paid her with interest, for I did not stir. Mademoiselle was in bed; Madame de Gêvres was therefore obliged to place herself at the lower end of the room, a provoking thing to be sure. The princess called for drink; somebody must present the napkin. I perceived Madame de Gêvres drawing the glove from her withered hand, upon which I gave Madame d'Arpajon, who was above me, a push, which she understood; and pulling off her glove, with the best grace in the world, advanced a step, got before the duchess, took the napkin, and presented it. The duchess was perfectly embarrassed; for she had reached the upper end of the room, and had pulled off her gloves, only to have the mortification of being a nearer witness of Madame d'Arpajon's presenting the napkin before her. My dear child, I am very wicked; this pleased me infinitely: it was uncommonly well done. Would anyone have thought of depriving

Madame d'Arpajon of a little piece of honour, which is naturally her due, as being one of the bedchamber? Madame de Puisieux was very much diverted at it. As for Mademoiselle, she did not dare look up, and my countenance was not the most settled. After this, a thousand kind things were said to me about you; and Mademoiselle was pleased to order me to tell you, that she is very glad you escaped drowning, and are in good health.

(Madame de Sévigné: *Letters to Her Daughter,*
the Countess de Grignan, March 30, 1671)

3

Crime Does Not Pay

A. THE GENTLEMAN AND THE ROBBERS

The inhuman treatment of prisoners described below will lead to protests in the eighteenth century by men like Beccaria and Voltaire. John Evelyn (1620–1706), of good family and educated at Oxford, traveled widely. He participated in the plot to return Charles II to the English throne and, after the Restoration, held various important government offices. The tone of his Diary is strikingly different from that of Pepys, whom he aided, however, when the latter fell into disgrace.

The weather being hot, and having sent my man on before, I rode negligently under favour of the shade, till, within three miles of Bromley, at a place called the Procession Oak, two cut-throats started out, and striking with long staves at the horse, and taking hold of the reins, threw me down, took my sword, and hauled me into a deep thicket, some quarter of a mile from the highway, where they might securely rob me, as they soon did. What they got of money, was not considerable, but they took two rings, the one an emerald with diamonds, the other an onyx, and a pair of buckles set with rubies and diamonds, which were of value, and after all bound my hands behind me, and my feet, having before pulled off my boots; they then set me up against an oak, with most bloody threats to cut my throat if I offered to cry out, or make any noise; for they should be within hearing, I not being the person they looked for. I told them that if they had not basely surprised me they should not have had so easy a prize, and that it would teach me never to ride near a hedge, since, had I been in the mid-way, they durst not have adventured on me; at which they cocked their pistols, and told me they had long guns, too, and were fourteen companions. I begged for my onyx, and told them it being engraved with my arms would betray them; but nothing prevailed. My horse's bridle they slipped, and searched the saddle, which they pulled off, but let the horse graze, and then turning again bridled him and tied him to a tree, yet so as he might graze, and thus left me bound. My horse was perhaps not taken, because he was marked and cropped on both ears, and well known on that road. Left in this manner, grievously was I tormented with flies, ants, and the sun, nor was my anxiety little how I should get loose in that solitary place, where I could neither hear nor see any creature but my poor horse and a few sheep straggling in the copse.

After near two hours attempting, I got my hands to turn palm to palm, having been tied back to back, and then it was long before I could slip the cord over my wrists to my thumb, which at last I did, and then soon unbound my feet, and saddling my horse and roaming a while about, I at last perceived dust to rise, and soon after heard the rattling of a cart, towards which I made, and, by the help of two countrymen, I got back into the highway. I rode to Colonel Blount's, a great justiciary of the times, who sent out hue and cry immediately. The next morning, sore as my wrists and arms were, I went to London, and got 500 tickets printed and dispersed by an officer of Goldsmiths' Hall, and within two days had tidings of all I had lost, except my sword, which had a silver hilt, and some trifles. The rogues had pawned one of my rings for a trifle to a goldsmith's servant, before the tickets came to the shop, by which means they escaped; the other ring was bought by a victualler, who brought it to a goldsmith, but he having seen the ticket seized the man. I afterwards discharged him on his protestation of innocence. Thus did God deliver me from these villains, and not only so, but restored what they took, . . .

(John Evelyn: *Diary*, June 11, 1652)

B. GALLEY SLAVES

We went then to visit the galleys, being about twenty-five in number; the Capitaine of the Galley Royal gave us most courteous entertainment in his cabin, the slaves in the interim playing both loud and soft music very rarely. Then he showed us how he commanded their motions with a nod, and his whistle making them row out. The spectacle was to me new and

9. Diego Rodriguez de Silva y Velásquez, *The Drunkards.*
Photo: Anderson-Giraudon.

strange, to see so many hundreds of miserably naked persons, their heads being shaven close, and having only high red bonnets, a pair of coarse canvas drawers, their whole back and legs naked, doubly chained about their middle and legs, in couples, and made fast to their seats, and all commanded in a trice by an imperious and cruel seaman. One Turk amongst the rest he much favoured, who waited on him in his cabin, but with no other dress than the rest, and a chain locked about his leg, but not coupled. This galley was richly carved and gilded, and most of the rest were very beautiful. After bestowing something on the slaves, the capitaine sent a band of them to give us music at dinner where we lodged. I was amazed to contemplate how these miserable caitiffs lie in their galley crowded together; yet there was hardly one but had some occupation, by which, as leisure and calms permitted, they got some little money, insomuch as some of them have, after many years of cruel servitude, been able to purchase their liberty. The rising-forward and falling-back at their oar, is a miserable spectacle, and the noise of their chains, with the roaring of the beaten waters, has something of strange and fearful in it to one unaccustomed to it. They are ruled and chastised by strokes on their backs and soles of their feet, on the least disorder, and without the least humanity, yet are they cheerful and full of knavery.

(John Evelyn: *Diary*, October 7, 1644)

C. TORTURE

I went to the Châtelet, or prison, where a malefactor was to have the question, or torture, given to him, he refusing to confess the robbery with which he was charged, which was thus: they first bound his wrist with a strong rope, or small cable, and one end of it to an iron ring made fast to the wall, about four feet from the floor, and then his feet with another cable, fastened about five feet farther than his utmost length to another ring on the floor of the room. Thus suspended, and yet lying but aslant, they slid a horse of wood under the rope which bound his feet, which so exceedingly stiffened it, as severed the fellow's joints in miserable sort, drawing him out at length in an extraordinary manner, he having only a pair of linen drawers on his naked body. Then, they questioned him of a robbery (the Lieutenant being present, and a clerk that wrote), which not confessing, they put a higher horse under the rope, to increase the torture and extension. In this agony, confessing nothing, the executioner with a horn (just such as they drench horses with) stuck the end of it into his mouth, and poured the quantity of two buckets of water down his throat and over him, which so prodigiously swelled him, as would have pitied and affrighted any one to see it; for all this, he denied all that was charged to him. They then let him down, and carried him before a warm fire to bring him to himself, being now to all appearance dead with pain. What became of him, I know not; but the gentleman whom he robbed constantly averred him to be the man, and the fellow's suspicious pale looks, before he knew he should be racked, betrayed some guilt; the Lieutenant was also of that opinion, and told us at first sight (for he was a lean, dry, black young man) he would conquer the torture; and so it seems they could not hang him, but did use in such cases, where the evidence is very presumptive, to send them to the galleys, which is as bad as death.

There was another malefactor to succeed, but the spectacle was so uncomfortable, that I was not able to stay the sight of another.

(John Evelyn: *Diary*, March 11, 1651)

4

The Scourges of the Century

A. WAR

Hans Jakob Christoffel von Grimmelshausen (1622(?)–1676) participated in the Thirty Years' War. He led an adventurous life which took him to Switzerland, Bohemia, the Netherlands and France. He was attached to various religious dignitaries, among whom was the Bishop of Strasbourg, and may have been converted to Catholicism. Although of low bourgeois origin, he was awarded a title of nobility. It is usually assumed that he depicts himself in his hero Simplicissimus.

In no time the air was humming with so many bullets that it seemed as if they had been fired especially as a salute for us. The fainthearted drew back thinking they could hide themselves; but the courageous ones, who had been through entertainment of that sort before, watched the bullets streak overhead without batting an eyelash. In the battle itself everybody tried to stay ahead of death by killing the closest enemy that was lunging for him. The horrible shooting, the clangor of the harness, the clashing of the pikes, and the cries both of the wounded and of the attacking soldiers — all this, mingled with trumpets, drums, and fifes, produced a dreadful music!

The air was filled with smoke and a thick dust that purposely seemed to cover the dreadful sight of the wounded and the dead. Our ears were ringing with the woeful screams of the dying and the hearty shouts of those still full of life. As time wore on, the horses seemed to gather strength in the defence of their masters, a duty they fulfilled with eagerness. Some of them were buried dead under their masters, bleeding from wounds they had received as compensation for their faithful services; others again, for the same reasons, fell on top of their riders thus receiving the honor, albeit in death, of being carried by those whom they had been obliged to carry in real life. Still others, having been relieved of the burden that had held

49

10. Jacques Courtois, *Cavalry Clash*. Photo: Giraudon.

them in check, left the humans to their rage and fury, and ran off to savor their first freedom in the open fields.

The earth that is wont to cover the dead was strewn itself with deceased soldiers who offered a variety of sights. Here lay heads that had lost their owners; there bodies that were short of heads. Some had their intestines hanging out, others had had their heads smashed and their brains spattered. Here the soul-bereaved bodies had been emptied of their blood; there the living were splashed with foreign blood. Here lay isolated arms whose fingers were still moving as if they wanted to get back into the fray; there men were running away who had not lost a drop of blood. Elsewhere one could see separated thighs which, even though relieved of the burden of the body, were now heavier than before. Finally, there were maimed soldiers begging to be finished off, while others pleaded for quarter in order to save their lives. All in all, it was nothing but a wretched and miserable sight.

(Grimmelshausen: *Der abenteuerliche Simplicissimus,*
Book II, Chap. 27; 1659)

B. THE PLAGUE

A maid servant of Mr. John Wright's falling sick of the plague, she was removed to an out-house, and a nurse appointed to look to her; who, being once absent, the maid got out of the house at the window, and ran away. The nurse coming and knocking, and having no answer, believed she was dead, and went and told Mr. Wright so; who and his lady were in great strait what to do to get her buried. At last resolved to go to Brentwood hard by, being in the parish, and there get people to do it. But they would not; so he went home full of trouble, and in the way met the wench walking over the common, which frightened him worse than before; and was forced to send people to take her, which he did; and they got one of the pest coaches and put her into it to carry her to the pest house. And passing in a narrow lane, Sir Anthony Browne, with his brother and some friends in the coach, met this coach with the curtain drawn close. The brother being a young man, and believing there might be some lady in it that would not be seen, and the way being narrow, he thrust his head out of his own into her coach, and to look, and there saw somebody look very ill, and in a sick dress, and stunk mightily; which the coachman also cried out upon. And presently they come up to some people that stood looking after it, and told our gallants that it was a maid of Mr. Wright's carried away sick of the plague; which put the young gentleman into a fright and had almost cost him his life, but is now well again.

(Samuel Pepys: *Diary*, August 3, 1665)

In the City died this week 7,496 and, of them 6,102 of the plague. But it is feared that the true number of the dead this week is near 10,000, partly from the poor that cannot be taken notice of, through the greatness of the number and partly from the Quakers and others that will not have any bell ring for them.

(Samuel Pepys: *Diary*, August 31, 1665)

C. THE GREAT FIRE OF LONDON, 1666

By and by Jane comes and tells me that she hears that above 300 houses have been burned down all Fish-Street, by London Bridge. So I made myself ready presently, and walked to the Tower, and there got up upon one

11. Micco Spadaro, *The Naples Plague*. Photo: Anderson-Giraudon.

12. L. P. Verschuier, *The Fire of London, 1666*. Photo: Hanfstaengl-Giraudon.

13. Diego Rodriguez de Silva y Velásquez, *The Surrender of Breda*, detail. Photo: Anderson-Giraudon.

of the high places . . . and there I did see the houses at that end of the bridge all on fire, and an infinite great fire on this and the other side the end of the bridge. . . . So down with my heart full of trouble, to the Lieutenant of the Tower, who tells me that it began this morning in the King's baker's house in Pudding Lane, and that it has burned St-Magnus Church and most part of Fish Street already. So I down to the water-side, and there got a boat and through bridge and there saw a lamentable fire. Poor Michell's house, as far as the Old Swan, already burned that way, and the fire running further, that in very little time it got as far as the Steel-Yard, while I was there. Everybody endeavouring to remove their goods, and flinging into the river or bringing them into lighters [3] that lay off; poor people staying in their houses as long as till the very fire touched them, and then running into boats, or clambering from one stair by the water-side to another. And among other things, the poor pigeons, I perceive, were loth to leave their houses, but hovered about the windows and balconies till they were, some of them burned, their wings, and fell down. Having staid, and in an hour's time seen the fire rage every way, and nobody, to my sight, endeavouring to quench it, but to remove their goods, and leave all to the fire, and having seen it get as far as the Steel-yard, and the wind mighty high and driving it into the City; and everything, after so long a drought, proving combustible, even the very stones of churches, . . . I to Whitehall and did tell the King and Duke of York what I saw, and that unless his Majesty did command houses to be pulled down nothing could stop the fire. . . . Walked along Watling-street, as well as I could, every creature coming away loaded with goods to save, and here and there sick people carried away in beds. . . . Walked home, seeing people all almost distracted, and no manner of means used to quench the fire. . . . And to see the churches all filling with goods by people who themselves should have been quietly there at this time. . . . Met with the King and Duke of York in their barge, and with them to Queenhithe. . . . When we could endure no more upon the water, we to a little ale-house on the Bankside . . . and there staid till it was dark almost, and saw the fire grow. . . . We saw the fire as only one entire arch of fire from this to the other side of the bridge, and in a bow up the hill for an arch of above a mile long: it made me weep to see it. The churches, houses, and all on fire and flaming at once; and a horrid noise the flames made, and the cracking of houses and their ruin. So home with a sad heart, . . . the news coming every moment of the growth of the fire; so that we were forced to begin to pack up our own goods, and prepare for their removal.

(Samuel Pepys: *Diary*, September 2, 1666)

About four o'clock in the morning my Lady Batten sent me a cart to carry away all my money, and plate, and best things to Bethnal-Green. Which I did, riding myself in my night-gown in the cart. . . . (September 3, 1666)

Now and then walking into the garden, and saw how horridly the sky looks, all on fire in the night, was enough to put us out of our wits; and, indeed, it was extremely dreadful, for it looks just as if it was at us, and the whole heaven on fire. (September 4, 1666)

Home, and whereas I expected to have seen our house on fire, it being now about seven o'clock, it was not. . . . Going to the fire, I find by the blowing up of houses, there is a good stop given to it . . . it having only burnt the dial of Barking Church. . . . I up the top of Barking steeple, and there saw the saddest sight of desolation that I ever saw; everywhere great fires, oil-cellars, and brimstone, and other things burning. . . . I walked into town, and find Fenchurch Street, Gracious Street and Lumbard Street all in dust. The exchange is a sad sight, nothing standing there, of all the statues or pillars but Sir Thomas Gresham's picture in the corner. Walked into Moorefields (our feet ready to burn, walking through the town among the hot coals), and find that full of people, and poor wretches carrying their goods there. . . . I also did see a poor cat taken out of a hole in the chimney, joining to the wall of the Exchange, with the hair all burnt off the body, and yet alive. So home at night, and find there good hopes of saving our office. (September 5, 1666)

Up by five o'clock, and, blessed be God, find all well.

(Samuel Pepys: *Diary*, September 7, 1666)

NOTES

1. William the Conqueror was Duke of Normandy before he became King of England and Eleanor of Aquitaine married Henry II of England. That is why the two French provinces are represented in the royal procession.
2. A derisive term for a tailor. Pepys' father had been a tailor.
3. A barge, a flat-bottomed river boat.

Heroism and Affectation

The first half of the seventeenth century attempts to find solutions to the problems created by long religious wars and the resultant social instability. Due to sheer exhaustion, people shy away from further religious quarrels, but the social disputes are far from over. Who shall rule: King or nobility? King or Parliament? In France, the measures taken by Louis XIII and Richelieu to contain the ambitions of the nobility lead to a gentlemanly but deeply serious conflict called the Slingshot War (la Fronde, 1648–1653); in England, royalty fared even worse: civil war raged between 1640 and 1660, Charles I was beheaded, and eventually Cromwell was named as Protector.

In these circumstances, a true nobleman is necessarily a brave soldier. But this is not enough. He must also be a gallant, dashing gentleman at court, for a severe reform of manners has taken place in noble society, where the ladies assume an increasingly important place. We shall therefore first attempt to define the ideal man of the century and compare him with a less perfect literary hero, Tirso de Molina's Don Juan. Next, we shall be concerned with the affectation and mannerisms that had developed in courtly society; and finally with the trends opposed to that movement.

1

The Heroic Ideal

THE IDEAL MAN OF THE SEVENTEENTH CENTURY.

It is always interesting to attempt to determine who, hypothetically, was the ideal man of a particular period and to judge the living or fictitious persons of that age by those yardsticks. During the seventeenth century, the most widely accepted image of the ideal man is perhaps represented by the French "honnête homme," a term that defies translation. Some of his essential traits are described below. To these must, of course, be added such basic requirements as generosity and good social behavior.

He Must Be of Noble Birth

First of all, it seems to me absolutely necessary that he who wishes to enter into court society be of noble birth and of a family marked by some noble distinction. . . . As for his profession, there is none more respectable or more essential for a gentleman than that of bearing arms.

He Must Be a Virtuous Man

The greatest ambition of one who carries a sword should be to be considered a generous and brave man, and consequently he ought to be a man of good conduct and of virtue. And, indeed, those who join malice to valor are usually feared and hated like ferocious beasts, because, having the power to do evil, they also have the will to do so. But those whose great courage is accompanied by good intentions are loved by every one and considered as guardian angels whom God has sent among us to oppose the oppressions of the wicked.

He Must Be Jealous of His Honor

Since everybody is concerned about his reputation, especially where his profession is involved, a gentleman has all the more reason to watch over the reputation of his weapons, which are truly the means of his nobility. In this respect he must be rigorous without being ostentatious, for, just as the reputation of a lady once blemished can never regain its original purity, so it is impossible that the esteem enjoyed by a soldier once tarnished by any lack of courage may be so completely re-established as to be above reproach.

Of Natural Gracefulness

One of the greatest gifts consists in a certain natural gracefulness which in all his movements, in his slightest actions must shine forth like a divine ray of light, a feature that is found in all those who are born to please courtly society.

Of Virtue

It is true, indeed, that virtue as such is greater in attraction and appeal when present in a person of good appearance and of quality than in one who is unattractive and of low condition. But nonetheless, even in the most illustrious and most handsome prince in the world, if he happens to be inclined to vice and of bad morals, the greatness of his birth would only make him hated all the more.

Of the Subjects of Which a Gentleman Should Not Be Ignorant

I feel that rather than get entangled in all the quarrels of philosophy, which would consume the entire life of a man, he would be wiser to study in the great book of experience than in Aristotle. It suffices for him to have a general idea of the most interesting matters that occupy the conversations of good society. I would rather have him be tolerably well informed in several subjects than solidly profound in only one. The reason is that life is too short to attain perfection in even the slightest of those specialties within our reach and that one who can speak only of one thing is too frequently obliged to keep silent.

He Must Respect Women

In consequence of all the efforts one must make to present a pleasant appearance, the first and foremost incumbent on one who wants to please women is to honor them with all the respect and all the submission that he is capable of and that are proper.

(Nicolas Faret: *The "Honnête Homme"* or
The Art of Pleasing at Court, 1630)

2
Hero with Some Defects

To illustrate the perfect hero, the best example might have been the Cid, either in the Spanish play of Guillén de Castro (1618) or in the French play by Pierre Corneille (1637), which established the classical theater in France. It is, however, often more interesting to compare the ideal man of a period with a character who, in many ways, serves as a negative example. Besides, the nobleman whom Tirso de Molina immortalized in The Trickster of Seville *(1630) is more than a hero. He stands at the origin of what has become one of the most fertile themes of modern times: the Don Juan legend. Molière, E. T. A. Hoffmann, Byron, Alfred de Musset, José Zorrilla, G. B. Shaw, Jean Anouilh, Henry de Montherlant, and hundreds of others have interpreted the subject since, each in his own way. Those who know primarily Mozart's opera* Don Giovanni *(1787) may be surprised to learn that Tirso de Molina's work is essentially a morality play with a religious message: Remember at all times that there is death and punishment. Do not delay repentance until the last moment. Tirso's Don Juan is not an atheist; he is a young gay blade who lives only for the present moment and whose game is the conquest of women. He gambles on the wide-spread belief that even the worst sinner can be saved by sincere repentance at the last minute. This was the problem foremost in the mind of the Spanish monk Gabriel Téllez (1583(?)–1648) who wrote several hundred plays under the name of Tirso de Molina. But the success of the Don Juan subject has been due to the spectacular stage effect of the animated statue and, most of all, to the character of the hero. The following excerpts concentrate on these two aspects of the play.*

Don Juan. Night spreads across the world. Silence is black.
    The Pleiades now tread the highest pole
    'Mid starry clusters. Now I set my trap.
    Love guides me to my joy — none can resist him.
    I've got to reach her bed. Aminta!

Aminta.   Who
    Calls for Aminta? Is it Batricio?
    He is at her door. She comes out, as from bed.

Don Juan. I'm not Batricio. No.

Aminta.   Then, who?

Don Juan.   Look slowly,
    And you'll see who I am.

Aminta.   Why, sir, I'm lost,
    With you outside my bedroom at these hours!

Don Juan. Such are the hours that I am wont to keep.

Aminta. Return, or I shall shout. Please don't exceed
    The courtesy you owe to my Batricio.
    You'll find, in Dos Hermanas, there are Romans —
    Emilias and Lucreces who avenge!

Don Juan. Just hear two words and hide the blushing scarlet
    Of your fair cheeks deep down within your heart!

AMINTA. Go, go! My husband's coming.

DON JUAN.   I'm your husband.
    So what have you to marvel at?

AMINTA.   Since when?

DON JUAN. From now on, and forever, I am he!

AMINTA. But who arranged the marriage?

DON JUAN.   My delight.

AMINTA. And who was it that married us?

DON JUAN.   Your eyes.

AMINTA. By what authority?

DON JUAN.   Why, that of sight!

AMINTA. But does Batricio know?

DON JUAN.   Yes! He forgets you.

AMINTA. Has he forgotten me?

DON JUAN.   Yes. I adore you.

AMINTA. How?

DON JUAN. Thus with all my heart I swoon before you.

AMINTA. Get out!

DON JUAN.   How can I when you see I'm dying
    With love for you alone?

AMINTA.   What shameless lying!

DON JUAN. Aminta, listen and you'll know the truth,
    Since women are the friends of truth. I am
    A noble knight, the heir of the Tenorios,
    The conquerors of Seville. And my father,
    Next to the king, is honoured and esteemed
    Beyond all men in court. Upon his lips
    Hang life or death according to his word.
    Travelling on my road, by merest chance,
    I came and saw you. Love ordains these things
    And guides them, so that even He, Himself,
    Forgets that they were anything but chance.
    I saw you, I adored you, I was kindled
    So that I am determined now to wed you.

Even though the king forbid it, and my father
In anger and with threats tries to prevent it,
I have to be your husband. What's your answer!

AMINTA. I don't know what to say. Your so-called "truths"
Are covered with deceitful rhetoric —
Because if I am married to Batricio
(As is well known) the fact is not annulled
Even if he deserts me.

DON JUAN.   Non-consummation,
Either by malice or deceit, is reason
For an annulment.

AMINTA.   In Batricio all
Was simple truth.

DON JUAN.   Tush! Come, give me your hand,
And let's confirm our vows.

AMINTA.   You're not deceiving?

DON JUAN. I'd be the one deceived.

AMINTA.   Then swear before me
To carry out your promised word.

DON JUAN.   I swear
By this white hand, a winter of pure snow.

AMINTA. Swear then, to God. Pray that he curse your soul
If you should fail!

DON JUAN.   If in my word and faith
I fail, I pray to God that by foul treason
I be murdered by a man!
Aside.
                        I mean a dead one,
For living man, may God forbid!

AMINTA.   This promise
Has made me your own wife.

DON JUAN.   My very soul
I offer you between my outstretched arms.

AMINTA. My life and soul are yours.

DON JUAN.   Ah, my Aminta,
Tomorrow you will walk in silver buskins

Studded with tacks of gold from heel to toe.
Your alabaster throat will be imprisoned
In necklaces of diamonds and rubies,
And your white fingers, in their flashing rings,
Will seem transparent pearls.

AMINTA.   From now to yours
My will bows down, and I am yours alone.

DON JUAN, *aside*. Little you know the Trickster of Seville!

.   .   .

Interior of the church

Enter DON JUAN *and* CATALINÓN.

CATALINÓN. It's very dark for such a great big church.
Oh, sir, protect me, someone grabbed my cloak!

DON GONZALO *comes in as before in the form of a statue.*

DON JUAN. Who's that?

DON GONZALO.   It is I.

CATALINÓN.   I am dead with fright!

DON GONZALO. I am the Dead Man: do not be afraid.
I did not think that you would keep your word
Since you delight in breaking it so often —

DON JUAN. I suppose that you imagine me a coward!

DON GONZALO. Why, yes! Because, that night, you fled from me
When you killed me.

DON JUAN.   I fled from recognition.
But here I stand before you. What's your will?

DON GONZALO. Why, only to invite you here to supper.

CATALINÓN. Pray let us be excused. Here all the victuals
They serve are cold — cold supper and cold lunches.

DON JUAN. We'll sup then.

DON GONZALO.   Well, to do so, you must lift
The lid, here, off this tomb.

DON JUAN.   Why, if you wish it
I'll lift these pillars too!

DON GONZALO.   You're very willing.

DON JUAN, *lifting by one end the lid of the tomb which folds back easily, leaving discovered a black table already laid and set.*

DON JUAN. Yes, I have strength and courage in my body. . . .
                You! Sit down!

CATALINÓN. What, me, sir? I've already fed this evening.

DON JUAN. Don't answer back!

CATALINÓN.   All right, I will not answer.
    Aside.
    O God, in safety get me out of this!
    They sing within.
        Let all those know who judge God's ways
        And treat his punishments with scorn
        There is no debt but that he pays,
        No date but it is bound to dawn.

CATALINÓN. How terrible! I've heard this tune before
    And now it is addressed to me.

DON JUAN, *aside.*   My breast
    Is frozen, and the ice tears me apart.
    They sing.
        While in the world one's flesh is lusting
        It is most wrong for men to say:
        "A long long time in me you're trusting"
        For very shortly dawns the day.

DON JUAN. Now I have eaten, let them clear the table.

DON GONZALO. Give me your hand. Don't be afraid! Your hand.

DON JUAN. Afraid, you say. *Me* frightened? Here's my hand.
    He gives it.
    I'm roasting, burning! Do not burn me so
    With your fierce fire!

DON GONZALO.   That's nothing to the fire
    Which you have sought yourself! The wondrous ways
    Of God, Don Juan, are not fathomable.
    And so He wishes now for you to pay

Your forfeits straight into the hands of death.
This is God's justice. What you've done, you pay for.

DON JUAN. I'm roasting. Do not grip my hand so hard!
I'll kill you with this dagger. But the blows
Strike only empty air. Look. With your daughter
I did no harm. She saw the hoax in time.

DON GONZALO. That does not matter. It was your intention.

DON JUAN. Then let me send for a confessor quickly,
So to absolve my soul before I die.

DON GONZALO. Impossible. You've thought of it too late.

DON JUAN. Oh, I am burning! Oh, I am roasting, burning!
I'm dying!
He falls dead.

(Tirso de Molina: *The Trickster of Seville,* 1630)

3
Literary Affectation

Along with heroism, the first half of the seventeenth century is dominated by affectation in literary style and manners. This had come about as a reaction to the rudeness of behavior that had been caused by prolonged religious wars. Although different in its manifestations from country to country, common tendencies can nonetheless be observed in Italy, England, France and Spain. The names given to these movements are usually derived from representative poets: Marinism in Italy, from Giambattista Marino (1569–1625); Gongorism in Spain, from Luis de Góngora (1561–1627); Euphuism in England, from John Lyly's Euphues (1578), which will serve as our principal illustration. In France this tendency is called "preciousness," and its outstanding representatives are Catherine de Rambouillet (1588–1665), Madeleine de Scudéry (1607–1701), and the poet Vincent Voiture (1598–1648).

The writings of these groups are addressed to small drawing-

room cliques that are anxious to distinguish themselves from the vulgar crowd, and hence meanings are not always clear on first sight. A long pastoral novel may describe well-known personages under the guise of shepherds and shepherdesses; a madrigal may hide a declaration of love to a lady whom one cannot address by her proper name; an object that may shock the overrefined senses of the ladies may be referred to by a far-fetched paraphrase. Thus, in France, "chair" became "the accommodation of conversation"; "shirt" was turned into "the eternal companion of the living and the dead"; or, more quaintly poetical, the eyes were renamed "the mirrors of the soul"; while music was raised to "the paradise of the ears."

This literature, then, tries to amuse rather than instruct, to surprise rather than analyze. It is not character depiction or deep philosophy that we must look for; but rather we must admire, even if it may be at times pushed to extremes, the ingenuity of the author, the way he arrives at an unexpected conceit, or the way he plays with antithesis or metaphor.

However much later generations may have ridiculed the excesses of these movements, their influence has remained a permanent one. We can still see it today in the exaggerated social courtesies in the countries that were affected by mannerism; and it is no less obvious in the devaluation of language that, in order to sound sincere, forces us to say that somebody is "madly" in love or that a play is "frightfully" interesting.

A. THE CONVERSATION OF WITTY PEOPLE

John Lyly (1553–1606) illustrates the kind of wit that was fashionable in certain circles of English court society in the late sixteenth and early seventeenth centuries. In the following excerpt Philautus, invited to supper by his beloved Lucilla, unexpectedly brings along his friend Euphues. In the text the spelling has been modernized, but otherwise a minimum of editing has been done.

It happened that Don Ferardo had occasion to go to Venice about certain of his own affairs, leaving his daughter the only stewart of his household, who spared not to feast Philautus her friend, with all kinds of delights and delicacies, reserving only her honesty as the chief stay of her honour.

Her father being gone, she sent for her friend to supper, who came not as he was accustomed solitarily alone, but accompanied with his friend Euphues. The Gentlewomen, whether it were for niceness or for niggardliness of courtesy, gave him such a cold welcome that he repented that he had come.

Euphues, though he knew himself worthy every way to have a good countenance, yet could he not perceive her willing any way to lend him a friendly look. At the last, supper being ready to come in, Philautus said unto her: "Gentlewomen, I was the bolder to bring my shadow with me (meaning Euphues) knowing that he should be the better welcome for my sake"; unto whom the gentlewoman replied: "Sir, as I never when I saw you thought that you came without your shadow, so now I cannot a little marvel to see you so overshot in bringing a new shadow with you." Euphues, though he perceived her coy nip, seemed not to care for it, but taking her hand said:

"Fair Lady, seeing the shade does often shield your beauty from the parching Sun, I hope you will the better esteem of the shadow, and by so much the less it is able to offend you, and by so much the more you ought to like it, by how much the more you used to lie in it."

"Well, gentleman," answered Lucilla, "in arguing of the shadow, we forgo the substance: please it you therefore to sit down to supper." And so they all sat down, but Euphues fed of one dish which ever stood before him: the beauty of Lucilla.

Here Euphues at first sight was so kindled with desire that almost he was like to burn to coals. Supper being ended, the order was in Naples that the gentlewoman would desire to hear some discourse, either concerning love or learning. And although Philautus was requested, yet he posted it over to Euphues, whom he knew most fit for that purpose. Euphues, being thus tied to the stake by their importunate entreaty, began as follows:

"He that worst may is always forced to hold the candle, the weakest must still to the wall, where none will, the Devil himself must bear the cross. But were it not, gentlewoman, that your desire stands for law, I would borrow so much leave as to resign my office to one of you, whose experience in love has made you learned, and whose learning has made you lovely. For me to entreat of the one, being a novice, or to discourse of the other, being a truant, I may well make you weary but never the wiser, and give you occasion rather to laugh at my rashness than to like my reasons. Yet I care the less to excuse my boldness to you, who were the cause of my blindness. And since I am at my own choice either to talk of love or of learning, I had rather for this time be deemed an unthrift in rejecting profit than a Stoic in renouncing pleasure.

"It has been a question often disputed but never determined, whether the qualities of the mind or the composition of the man cause women most to like, or whether beauty or wit move men most to love. Certainly, by how much the more the mind is to be preferred before the body, by so much the more the graces of the one are to be preferred before the gifts of the other; which, if it be so: that the contemplation of the inward quality ought to be respected more than the view of the outward beauty, then doubtless women either do or should love those best whose virtue is best, not measuring the deformed men with the reformed mind. The foul Toad has a fair stone in his head, the fine gold is found in the filthy earth, the sweet kernel lies in the hard shell. Virtue is harbored in the heart of him that most men esteem misshapen; contrariwise, if we respect more the outward shape than the inward habit, good God, into how many mischiefs do we fall? into what blindness are we led? Do we not commonly see that in painted pots is hidden the deadliest poison? that in the greenest grass is the greatest serpent? in the clearest water the ugliest toad? Does not experience teach us that in the most curious Sepulchre are enclosed rotten bones? that the cypress tree bears a fair leaf but not fruit? that the ostrich carries fair feathers but rank flesh? How frantic are those lovers which are carried away with the gay glistering of the fine face? the beauty whereof is parched with the Summer's blaze and chipped with the Winter's blast, which is of so short continuance that it fades before one perceive it flourish, or so small profit that it poisons those that possess it, of so little value with the wise that they account it a delicate bait with a deadly hook, a sweet Panther with a devouring paunch, a sour poison in a silver pot . . ."

It does not suffice to be handsome. One must also know how to speak well, as illustrated by Euphues who declares his love to Lucilla.

"Gentlewoman, my acquaintance being so little, I am afraid my credit will be less, for that they commonly are soonest believed that are best beloved, and they liked best whom we have known longest. Nevertheless, the noble mind suspects no guile without cause, neither condemns any creature without proof. Having therefore noticed of your heroical heart, I am the better persuaded of my good chance. So it is, Lucilla, that, coming to Naples but to fetch fire, as the byword is, not to make my place of abode, I have found such flames that I can neither quench them with

14. Diego Rodriguez de Silva y Velásquez, *The Duke d'Olivares*,
detail. Photo: Anderson-Giraudon.

15. Abraham Bosse, *Precious Ladies*.

16. Jacques Callot, *Nobility.*

17. Peter Paul Rubens, *Rainbow Landscape.* Photo: Giraudon.

the water of free will nor cool them with wisdom. For . . . as the dry Beech, kindled at the root, never leaves until it comes to the top, or as one drop of poison disperses itself into every vein, so affection having caught hold of my heart and the sparkles of love kindled my liver, will suddenly though secretly flame up into my head and spread itself into every sinew. It is your beauty (pardon my abrupt boldness), Lady, that has taken every part of me prisoner, and brought me to this deep distress. But seeing women, when one praises them for their deserts, deem that he flatters them to obtain his desire, I am here present to yield myself to such trial as your courtesy in this behalf shall require . . ."

(John Lyly: *Euphues, The Anatomy of Wit*, 1578)

B. POETIC MANNERISM

Literary affectation attained its perfection in poetry in which mythological allusions, complicated metaphors, and involved play on words provided the intended obscurity that would limit appreciation of the poem to an intimate group. The difficulties in translation are, of course, considerable; but the samples of poetry below will at least give some idea of this type of literature, which has not disappeared in our times. An intended obscurity, for example, can be found in the poems of Stéphane Mallarmé; and mythological allusions are rather frequent in the poetic works of T. S. Eliot.

O Noble and Most High in Beauty, Thou . . .
Illustre y hermosísima María . . .

O noble and most high in beauty, thou,
María, while every hour there royally grows
Rosial Aurora on thy cheek's pale rose,
And Phoebus breaks through those eyes, the contour of thy brow;

While in insolent lenity Zephyrus' hands
The gold of that glib-hanging hair profanes,
Arabia's avarice hides in her veins,
Or opulent Tagus filters through his sands.

Ere Phoebus shall be all eclipsed by time,
Ere day be lost and night be all thy prime,
To fly that unhued and last dawn, O be bold!

Ere that which burns, precarious rubies now,
Be stifled by the long hands of the snow,
Enjoy, enjoy the gusts of color, light, and gold!

(Luis de Góngora)

Leave-Taking

Already the Sun pulls out his coursers from the waves,
The time has come for us to part and say good-byes.
Lilla, the while, since Love our sweet desire braves,
Let our messages be couched in faithful sighs.
And, as by paths unknown and vast
Alpheus and Arethusa join again at last,
So, while our bodies live thus separate,
Let our thoughts pay visits in their stead.
Often two stars glittering in the firmament,
However differently their course advances,
At last will meet with glad and loving glances;
And if two plants quite separated stand,
Yet underground, if not their branches,
At least their roots go hand in hand.

(Giambattista Marino)

On His Mistress, Encountered in Boy's Clothes One Carnival Evening

One evening, while waiting for my mistress,
Who, two years now, my heart bewitches,
I saw, as if fallen from the skies,
This Narcissus, my unswerving goal;
And, as he appeared before my eyes,
I felt him deep inside my soul.

His face, smiling 'bove naïve attire,
Cast off such a lively fire
And threw so many rays above,
That by the splendor of that light

I almost thought that it was Love
With Venus' eyes full of delight.

A thousand flowers freshly spread,
Lilies, camelias, and roses red,
Covered the snow of his complexion;
But 'neath those flowers in a heap,
The serpent, cause of my distraction,
Lay in ambush ready to leap.

On a brow of ivory white
Two black arcs spring into sight,
Sweetly curved as if by painter put,
Whence this god in war perverse,
Trampling my dear freedom underfoot,
Triumphs over all the universe.

His eyes, of souls the paradise,
Full of laughter, lure, of sunrise,
Turned dark night into bright day:
Stars divine shining high above,
Which exert benevolent sway
O'er the beauteous realm of love.

A grace, above all, he possessed
(In what terms could it be expressed?)
That outshines Love's most luscious luster,
A smile how sweet I cannot say,
An air that others fain would muster,
That one may see but never can portray . . .

(Vincent Voiture)

4

Countertrends

Exaggeration of manners invites reactions. In the case of mannerism these reactions took two principal forms: satire and low-life novels. Just as the overly idealistic Don Quixote is counterbalanced by the overly earthly Sancho Panza, or as the passionate and noble hero of the Spanish comedia is flanked by his lowly servant, so the high-flown but affected literature of the first half of the seventeenth century produced a contrary effect, expressed in novels that emphasized low life and bad manners. Whether the reaction is expressed in Furetière's "burlesque" novel or in Grimmelshausen's picaresque adventure story, it tends to rely on farcical situations.

A. AN ILL-FATED SUITOR

Along with Paul Scarron, Antoine Furetière (1619–1688) was one of the principal writers of bourgeois and low-life novels. Below, Nicomède, the suitor, arrives at the house of his fiancée Javotte. But the latter and her mother have learned that Nicomède has promised marriage to another woman.

Meanwhile Nicomède, who was unaware of what had happened, went to visit Javotte, his true love. Having put on white-ribboned breeches, well-combed and powdered, he arrived in a chair, very gay, twirling his mustache and humming a new tune. In the house he found mother and daughter busy with needle-work to complete the trousseau of his fiancée. A bit surprised by their cold reception, he began the conversation by referring to the work they were engaged in: "I am sure, my dear mother," he said, "that your daughter will be obliged to you, for I do suspect that the linen you are embroidering is meant for her." His mother-in-law to-be replied rather harshly: "Indeed, Sir, it is for her, but as for the rest, you are off the mark. I find you impudent to dare come into this house after the affront you have committed. Look here, my daughter is young and does not lack marriage offers, and we are not the kind of people who go to court over a broken promise of marriage. Go back to your other woman whom you have promised marriage. We would not want her to be dishonored because of us." Nicomède, aghast, swore that he was engaged to nobody except her daughter. "Is that so?" the mother replied. "He might convince us of his innocence, if we did not have definite proof." And calling her servant, she said to her: "Julienne, go and fetch the paper that is on the mantle-piece upstairs, so I can show him up." The servant brought the paper. "Have a look at this," she said, "and see whether I know what I'm talking about." Nicomède gasped upon reading the paper, for he could not image that so proud a person as Lucrèce would go to

19. Antoine Le Nain, *Family Reunion*. Photo: Giraudon.

20. Gabriel Metsu,
*Soldier Receiving a
Young Woman.*
Photo: Giraudon.

21. Francisco Zurbaran, *Kitchen*. Photo: Giraudon.

court in order to get herself a husband. He knew, furthermore, that she had received his promise with laughter and without any hope or design of marriage. The fact that she had not spoken of it since made him conclude that all this had been done without her knowledge. So he said to the mother: "It must be a dirty trick by some enemy of mine. If that is what's worrying you, I'll bring you by tomorrow a notarized order nullifying that legal objection."

"I don't care about notaries or lawyers," the mother said. "I don't want to entrust my daughter to a debauchee who only wants to dishonor virgins. I want her to marry a man who will be a good husband and who will make a good living."

Nicomède, who was not particularly pleased by this conversation and impatient to find out what was really behind this quarrel, decided to take leave shortly after. He was not bold enough to salute his fiancée the way engaged people may. As for Javotte, she merely curtsied silently. But, on rising, she dropped a ball of thread and the scissors that she had held on her skirt. Nicomède bounded to her feet to pick them up. Javotte, however, bent down to beat him to it. But as both straightened up at the same time, their heads met with such violence that each received a bump. Nicomède, desperate about this mishap, wanted to leave promptly, but he did not watch out for an uneven buffet into which he bumped so heavily that he broke a porcelain plate, a unique treasure held in great esteem in the house. Thereupon the mother began to swear at him. He excused himself profusely and started to pick up the pieces so that he could replace the plate. But walking rapidly with his new shoes on a floor especially waxed for the engagement, he slipped. And since, in these circumstances, one tries to hold on to the first thing, he grabbed the ends of the cords with which the mirror was fastened. The weight of his body broke them and both the mirror and Nicomède came crashing down together. Still, the more seriously injured was the mirror which broke into a thousand pieces. Nicomède suffered no more than two light bruises. The mother, screaming ever more loudly, said to him: "What ill fate has sent me this house-destroyer, this bull in a china shop?" And she picked up a broom to chase him out. Nicomède, filled with shame, ran to the door which, in his anger, he opened with such force that it struck a lute that a neighbor had left leaning against the wall and which was completely smashed. Fortunately for him it was dark already, for, in daylight, what with the hullabaloo the mother was making, he would have been followed by all the children in the street. So he went off red both with shame and anger.

(Antoine Furetière: *The Bourgeois Novel,* 1666)

B. A DISGUISE THAT CAUSED SOME CONFUSION AND MUCH TROUBLE

Grimmelshausen's young hero Simplicissimus runs into trouble when, during the Thirty Years' War, he exchanges his fool's outfit for a woman's dress.

One day, when we were coming into a large village, I stole away to see if perhaps I could exchange my fool's outfit for a peasant suit. But unable to find what I was looking for, I had to be content with a woman's dress. I put it on and threw away my old outfit thinking that this would be the end of all my troubles. Thus dressed I crossed the street and walked with small steps toward some officers' wives. But no sooner had I come out into the open when several soldiers saw me and taught me to jump fast. For when they shouted: "Stop, stop!" I ran the faster and got to the officers' wives before they did. I fell to my knees before the women and begged them, in the name of all women's honor and virtue, to protect my innocence against these wicked men. Not only was my request granted but a captain's wife took me on as a maid.

The captain's wife, although young, was no longer a child and took such a fancy to my smooth face and straight body that finally, after many efforts and veiled allusions, she made me understand only too clearly where the shoe hurt her most. At that time I was still too innocent, pretended that I had noticed nothing and behaved as a God-fearing virgin should.

The captain and his valet were both sick in the hospital; so the former ordered his wife to get better clothes for me, so that she would not have to be ashamed of my peasant dress. She went further than that. She dressed me up like a French doll, which increased the passion in all of them. It reached such proportions that both master and valet eagerly desired of me what I could not grant them and what I courteously refused to his wife. Finally the captain began to seek an opportunity to obtain from me by force what he could not obtain in any manner. But his wife noticed his designs and, since she had not given up all hope to overcome my resistance, she blocked all his paths, so that he nearly lost his mind.

One night, when husband and wife were asleep, the valet appeared before the wagon in which I had to sleep, protested his love with warm tears and begged me insistently to be merciful. But I showed myself harder than stone and made it clear to him that I intended to keep my virginity until marriage. But, when he offered to marry me a thousand times and I replied only that it was impossible for me to marry him, he finally fell into despair or at least he pretended. So he pulled out his sword, placed the end against his chest and seemed to prepare to kill himself. I thought: "The devil is full of tricks," and consoled him saying I would give him a definite answer in the morning. This calmed him and he went to bed. But I stayed awake a long time thinking about my strange situation.

I considered that not much good could come of all this, for the wife was getting increasingly importunate with her teasing, the captain bolder in his allusions, and the valet more desperate in his faithful love. My mistress ordered me frequently, in full daylight, to rid her of her fleas, merely so I could see her snow-white breasts and touch her entire body. Being made of flesh and blood, this caused me no small distress. When the wife left me in peace, the captain started to bother me and, at night when both left me alone, the valet would annoy me. As a result, the woman's dress turned out to be more trouble than my old fool's outfit had been, for the dress kept me imprisoned, since I could not run away in it; and the captain would have made me rue the day he found out what I really was and that I was ridding his wife of fleas. What was I to do? I decided to tell the valet the truth at daybreak thinking: "His passion will subside, and if you give him some of your money, he will get you a man's suit and that will be the end of your troubles." It might have turned out that way if fate had been on my side; but it was not.

At midnight, just when I was fast asleep, up comes the valet and knocks at the wagon, calling somewhat too loudly: "Sabina, Sabina, my treasure, get up and keep your promise!" which woke up the captain whose tent was right next to the wagon. The captain, who turned green with jealousy, did not come out but only got up in order to see what would happen. Finally the valet's urgings woke me up and forced me either to leave the wagon or to let him come in with me. But I scolded him and asked him whether he thought I was a whore and added that my promise yesterday referred only to marriage and that he could not have me any other way. He replied I should get up because it was getting light and I would have to prepare breakfast. . . .

When I stepped out of the wagon with my sleeves rolled up, my white arms inflamed the valet so much that he could not resist trying to kiss me, and as I was not putting up any special resistance, the captain could stand it no longer and jumped out of his tent with drawn sword. My suitor preferred to take to his heels, and the captain said to me: "You filthy whore, I'll teach you . . ." His voice choked, so he began beating me as if he had lost his senses. I started to scream which forced him to stop for fear that the alarm might be sounded, for the Saxon and the Imperial armies were camping close together, because the Swedes were approaching.

When it had become light, the captain turned me over to the stable-boys, just as the two armies were breaking camp. These boys were a band of scoundrels and hence I was frightened to death at what awaited me. They dragged me toward some bushes to satisfy their beastly desires, as these little devils are wont to do when a woman is given into their power. They were followed by a number of servants who wanted to watch the fun; among these was the valet. He did not take his eyes off me, and when he saw that I was in serious trouble, he attempted to save me by force, even if he were to lose his life in the process. He received support from some of the bystanders who felt pity for him and me, because he said that I was his promised bride. But this angered the stable-boys who thought they had a better right over me and who did not wish to give up such a good prey; so they decided to answer force with force. The two parties soon came to blows and, as the fight continued, the crowd and the noise increased. It all resembled a knightly tournament in which everybody does his best in order to please a beautiful lady. The tumult finally attracted the captain of the guards who arrived on the scene just at the moment when my clothes had been torn off my body, revealing that I was not a woman. His presence imposed an immediate silence, for he was more feared than the devil himself. All those who had been involved in the fighting scampered off hastily. In a few words he informed himself of what had happened, but contrary to my hope that he would save me, he ordered me to be taken prisoner, because he found it unusual and almost suspicious that a man in woman's clothing should be found among soldiers.

(Grimmelshausen: *Der abenteuerliche Simplicissimus,*
Book II, Chaps. 25, 26; 1659)

III

The Rational Revolution

Periodically, throughout the history of mankind, old (and what had seemed permanent) notions, values, and explanations have been questioned by a new generation. Such a period was the seventeenth century, when the most vital and thorough reappraisal of medieval philosophy ushered in the modern era.

When reading the philosophical works of the century, one is struck by the insistent and urgent demand for certainty. What is truth? What is reality? What is the universe "really" like? These are not new questions, but the answer expected is different.

It is important to remember that the seventeenth century was not only the age of reason but also of science. Due to the important progress achieved in the fields of mathematics, geometry, astronomy, and physics, a new, measurable certainty had been discovered. Why could this same type of explanation, of proof not be applied to philosophy? This is the challenge the new generation hurls at then accepted authorities (Aristotle and scholasticism, in particular) and it finds that they cannot pass the test.

Everything, it seems to the new rationalists, needs to be redefined; an orderly process of cleaning up will be necessary before they will be able to rebuild philosophy on a new basis. Hence it must be ascertained into which fields human thought may legitimately inquire, which avenues of approach promise results, and how demonstrable certainty can be attained.

The new school, as can be seen, is mathematically and scientifically oriented. It exposes methods that are based on reason, that will open up new fields of inquiry, permit new experiments, and lead to new discoveries. The seventeenth-century philosophers may strongly differ on any given question, but they hold in common a belief in the universality of human reason and a respect for the "scientific" approach to solving problems. Their methods and ideas were perhaps not entirely new, but their influence in shaping modern thought is enormous. The excitement of explorers in discovering new lands can have been no greater than that of the new philosophers as they were striking out on new paths.

1
The Attack on Past Authority

Medieval philosophy was dominated by scholasticism, the philosophy practiced by clerics. Even though they often engaged in violent disputes, they shared a common basis and a common method. The basis was the attempt to explain philosophical problems and physical phenomena in terms consistent with an authoritative source of knowledge: the Scriptures; their method was the syllogism, of which more later. The principal concern of the scholastics (or the schoolmen, as they are often called) was not to investigate how things work; it was rather metaphysical in nature: the inquiry into cause and end, essence and being. Hence this philosophical approach was not very profitable to scientific investigation or to new discoveries.

The greatest of the scholastics was St. Thomas Aquinas (1225–1274) who created the synthesis of Aristotle's metaphysics and Christian revelation in his monumental works Summa contra Gentiles *and* Summa theologica.

Very briefly, St. Thomas teaches that God created and sustains the world by eternal laws. To everything created he has given a "nature" or "form" which determines not only what it is but also what it strives to become. Heavy bodies tend to move downward, light ones upward. God has endowed man with reason and free will. He is therefore subject to error, but St. Thomas insists that if man exercises his reason properly, he is able to understand the existence of God and finally to arrive at faith.

The attack against scholasticism is, of course, not a dispassionate one and we must therefore not expect to get a fair appraisal of that philosophy below.

Convinced that scholasticism was stifling fresh inquiry, the seventeenth-century philosophers directed their attack prima-

rily against its explanation of physical laws and against its method of reasoning.

The works already known are due to chance and experiment rather than to science; for the sciences we now possess are merely systems for the nice ordering and setting forth of things already invented; not methods of invention or directions for new works.

As the sciences which we now have do not help us in finding out new works, so neither does the logic which we now have help us in finding out new sciences.

It is idle to expect any great advancement in science from the super-inducing and engrafting of new things upon old. We must begin anew from the very foundations, unless we would revolve for ever in a circle with mean and contemptible progress.

In times no less than in regions there are wastes and deserts. For only three revolutions and periods of learning can properly be reckoned; one among the Greeks, the second among the Romans, and the last among us, that is to say, the nations of Western Europe; and to each of these hardly two centuries can justly be assigned. The intervening ages of the world, in respect of any rich or flourishing growth of the sciences, were un-prosperous. For neither the Arabians nor the Schoolmen need be mentioned; who in the intermediate times rather crushed the sciences with a multitude of treatises, than increased their weight. And therefore the first cause of so meagre a progress in the sciences is duly and orderly referred to the narrow limits of the time that has been favourable to them.

And an astonishing thing it is to one who rightly considers the matter, that no mortal should have seriously applied himself to the opening and laying out of a road for the human understanding direct from the sense, by a course of experiment orderly conducted and well built up; but that all has been left either to the mist of tradition, or the whirl and eddy of argument, or the fluctuations and mazes of chance and of vague and ill-digested experience.

The logic now in use serves rather to fix and give stability to the errors which have their foundation in commonly received notions than to help the search after truth. So it does more harm than good.

The syllogism consists of propositions, propositions consist of words, words are symbols of notions. Therefore if the notions themselves (which is the root of the matter) are confused and over-hastily abstracted from

22. Rembrandt van Ryn, *Mayor Six Reading*. Photo: Giraudon.

the facts, there can be no firmness in the superstructure. Our only hope therefore lies in a true induction.

The axioms now in use, having been suggested by a scanty and manipular experience, are made for the most part just large enough to fit and take these in: and therefore it is no wonder if they do not lead to new particulars. And if some opposite instance, not observed or not known before, chance to come in the way, the axiom is rescued and preserved by some frivolous distinction; whereas the truer course would be to correct the axiom itself.

(Francis Bacon: *Novum Organum,* the first book of aphorisms; 1620)

2

Truth, Certainty and Reason

If wild speculation and meaningless terms are to be avoided, one has to resort to careful definitions, to strictly controlled chains of reasoning. Thus truth and certainty can best be found in mathematics and geometry. But can these methods be applied to human affairs, to moral problems, to philosophical disputes? After destroying the prestige of Aristotle and scholasticism, the new philosophers, in their turn, have to assume the burden of proof.

Philosophy is written in that vast book which stands forever open before our eyes, I mean the universe; but it cannot be read until we have learned the language and become familiar with the characters in which it is written. It is written in mathematical language, and the letters are triangles, circles and other geometrical figures, without which means it is humanly impossible to understand a single word.

(Galileo Galilei: *Il Saggiatore*, Question 6; 1624)

It is manifest that if we could find characters or signs appropriate to the expression of all thoughts as definitely and as exactly as numbers are expressed by arithmetic or lines by geometrical analysis, we could in all subjects, in so far as they are amenable to reasoning, accomplish what is done in Arithmetic and Geometry.

All inquiries which depend on reasoning would be performed by the transposition of characters and by a kind of calculus which would directly assist the discovery of elegant results. We should not have to puzzle our heads as much as we have to-day, and yet we should be sure of accomplishing everything the given facts allowed.

Moreover, we should be able to convince the world of what we had discovered or inferred, since it would be easy to verify the calculation

88

either by doing it again or by trying tests similar to that of casting out nines in arithmetic. And if someone doubted my results, I should say to him "Let us calculate, Sir," and so by taking pen and ink we should soon settle the question.

(Gottfried Wilhelm von Leibnitz: *On Method,*
Preface to the General Science; 1677)

Reason is not the exclusive tool employed by the rationalists, but it is the principal one. With the problem this caused in religious questions we shall deal later. The use of reason was, of course, nothing new in philosophy; what is new is the zest with which reason is praised and applied, and the conviction that the proper use of reason will not only solve most problems but lead man to happiness.

Baruch Spinoza (1632–1677) was born in Amsterdam of a prosperous Jewish family. Educated in a Jewish school, he became increasingly interested in philosophy. His reputation as a freethinker led to his exclusion from the Jewish community in 1656. He earned his living by polishing lenses, published very little, and kept up an enormous correspondence with numerous philosophers. His major philosophical works were not published until after his death.

PROP. XXVI. Whatever we endeavour to do under the guidance of reason is nothing else than to understand; nor does the mind, in so far as it uses reason, judge anything useful to itself save what is conducive to understanding.

Proof. — The endeavour to preserve oneself is nothing else than the essence of the thing which, in so far as it exists as such, is conceived to have force for persisting in existing, and for doing those things which necessarily follow from its given nature. But the essence of reason is nothing else than the mind itself in so far as it understands clearly and distinctly. Therefore, whatever we endeavour to do under the guidance of reason is nothing else than to understand. Again, as this endeavour of the mind, whereby, in so far as it reasons, it tries to preserve its own being, is nothing other than to understand (first part of this Prop.), therefore this endeavour to understand is the first and only basis of virtue. Nor do we endeavour to understand for the sake of any end, but, on the contrary, the mind, in so far as it reasons, cannot conceive anything as good to itself save what is conducive to understanding.

PROP. XXXV. In so far as men live under the guidance of reason, thus far only they always necessarily agree in nature.

Proof. — In so far as men are assailed by emotions which are passions they can be different in nature and contrary one to the other. But men are said to be active only in so far as they live under the guidance of reason, and therefore whatever follows from human nature, in so far as it is defined by reason, must be understood through human nature alone as its proximate cause. But inasmuch as each one desires according to the laws of his own nature what is good, and endeavours to remove what he thinks to be bad, and inasmuch as that which we judge to be good or bad, according to the dictate of reason, is necessarily good or bad, therefore men, in so far as they live according to the dictates of reason, do those things which are necessarily good to human nature, and consequently to each man, that is, which agree with the nature of each man. And therefore men also necessarily agree one with the other in so far as they live according to the mandate of reason. *Q.e.d.*

Corollary I. — There is no individual thing in nature more useful to man than one who lives under the guidance of reason. For that is most useful to man which mostly agrees with his nature, that is (as is self-evident), man. But man is absolutely active according to the laws of his nature when he lives under the guidance of reason, and thus far only can he agree necessarily with the nature of another man. Therefore there is nothing more useful to man than a man, etc. *Q.e.d.*

Corollary II. — As each man seeks that most which is useful to him, so men are most useful one to the other. For the more each man seeks what is useful to him and endeavours to preserve himself, the more he is endowed with virtue, or, what is the same thing, the more power he is endowed with to act according to the laws of his nature, that is, to live under the guidance of reason. But men agree most in nature when they live under the guidance of reason. Therefore men are most useful one to the other when each one most seeks out what is useful to himself. *Q.e.d.*

Note. — What we have just shown is borne witness to by experience daily with such convincing examples that it has become a proverb: Man is a God to man. Yet it rarely happens that men live according to the instructions of reason, but among them things are in such a state that they are usually envious of or a nuisance to each other. But nevertheless they are scarcely able to lead a solitary life, so that to many the definition that man is a social animal must be very apparent; and in truth things are so ordered that from the common society of men far more conveniences arise than the contrary. Let satirists therefore laugh to their hearts' content at human affairs, let theologians revile them, and let the melancholy praise as much as they can the rude and barbarous isolated life: let them despise men and admire the brutes — despite all this, men will find that they can prepare with mutual aid far more easily what they need, and avoid far more easily the perils which beset them on all sides, by united forces: to say nothing of how much better it is, and more worthy of our knowledge, to regard the deeds of men rather than those of brutes.

PROP. LXV. Under the guidance of reason we follow the greater of two things which are good and the lesser of two things which are evil.

Proof. — A good thing which prevents us from enjoying a greater good is in truth an evil, for good and bad is said of things in so far as we compare them one with the other, and (for the same reason) a lesser evil is in truth a good. Wherefore under the guidance of reason we desire or follow only the greater of two things which are good and the lesser of two which are evil. *Q.e.d.*

Corollary. — We may follow under the guidance of reason the lesser evil as if it were the greater good, and neglect the lesser good as the cause of a greater evil. For the evil which is here called lesser is in truth good, and, on the other hand, the good is evil. Wherefore we desire the former and avoid the latter. *Q.e.d.*

PROP. LXXIII. A man who is guided by reason is more free in a state where he lives according to common law than in solitude where he is subject to no law.

Proof. — A man who is guided by reason is not held in subjection by fear, but in so far as he endeavours to preserve his being according to the dictates of reason, that is, in so far as he endeavours to live freely, he desires to have regard for common life and advantage, and consequently he desires to live according to the ordinary decrees of the state. Therefore a man guided by reason desires, so as to live with more freedom, to regard the ordinary laws of the state. *Q.e.d.*

Note. — These and such things which we have shown of the true freedom of man have reference to fortitude, that is, to courage and nobility. Nor do I think it worth while to show here separately all the properties of fortitude, and far less that a strong man hates no one, is enraged with no one, envies no one, is indignant with no one, despises no one, and is in no wise proud. For . . . hatred should be overcome by love, and every one led by reason desires for his fellows the good he desires for himself. To which must be added what we noted in the Note of Prop. 50, Part IV., and in other places, namely, that a strong man considers this above all things, that everything follows from the necessity of divine nature; and accordingly, whatever he thinks to be a nuisance or evil, and whatever, moreover, seems to him impious, horrible, unjust, or disgraceful, arises from the fact that he conceives these things in a disturbed, mutilated, and confused manner: and on this account he endeavours to conceive things as they are in themselves, and to remove obstacles from true knowledge, as, for example, hatred, rage, envy, derision, pride, and the other emotions of this kind which we have noted in the previous propositions: and therefore he endeavours as much as he can, as we said, to act well and rejoice. How far human virtue lends itself to the attainment of this, and what it is capable of, I shall show in the next part.

Appendix

What I have said in this part concerning the right manner of life is not so arranged that it can be seen at one glance, but has been proved by me in parts, for then I could easily prove one from another. I have determined, therefore, to collect the parts here and reduce them to their principal headings.

I. All our endeavours or desires follow from the necessity of our nature in such a manner that they can be understood either through this alone, as through their proximate cause, or in so far as we are a part of nature which cannot be adequately conceived through itself without other individuals.

II. Desires which follow from our nature in such a way that they can be understood through it alone are those which have reference to the mind in so far as this is conceived to consist of adequate ideas; the remaining desires have no reference to the mind save in so far as it conceives things inadequately, and their force and increase are not defined by human power, but by power which is outside us. Therefore the first are called actions, while the second, passions. For the former always indicate our power, and the latter, on the contrary, indicate our want of power and our mutilated knowledge.

III. Our actions, that is, those desires which are defined by the power or reason of man, are always good: the others can be both good and bad.

IV. It is therefore extremely useful in life to perfect as much as we can the intellect or reason, and of this alone does the happiness or blessedness of man consist: for blessedness (*beatitudo*) is nothing else than satisfaction of mind which arises from the intuitive knowledge of God. But to perfect the intellect is nothing else than to understand God and his attributes and actions which follow from the necessity of his nature. Wherefore the ultimate aim of a man who is guided by reason, that is, his greatest desire by which he endeavours to moderate all the others, is that which brings him to conceive adequately himself and all things which can come within the scope of his intelligence.

V. Accordingly no rational life is without intelligence, and things are only good in so far as they help man to enjoy intellectual life, which is defined intelligence (*intelligentia*). But those things which prevent a man from perfecting his reason and enjoying a rational life — these things, I say, alone we call evil.

(Baruch Spinoza: *Ethics,* Part IV; 1677)

3
The Methods of Reason

A. BACON: THE INDUCTIVE METHOD

Francis Bacon (1561–1626), whose family had connections with both court and governmental circles, studied law at Gray's Inn. He did not succeed fully until the accession of James I, but then his career was brilliant. Knighted in 1603, be became attorney general in 1613 and lord chancellor in 1618; he was given the title of Viscount St. Albans in 1621. After that he lost favor, was accused of having taken bribes and was imprisoned for a short time. He retired to the country for the rest of his life. Although in many ways exposing sixteenth-century views, Bacon was among the first to reveal the weaknesses of the syllogistic method. His writings were widely read and he pointed out one method by which science could advance in his time.

There are and can be only two ways of searching into and discovering truth. The one flies from the senses and particulars to the most general axioms, and from these principles, the truth of which it takes for settled and immovable, proceeds to judgment and to the discovery of middle axioms. And this way is now in fashion. The other derives axioms from the senses and particulars, rising by a gradual and unbroken ascent, so that it arrives at the most general axioms last of all. This is the true way, but as yet untried.

Both ways set out from the senses and particulars, and rest in the highest generalities; but the difference between them is infinite. For the one just glances at experiment and particulars in passing, the other dwells duly and orderly among them. The one, again, begins at once by establishing certain abstract and useless generalities, the other rises by gradual steps to that which is prior and better known in the order of nature.

It cannot be that axioms established by argumentation should avail for the discovery of new works; since the subtlety of nature is greater many times over than the subtlety of argument. But axioms duly and orderly formed from particulars easily discover the way to new particulars, and thus render sciences active.

One method of delivery alone remains to us; which is simply this: We must lead men to the particulars themselves, and their series and order; while men on their side must force themselves for awhile to lay their notions by and begin to familiarise themselves with facts.

The human understanding when it has once adopted an opinion (either as being the received opinion or as being agreeable to itself) draws all things else to support and agree with it. And though there be a greater number and weight of instances to be found on the other side, yet these it either neglects and despises, or else by some distinction sets aside and rejects; in order that by this great and pernicious predetermination the authority of its former conclusions may remain inviolate. And therefore it was a good answer that was made by one who when they showed him hanging in a temple a picture of those who had paid their vows as having escaped shipwreck, and would have him say whether he did not now acknowledge the power of the gods,—"Aye," asked he again, "but where are they painted that were drowned, after their vows?" And such is the way of all superstition, whether in astrology, dreams, omens, divine judgments, or the like; wherein men, having a delight in such vanities, mark the events where they are fulfilled, but where they fail, though this happen much oftener, neglect and pass them by. But with far more subtlety does this mischief insinuate itself into philosophy and the sciences; in which the first conclusion colours and brings into conformity with itself all that come after, though far sounder and better. Besides, independently of that delight and vanity which I have described, it is the peculiar and perpetual error of human intellect to be more moved and excited by affirmatives than by negatives; whereas it ought properly to hold itself indifferently disposed towards both alike. Indeed in the establishment of any true axiom, the negative instance is the more forcible of the two.

But not only is a greater abundance of experiments to be sought for and procured, and that too of a different kind from those hitherto tried; an entirely different method, order, and process for carrying on and advancing experience must also be introduced. For experience, when it wanders in its own track, is, as I have already remarked, mere groping in the dark, and confounds men rather than instructs them. But when it shall proceed in accordance with a fixed law, in regular order, and without interruption, then may better things be hoped of knowledge.

The understanding must not however be allowed to jump and fly from particulars to remote axioms and of almost the highest generality (such as the first principles, as they are called, of arts and things), and taking stand upon them as truths that cannot be shaken, proceed to prove and frame the middle axioms by reference to them; which has been the practice hitherto; the understanding being not only carried that way by a natural impulse, but also by the use of syllogistic demonstration trained and inured to it. But then, and then only, may we hope well of the sciences, when in a just scale of ascent, and by successive steps not interrupted or broken, we rise from particulars to lesser axioms; and then to middle axioms, one above the other; and last of all to the most general. For the lowest axioms differ but slightly from bare experience, while the highest and most general (which we now have) are notional and abstract and without solidity. But the middle are the true and solid and living axioms, on which depend the affairs and fortunes of men; and above them again, last of all, those which are indeed the most general; such I mean as are not abstract, but of which those intermediate axioms are really limitations.

The understanding must not therefore be supplied with wings, but rather hung with weights, to keep it from leaping and flying. Now this has never been done; when it is done, we may entertain better hopes of the sciences.

In establishing axioms, another form of induction must be devised than has hitherto been employed; and it must be used for proving and discovering not first principles (as they are called) only, but also the lesser axioms, and the middle, and indeed all. For the induction which proceeds by simple enumeration is childish; its conclusions are precarious, and exposed to peril from a contradictory instance; and it generally decides on too small a number of facts, and on those only which are at hand. But the induction which is to be available for the discovery and demonstration of sciences and arts, must analyse nature by proper rejections and exclusions; and then, after a sufficient number of negatives, come to a conclusion on the affirmative instances; which has not yet been done or even attempted, save only by Plato, who does indeed employ this form of induction to a certain extent for the purpose of discussing definitions and ideas. But in order to furnish this induction or demonstration well and duly for its work, very many things are to be provided which no mortal has yet thought of: insomuch that greater labour will have to be spent in it than has hitherto been spent on the syllogism. And this induction must be used not only to discover axioms, but also in the formation of notions. And it is in this induction that our chief hope lies.

But in establishing axioms by this kind of induction, we must also examine and try whether the axiom so established be framed to the measure of those particulars only from which it is derived, or whether it be larger and wider. And if it be larger and wider, we must observe whether by indicating to us new particulars it confirm that wideness and largeness as by a collateral security; that we may not either stick fast in things already known, or loosely grasp at shadows and abstract forms; not at things solid and realised in matter. And when the process shall have come into use, then at last shall we see the dawn of a solid hope.

(Francis Bacon: *Novum Organum,* first book of aphorisms; 1620)

B.   DESCARTES: THE DEDUCTIVE METHOD

René Descartes (1596–1650) has had a more lasting influence on modern thought than any of his contemporaries. He was educated in a Jesuit school at La Flèche and studied law at Poitiers. In order to educate himself further by traveling he joined a force under Maurice of Nassau as a soldier of fortune during the Thirty Years' War. Fascinated by mathematics, he invented the co-ordinates of analytical geometry which are named after him. In 1619, he had two visions during which, in a dream, his entire philosophy was revealed to him. In 1637, he decided to settle in Holland in order to study and write. Upon the invitation of Queen Christina of Sweden, Descartes went to Stockholm in 1649; there he died the next year of pneumonia.

Descartes stands at the beginning of modern philosophy. His influence, although greatest during the eighteenth century, was immediate because he wrote his Discourse on Method *not in Latin but in French and in a style that could be read by laymen. Descartes is one of those rare thinkers who show that age-old problems can be attacked in a new and different way. In his* Discourse on Method *we find most of the major ideas of the seventeenth-century rationalists. He refuses to accept any previous authority; although respecting revealed religion, he resolutely directs his inquiries to problems that offer the possibility of being dealt with by human reason and turns what had in many ways been a mysterious universe into one that is governed by rational laws and hence permits scientific optimism. As for the question of our existence, Descartes finds a simple solution in his affirmation "I think, therefore I am"; finally, he exposes his four-point method which succinctly states an orderly way of dealing with problems.*

It is evident that Descartes was heavily influenced by his mathematical and scientific studies. It is he who first made the revolutionary proposal to apply mathematical principles to the solution of philosophical problems. Of course, Descartes did not solve all problems; in fact, he created some new ones, such as his metaphysical dualism (the division of reality into two distinct substances — body and soul, extension and thought), a problem that we shall consider later.

There remains Descartes the man. We must not be deceived by his conversational tone and apparent humility which, incidentally, is contradicted by his statements at the end of the Discourse on Method. *The philosophy Descartes proposes is revolutionary, at least in its implications. The reference to tearing down the old house in order to rebuild it is probably more than a convenient illustration. If methodical doubt, if rules of reason and evidence are to prevail, these will inevitably sooner or later be applied to judge existing institutions and religious beliefs.*

Was Descartes aware of these implications? Or did he believe he was merely cleaning away the useless aspects of scholasticism while keeping intact the essential fabric of the faith? On the one hand, Descartes bases his idea of certainty on the existence of God; he also maintained excellent relations with members of various religious orders. On the other hand, he was a cautious man who did not wish to be disturbed in his research by

*civil or religious persecution; moreover, it has been argued that
his system does not necessarily require his proof of the existence
of God (which can be found in the next section). We do not
possess enough evidence to supply answers to these questions;
however, subsequent history leaves no doubt about the profound effects of the* Discourse on Method, *one of the great
monuments in philosophy.*

Good sense is mankind's most equitably divided endowment, for everyone
thinks that he is so abundantly provided with it that even those most difficult to please in other ways do not usually want more than they have of
this. As it is not likely that everyone is mistaken, this evidence shows that
the ability to judge correctly, and to distinguish the true from the false —
which is really what is meant by good sense or reason — is the same by
nature in all men; and that differences of opinion are not due to differences in intelligence, but merely to the fact that we use different ap-
proaches and consider different things. For it is not enough to have a good
mind: one must use it well. The greatest souls are capable of the greatest
vices as well as of the greatest virtues; and those who walk slowly can, if
they follow the right path, go much farther than those who run rapidly in
the wrong direction.

As for myself, I have never supposed that my mind was above the ordinary. On the contrary, I have often wished to have as quick a wit or as
clear and distinct an imagination, or as ready and retentive a memory, as
another person. And I know of no other qualities which make for a good
mind, because as far as reason is concerned, it is the only thing which
makes us men and distinguishes us from the animals, and I am therefore
satisfied that it is fully present in each one of us. In this I follow the general opinion of philosophers, who say that there are differences in degree
only in the *accidental* qualities, and not in the *essential* qualities or natures of individuals of the same species.

.   .   .

I was especially pleased with mathematics, because of the certainty and
self-evidence of its proofs; but I did not yet see its true usefulness and,
thinking that it was good only for the mechanical arts, I was astonished
that nothing more noble had been built on so firm and solid a foundation.
On the other hand, I compared the ethical writings of the ancient pagans
to very superb and magnificent palaces built only on mud and sand: they
laud the virtues and make them appear more desirable than anything else

in the world; but they give no adequate criterion of virtue, and often what they call by such a name is nothing but apathy, parricide, pride or despair.

I revered our theology, and hoped as much as anyone else to get to heaven, but having learned on great authority that the road was just as open to the most ignorant as to the most learned, and that the truths of revelation which lead thereto are beyond our understanding, I would not have dared to submit them to the weakness of my reasonings. I thought that to succeed in their examination it would be necessary to have some extraordinary assistance from heaven, and to be more than a man.

* * *

It is true that we never tear down all the houses in a city just to rebuild them in a different way and to make the streets more beautiful; but we do see that individual owners often have theirs torn down and rebuilt, and even that they may be forced to do so when the foundation is not firm and it is in danger of collapsing. By this example I was convinced that a private individual should not seek to reform a nation by changing all its customs and destroying it to construct it anew, nor to reform the body of knowledge or the system of education. Nevertheless, as far as the opinions which I had been receiving since my birth were concerned, I could not do better than to reject them completely for once in my lifetime, and to resume them afterwards, or perhaps accept better ones in their place, when I had determined how they fitted into a rational scheme. And I firmly believed that by this means I would succeed in conducting my life much better than if I built only upon the old foundations and gave credence to the principles which I had acquired in my childhood without ever having examined them to see whether they were true or not.

* * *

I cannot at all approve those mischievous spirits who, not being called either by birth or by attainments to a position of political power, are nevertheless constantly proposing some new reform. If I thought the slightest basis could be found in this *Discourse* for a suspicion that I was guilty of this folly, I would be loath to permit it to be published. Never has my intention been more than to try to reform my own ideas, and rebuild them on foundations that would be wholly mine.

* * *

Among the branches of philosophy, I had, when younger, studied logic, and among those of mathematics, geometrical analysis and algebra; three arts or sciences which should be able to contribute something to my design. But in examining them I noticed that as far as logic was concerned its syllogisms and most of its other methods serve rather to explain to another what one already knows, or even, as the art of Lully, to speak without judgment of what one does not know, than to learn new things. Although it does contain many true and good precepts, they are interspersed among so many others that are harmful or superfluous that it is almost as difficult to separate them as to bring forth a Diana or a Minerva from a block of virgin marble. Then, as far as the analysis of the Greeks and the algebra of the moderns is concerned, besides the fact that they deal with abstractions and appear to have no utility, the first is always so limited to the consideration of figures that it cannot exercise the understanding without greatly fatiguing the imagination, and the last is so limited to certain rules and certain numbers that it has become a confused and obscure art which perplexes the mind instead of a science which educates it. In consequence I thought that some other method must be found to combine the advantages of these three and to escape their faults. Finally, just as the multitude of laws frequently furnishes an excuse for vice, and a state is much better governed with a few laws which are strictly adhered to, so I thought that instead of the great number of precepts of which logic is composed, I would have enough with the four following ones, provided that I made a firm and unalterable resolution not to violate them even in a single instance.

The first rule was never to accept anything as true unless I recognized it to be evidently such: that is, carefully to avoid precipitation and prejudgment, and to include nothing in my conclusions unless it presented itself so clearly and distinctly to my mind that there was no occasion to doubt it.

The second was to divide each of the difficulties which I encountered into as many parts as possible, and as might be required for an easier solution.

The third was to think in an orderly fashion, beginning with the things which were simplest and easiest to understand, and gradually and by degrees reaching toward more complex knowledge, even treating as though ordered materials which were not necessarily so.

The last was always to make enumerations so complete, and reviews so general, that I would be certain that nothing was omitted.

.   .   .

23. Franz Hals, *René Descartes*, detail. Photo: Giraudon.

What pleased me most about this method was that it enabled me to reason in all things, if not perfectly, at least as well as was in my power. In addition, I felt that in practicing it my mind was gradually becoming accustomed to conceive its objects more clearly and distinctly, and since I had not directed this method to any particular subject matter, I was in hopes of applying it just as usefully to the difficulties of other sciences as I had already to those of algebra. Not that I would dare to undertake to examine at once all the difficulties that presented themselves, for that would have been contrary to the principle of order. But I had observed that all the basic principles of the sciences were taken from philosophy, which itself had no certain ones. It therefore seemed that I should first attempt to establish philosophic principles, and that since this was the most important thing in the world and the place where precipitation and prejudgment were most to be feared, I should not attempt to reach conclusions until I had attained a much more mature age than my then twenty-three years, and had spent much time in preparing for it. This preparation would consist partly in freeing my mind from the false opinions which I had previously acquired, partly in building up a fund of experiences which should serve afterwards as the raw material of my reasoning, and partly in training myself in the method which I had determined upon, so that I should become more and more adept in its use.

I do not know whether I ought to touch upon my first meditations here, for they are so metaphysical and out of the ordinary that they might not be interesting to most people. Nevertheless, in order to show whether my fundamental notions are sufficiently sound, I find myself more or less constrained to speak of them. I had noticed for a long time that in practice it is sometimes necessary to follow opinions which we know to be very uncertain, just as though they were indubitable, as I stated before; but inasmuch as I desired to devote myself wholly to the search for truth, I thought that I should take a course precisely contrary, and reject as absolutely false anything of which I could have the least doubt, in order to see whether anything would be left after this procedure which could be called wholly certain. Thus, as our senses deceive us at times, I was ready to suppose that nothing was at all the way our senses represented them to be. As there are men who make mistakes in reasoning even on the simplest topics in geometry, I judged that I was as liable to error as any other, and rejected as false all the reasoning which I had previously accepted as valid demonstration. Finally, as the same precepts which we have when awake may come to us when asleep without their being true, I decided to suppose that nothing that had ever entered my mind was more real than the illusions of my dreams. But I soon noticed that while I thus wished to think everything false, it was necessarily true that I who thought so was something. Since this truth, *I think, therefore I am,* was so firm and assured that all the most extravagant suppositions of the sceptics were unable to shake it, I judged that I could safely accept it as the first principle of the philosophy I was seeking.

I then examined closely what I was, and saw that I could imagine that I had no body, and that there was no world nor any place that I occupied, but that I could not imagine for a moment that I did not exist. On the contrary, from the very fact that I doubted the truth of other things, it followed very evidently and very certainly that I existed. On the other hand, if I had ceased to think while all the rest of what I had ever imagined remained true, I would have had no reason to believe that I existed; therefore I concluded that I was a substance whose whole essence or nature was only to think, and which, to exist, has no need of space nor of any material thing. Thus it follows that this ego, this soul, by which I am what I am, is entirely distinct from the body and is easier to know than the latter, and that even if the body were not, the soul would not cease to be all that it now is.

Next I considered in general what is required of a proposition for it to be true and certain, for since I had just discovered one to be such, I thought I ought also to know of what that certitude consisted. I saw that there was nothing at all in this statement, "I think, therefore I am," to assure me that I was saying the truth, unless it was that I saw very clearly that to think one must exist. So I judged that I could accept as a general rule that the things which we conceive very clearly and very distinctly are always true, but that there may well be some difficulty in deciding which are those which we conceive distinctly.

(René Descartes: *Discourse on Method,* 1637)

4

Science and the New Universe

Scholasticism had not only adopted Aristotle; it had also incorporated in its system the Ptolemaic universe, one that seemed especially created for man. The earth immobile in the center of the world; all heavenly bodies turning around the earth in circular movement, a sign of nobility and perfection; contrary to sublunary bodies, the heavenly ones are pure and incorruptible. To this system scholasticism had linked an intricate symbolism which established parallels between the universe and the reflection of divine intelligence and purposes. Thus an attack on the Ptolemaic system amounted to an attack on the Catholic Church.

However, Copernicus (1473–1543), Johannes Kepler (1571–1630), and Galileo (1564–1642) successively demonstrated that the earth turned around the sun, that the movements of heavenly bodies were not circular but elliptic, and that they too were subject to corruption and impurities, such as sunspots. Galileo had furthermore proved by the principle of inertia that, once the planets had been set in motion, no further effort on the part of God was required to keep them going. In 1616, the Holy Office in Rome stated: "The view that the sun is immobile in the center of the universe is insane, philosophically false and completely opposed to Holy Scripture. The view that the earth is not in the center of the universe and that it even has a daily rotation is philosophically false and, at the least, an erroneous belief." In 1633, Galileo was arrested by the Inquisition and forced to recant his "heretical" findings.

A. THE MECHANICAL UNIVERSE

Bernard Le Bovier de Fontenelle (1657–1757) was secretary of the French Academy of Sciences. Although he wrote literary works, he obtained his greatest success as a popularizer of new scientific views. In the excerpt below he gallantly explains the new universe to a noble French lady while they are walking in a garden.

I fancy to my self, that Nature very much resembleth an Opera, where you stand, you do not see the Stage as really it is; but it is plac'd with advantage, and all the Wheels and Movements are hid, to make the Representation the more agreeable: Nor do you trouble your self how, or by what means the Machines are moved, tho' certainly an Engineer in the Pit is affected with what doth not touch you; he is pleas'd with the motion, and is demonstrating to himself on what it depends, and how it comes to pass. This Engineer then is like a Philosopher, tho' the difficulty is greater on the Philosopher's part, the Machines of the Theatre being nothing so curious as those of Nature, which disposeth her Wheels and Springs so out of sight, that we have been long a guessing at the Movement of the Universe. Suppose then the Sages at an Opera, the *Pithagoras's,* the *Plato's,* the *Aristotle's,* and all the Wise Men, who have made such a noise in the World, for these many Ages: We will suppose 'em at the Representation of *Phaeton,* where they see the aspiring Youth lifted up by the Winds, but do not discover the Wires by which he mounts, nor know they any thing of what is done behind the Scenes. Would you have all these Philosophers own themselves to be stark Fools, and confess ingenuously they know not how it comes to pass: No, no, they are not called Wise Men for nothing; tho', let me tell you, most of their Wisdom depends upon the ignorance of their Neighbours. Every man presently gives his Opinion, and how improbable so ever, there are Fools enough of all sorts to believe 'em: One tells you *Phaeton* is drawn up by a hidden Magnetick Vertue, no matter where it lies; and perhaps the grave Gentleman will take pet, if you ask him the Question. Another says, *Phaeton* is compos'd of certain Numbers that make him mount; and after all, the Philosopher knows no more of those numbers than a sucking Child of *Algebra:* A third tells you,

Phaeton hath a secret love for the top of the Theatre, and like a true Lover cannot be at rest out of his Mistresses Company, with an hundred such extravagant fancies, that a Man must conclude the Old Sages were very good Banterers: But now comes Monsieur *Descartes,* with some of the Moderns, and they tell you *Phaeton* ascends, because a greater weight than he descends; so that now we do not believe a Body can move without it is push'd and forc'd by another body, and as it were drawn by Cords, so that nothing can rise or fall but by the means of a Counterpoise; he then that will see Nature really as she is, must stand behind the Scenes at the Opera. I perceive, *said the Countess,* Philosophy is now become very Mechanical. So Mechanical, *said I,* that I fear we shall quickly be asham'd of it; they will have the World to be in great, what a Watch is in little; which is very regular, and depends only upon the just disposing of the several parts of the Movement. But pray tell me, Madam, had you not formerly a more sublime Idea of the Universe? Do you not think you did then honour it more than it deserv'd? For most have the less esteem of it since they have pretended to know it. I am not of their opinion, *said she,* I value it the more since I know it resembles a Watch, and the whole order of Nature the more plain and easie it is, to me it appears the more admirable.

I know not, *said I,* who hath inspir'd you with these solid Notions, but I am certain there are few that have them besides your self, People generally admire what they do not comprehend, they have a Veneration for Obscurity, and look upon Nature while they do not understand her, as a kind of Magick, and despise her below Legerdemain, when once they are acquainted with her; but I find you, Madam, so much better dispos'd, that I have nothing to do but to draw the Curtain, and shew you the World.

. . . before I expound the first Systeme, I would have you observe, we are all naturally like that Mad-man at *Athens,* who fancy'd all the Ships were his that came into the Port *Pyraeum:* Nor is our Folly less extravagant, we believe all things in Nature design'd for our use; and do but ask a Philosopher, to what purpose there is that prodigious company of fix'd Stars, when a far less number would perform the service they do us? He answers coldly, they were made to please our Sight, Upon this Principle they imagin'd the Earth rested in the Centre of the Universe, while all the Celestial Bodies (which were made for it) took the pains to turn round to give light to it. . . . But why, *said the Countess,* interrupting me, do you dislike this Systeme? It seems to me very Clear and Intelligible. However, Madam, *said I,* I will make it plainer; for should I give it you as it came from *Ptolomy* its Author, or from some who have since study'd it, I should fright you, I fancy, instead of diverting you. Since the Motions of the Planets are not so regular, but that sometimes they go faster, sometimes slower, sometimes are nearer the Earth, and sometimes farther from it; the Ancients did invent I do not know how many Orbs or Circles involv'd one within another, which they thought would salve all Objections; this confusion of Circles was so great, that at that time when they knew no better, a certain King of *Arragon,* a great Mathematician, but not much troubled with Religion, said, *That had God consulted him when he made the World, he would have told him how to have fram'd it better.* The fancy was very Atheistical, and no doubt the Instructions he would have given the Almighty, was the suppressing those Circles with which they had clog'd the Celestial Motions, and the taking away two or three superfluous Heavens which they had placed above the fixed Stars; for these Philosophers to explain the Motion of the Celestial Bodies, had above the uppermost Heaven (which we see,) found another of Crystal, to influence and give Motion to the inferior Heavens; and wherever they heard of another Motion, they presently clap'd up a Crystal Heaven which cost 'em nothing. . . . [but] by the observations of these latter Ages it is now out of doubt, that *Venus* and *Mercury* turn round the Sun, and not round the Earth, according to the Antient Systeme, which is now every where exploded, and all the *Ipse Dixits* not worth a rush. But that which I am going to lay down, will salve all, and is so clear, that the King of *Arragon* himself may spare his Advice. Methinks, *saith the Countess,* your Philosophy is a kind of Out-cry, where he that offers to do the work cheapest, carries it from all the rest. 'Tis very true, *said I,* Nature is a great Huswife, she always makes use of what costs least, let the difference be never so inconsiderable; and yet this frugality is accompany'd with an extraordinary magnificence, which shines thro' all her works; that is, she is magnificent in the Design, but frugal in the Execution; and what can be more praise-worthy, than a great design accomplish'd with a little Expence? But in our Ideas we turn things topsy-turvy, we place our thrift in the Design, and are at ten times more charge in Workmanship than it requires, which is very ridiculous: Imitate Nature then, *saith she,* in your Systeme, and give me as little trouble as you can to comprehend you. Fear it not, Madam, *said I,* we have done with our impertinencies: Imagine then a German call'd *Copernicus* confounding every thing, tearing in pieces the beloved Circles of Antiquity, and shattering their Crystal Heavens like so many Glass-Windows, seiz'd with the noble Rage of Astronomy, he snatcheth up the Earth from the Centre of the Universe, sends her packing, and placeth the Sun in the

Centre to which it did more justly belong, the Planets no longer turn round the Earth, and do not inclose it in the Circles they describe; if they give us light, it is but by chance, and as they meet us in their way. All now turns round the Sun, the Earth her self goes round the Sun, and *Copernicus* to punish the Earth for her former Lazyness, makes her contribute all he can to the Motion of the Planets and Heavens, and now stripp'd of all the heavenly Equipage with which she was so gloriously attended, she hath nothing left her but the Moon, which still turns round about her. . . .

. . . the Earth, at the same time that she advanceth on the Circle which in a Years space she makes round the Sun, in twenty four hours she turns round her self; so that in twenty four hours every part of the Earth loseth the Sun, and recovers him again, and as it turns towards the Sun, it seems to rise, and as it turns from him, it seems to fall. It is very pleasant, *said she,* that the Earth must take all upon her self, and the Sun do nothing. And when the Moon, the other Planets, and the fix'd Stars seem to go over our Heads every twenty four hours, you'll say that too is only Fancy? Pure Fancy, *said I,* which proceeds from the same cause, for the Planets compleat their Courses round the Sun at unequal times, according to their unequal distances, and that which we see to Day answer to a certain Point in the Zodiack or Circle of the fix'd Stars, to morrow we see answer to another point, because it is advanced on its own Circle as well as we are advanced upon ours. We move, and the Planets move too, which must make a great alteration; so that what seems irregular in the Planets, proceeds only from our Motion, when in truth they are all very irregular: I will suppose 'em so, *said the Countess,* but I would not have their Regularity put the Earth to so great trouble; methinks you exact too much Activity from so ponderous a Mass. But, *said I,* had you rather that the Sun and all the Stars, which are vast great Bodies, should in twenty four Hours travel such an infinity of Miles, and make so prodigious a *Tour* as they needs must, if the Earth did not turn round it self every twenty four Hours?

Ticho Brahe, who had fix'd the Earth in the Centre of the World, turn'd the Sun round the Earth, and the rest of the Planets round the Sun; for since the new discoveries, there was no way left to have the Planets turn round the Earth. But the Countess, who had a quick apprehension, said, she thought it was too affected, among so many great Bodies, to exempt the Earth only from turning round the Sun; that it was improper to make the Sun turn round the Earth, when all the Planets turn round the Sun; and that tho' this Systeme was to prove the immobility of the Earth, yet she thought it very improbable: So we resolv'd to stick to *Copernicus,* whose Opinion we thought most Uniform, Probable, and Diverting.

.   .   .

Well, Madam, *said I,* Since the Sun, which is now immoveable, hath left off being a Planet; and the Earth, which turns round him, is now become one, you will not be surprized when you hear that the Moon is an Earth too, and that she is inhabited as ours is.

.   .   .

The Moon, to all appearance, is inhabited, why should not *Venus* be so too? You are so full of your Whys, and your Wherefores, *says she,* interrupting me, that I fancy you are sending Colonies to all the Planets. You may be certain, so I will, *I reply'd,* for I see no reason to the contrary; we find that all the Planets are of the same nature, all obscure Bodies, which receive no Light but from the Sun, and then send it to one another; their Motions are the same, so that hitherto they are alike; and yet if we are to believe that these vast Bodies are not inhabited, I think they were made but to little purpose; why should Nature be so partial, as to except only the Earth?

.   .   .

I perceive, *says the Countess,* where you would carry me; you are going to tell me, that if the fix'd Stars are so many Suns, and our Sun the Centre of a Vortex that turns round him, why may not every fix'd Star be the Centre of a Vortex that turns round the fix'd Star? Our Sun enlightens the Planets; why may not every fix'd Star have Planets to which they give light? You have said it, *I reply'd,* and I will not contradict you.

You have made the Universe so large, *says she,* that I know not where I am, or what will become of me; what is it all to be divided into heaps confusedly, one among another? Is every Star the Centre of a Vortex, as big as ours? Is that vast space which comprehends our Sun and Planets, but an inconsiderable part of the Universe? and are there as many such spaces, as there are fix'd Stars? I protest it is dreadful. Dreadful, Madame, *said I;* I think it very pleasant, when the Heavens were a little blue Arch, stuck with Stars; methought the Universe was too strait and close, I was almost stifled for want of Air, but now it is enlarg'd in height and breadth, and a thousand Vortex's taken in; I begin to breathe with more freedom, and think the Universe to be incomparably more magnificent than it was before. Nature hath spar'd no cost, even to profuseness, and nothing can be so glorious, as to see such a prodigious number of Vortex's, whose several centres are possess'd by a particular Sun, which makes the Planets turn round it.

.   .   .

Oh, Madam, *said I,* there is a great deal of time required to ruine a World. Grant it, *said she,* yet 'tis but time that is required. I confess it, *said I;* all this immense mass of Matter that composes the Universe, is in perpetual Motion, no part of it excepted; and since every part is moved, you may be sure that changes must happen sooner or later; but still in times proportioned to the Effect. The Ancients were pleasant Gentlemen, to imagine that the Celestial Bodies were in their own Nature unchangeable, because they observed no change in them; but they did not live long enough to confirm their Opinion by their own Experience; they were Boys in comparison of us.

(Fontenelle: *A Plurality of Worlds,* 1686)

B. THE NEW SCIENCE

It would be an exaggeration to say that Bacon's call to induction led to immediate scientific progress in the seventeenth century, or that the advance was uniform in all the sciences. Nevertheless, the scientific record of the century is impressive, to say the least. Two important societies were founded: the Royal Society in 1660 and the French Academy of Science in 1666. The roster of great scientists is brilliant. Aside from those already mentioned (Galileo, Descartes), Robert Hooke (1635–1703) established the definition of the structure of plants; John Ray (1628–1705) set up the classification of plants and birds; Marcello Malpighi (1628–1694) created the science of microbiology and also was able to observe and prove Harvey's theory of blood circulation. Anton van Leeuwenhoek (1632–1723) went beyond his predecessors in microbiology in discovering bacteria and spermatozoa. Christian Huygens (1629–1695) gained fame for his studies of the pendulum. Besides Boyle and Harvey, who will illustrate the new science below, two great names remain: Isaac Newton (1642–1727), whose discovery of the law of gravity completed the work of Copernicus and Kepler and who, along with but independent of Leibnitz (1646–1716), invented calculus, which opened up undreamed-of possibilities to mathematicians and scientists.

1. BOYLE: THE CORPUSCULAR PHILOSOPHY

Robert Boyle (1627–1691), best known for his law concerning the pressure of gases and for his book, The Sceptical Chemist *(1661), was a member of the Royal Society.*

I considered, that the Atomical and Cartesian hypotheses, though they differed in some material points from one another, yet in opposition to the Peripatetic and other vulgar doctrines they might be looked upon as one philosophy: for they agree with one another, and differ from the schools in this grand and fundamental point, that not only they take care to explicate things intelligibly; but that whereas those other philosophers give only a general and superficial account of the phaenomena of nature from certain substantial forms, which the most ingenious among themselves confess to be incomprehensible, and certain real qualities, which knowing men of other persuasions think to be likewise unintelligible; both the Cartesians and the Atomists explicate the same phaenomena by little bodies variously figured and moved. I know, that these two sects of modern naturalists disagree about the notion of body in general, and consequently about the possibility of a true vacuum; as also about the origin of motion, the indefinite divisibleness of matter, and some other points of less importance than these: but in regard that some of them seem to be rather metaphysical than physiological notions, and that some others seem rather to be requisite to the explication of the first origin of the universe, than of the phaenomena of it, in the state wherein we now find it; in regard of these, I say, and some other considerations, and especially for this reason, that both parties agree in deducing all the phaenomena of nature from matter and local motion; I esteemed that, notwithstanding these things, wherein the Atomists and the Cartesians differed, they might be thought to agree in the main, and their hypotheses might by a person of a reconciling disposition be looked on as, upon the matter, one philosophy. Which because it explicates things by corpuscles, or minute bodies, may (not very unfitly) be called corpuscular; though I sometimes style it the Phaenician philosophy, because some antient writers inform us, that not only before *Epicurus* and *Democritus,* but even before *Leucippus* taught in *Greece,* a Phaenician naturalist was wont to give an account of the phaenomena of nature by the motion and other affections of the minute particles of matter. Which because they are obvious and very powerful in mechanical engines, I sometimes also term it the mechanical hypothesis or philosophy.

By such considerations then, and by this occasion, I was invited to try, whether, without pretending to determine the above-mentioned controverted points, I could, by the help of the corpuscular philosophy, in the sense newly given of that appellation, associated with chymical experiments, explicate some particular subjects more intelligibly, than they are wont to be accounted for, either by the schools or the chymists. And however since the vulgar philosophy is yet so vulgar, that it is still in great request with the generality of scholars; and since the mechanical philosophers have brought so few experiments to verify their assertions: and the chymists are thought to have brought so many on the behalf of theirs, that of those, that have quitted the unsatisfactory philosophy of the schools, the greater number, dazzled as it were by the experiments of Spagyrists, have imbraced their doctrines instead of those they deserted: for these reasons, I say, I hoped I might at least do no unseasonable piece of service to the corpuscular philosophers, by illustrating some of their notions with sensible experiments, and manifesting, that the things by me treated of may be at least plausibly explicated without having recourse to inexplicable forms, real qualities, the four peripatetic elements, or so much as the three chymical principles.

·   ·   ·

That, before I descend to particulars, I may, *Pyrophilus,* furnish you with some general apprehension of the doctrine (or rather the hypothesis) which is to be collated with, and to be either confirmed or disproved by the historical truths that will be delivered concerning particular qualities (and forms); I will assume the person of a Corpuscularian, and here at the entrance give you (in a general way) a brief account of the hypothesis itself, as it concerns the origin of qualities (and forms). . . .

I. I agree with the generality of philosophers so far as to allow, that there is one catholick or universal matter common to all bodies, by which

I mean a substance extended, divisible, and impenetrable.

II. But because this matter being in its own nature but one, the diversity we see in bodies must necessarily arise from somewhat else than the matter they consist of. And since we see not how there could be any change in matter, if all its (actual or designable) parts were perpetually at rest among themselves, it will follow, that to discriminate the catholick matter into variety of natural bodies, it must have motion in some or all its designable parts: and that motion must have various tendencies, that which is in this part of the matter tending one way, and that which is in that part tending another; as we plainly see in the universe or general mass of matter, there is really a great quantity of motion, and that variously determined, and that yet divers portions of matter are at rest.

That there is local motion in many parts of matter is manifest to sense; but how matter came by this motion was of old, and is still hotly disputed of: for the antient Corpuscularian philosophers (whose doctrine in most other points, though not in all, we are most inclinable to) not acknowledging an Author of the universe, were thereby reduced to make motion congenite to matter, and consequently coeval with it. But since local motion, or an endeavour at it, is not included in the nature of matter, which is as much matter when it rests as when it moves; and since we see that the same portion of matter may from motion be reduced to rest, and after it hath continued at rest, as long as other bodies do not put it out of that state, may by external agents be set a moving again; I, who am not wont to think a man the worse naturalist for not being an atheist, shall not scruple to say with an eminent philosopher of old, whom I find to have proposed among the *Greeks* that opinion (for the main) that the excellent *Des Cartes* has revived amongst us, that the origin of motion in matter is from God; and not only so, but that thinking it very unfit to be believed that matter barely put into motion, and then left to itself, should casually constitute this beautiful and orderly world: I think also further, that the wise Author of things did, by establishing the laws of motion among bodies, and by guiding the first motions of the small parts of matter, bring them to convene after the manner requisite to compose the world, and especially did contrive those curious and elaborate engines, the bodies of living creatures, endowing most of them with a power of propagating their species. But though these things are my persuasions, yet, because they are not necessary to be supposed here, where I do not pretend to deliver any compleat discourse of the principles of natural philosophy, but only to touch upon such notions as are requisite to explicate the origin of qualities and forms, I shall pass on to what remains, as soon as I have taken notice that local motion seems to be indeed the principal amongst second causes, and the grand agent of all that happens in nature: for though bulk, figure, rest, situation, and texture do concur to the phaenomena of nature, yet in comparison of motion they seem to be in many cases, effects, and in many others little better than conditions, or requisites, or causes *sine quibus non,* which modify the operation that one part of matter by virtue of its motion hath upon another; as in a watch, the number, the figure, and coaptation of the wheels and other parts is requisite to the shewing the hour, and doing the other things that may be performed by the watch; but till these parts be actually put into motion, all their other affections remain inefficacious. . . .

III. These two grand and most catholick principles of bodies, matter and motion, being thus established, it will follow, both that matter must be actually divided into parts, that being the genuine effect of variously determined motion, and that each of the primitive fragments, or other distinct and intire masses of matter, must have two attributes, its own magnitude, or rather size, and its own figure or shape. And since experience shews us (especially that which is afforded us by chymical operations, in many of which matter is divided into parts too small to be singly sensible) that this division of matter is frequently made into insensible corpuscles or particles, we may conclude, that the minutest fragments, as well as the biggest masses of the universal matter, are likewise endowed each with its peculiar bulk and shape. For being a finite body, its dimensions must be terminated and measurable: and though it may change its figure, yet for the same reason it must necessarily have some figure or other. So that now we have found out, and must admit three essential properties of each intire or undivided, though insensible part of matter; namely, magnitude (by which I mean not quantity in general, but a determined quantity, which we in *English* oftentimes call the size of a body) shape, and either motion or rest (for betwixt them two there is no mean). . . .

.   .   .

For though I do as freely and heartily, as the doctor himself, who, I dare say, does it very sincerely, admit, or rather assert an incorporeal being, that made and governs the world; yet all that I have endeavoured to do in the explication of what happens among inanimate bodies, is to shew, that supposing the world to have been at first made, and to be continually preserved by God's divine power and wisdom; and supposing his general concourse to the maintenance of the laws he has established in it, the phaenomena, I strive to explicate, may be solved mechanically, that is, by the mechanical affections of matter, without recourse to nature's abhorrence of a vacuum, to substantial forms, or to other incorporeal creatures. And therefore, if I have shewn, that the phaenomena, I have endeavoured to account for, are explicable by the motion, bigness, gravity, shape, and other mechanical affections of the small parts of liquors, I have done what I pretended; which was not to prove, that no angel or other immaterial creature could interpose in these cases; for concerning such agents, all that I need say, is, that in the cases proposed we have no need to recur to them. And this being agreeable to the generally owned rule about hypotheses, that *entia non sunt multiplicanda absque necessitate,* has been by almost all the modern philosophers of different sects thought a sufficient reason to reject the agency of intelligences, after *Aristotle,* and so many learned men, both mathematicians and others, had for many ages believed them the movers of the celestial orbs.

.   .   .

And now at length I come to consider that, which I observe the most to alienate other sects from the mechanical philosophy; namely, that they think it pretends to have principles so universal and so mathematical, that no other physical hypothesis can comport with it, or be tolerated by it.

But this I look upon as an easy, indeed, but an important mistake; because by this very thing, that the mechanical principles are so universal, and therefore applicable to so many things, they are rather fitted to include, than necessitated to exclude, any other hypothesis, that is founded in nature, as far as it is so. And such hypotheses, if prudently considered by a skilful and moderate person, who is rather disposed to unite sects than multiply them, will be found, as far as they have truth in them, to be either legitimately (though perhaps not immediately) deducible from the mechanical principles, or fairly reconcileable to them. For, such hypotheses will probably attempt to account for the phaenomena of nature, either by the help of a determinate number of material ingredients, such as the *tria prima* of the chymists, by participation whereof other bodies obtain their qualities; or else by introducing some general agents, as the Platonic soul of the world, or the universal spirit, asserted by some spagyrists; or by both these ways together.

Now, to dispatch first those, that I named in the second place; I consider, that the chief thing, that inquisitive naturalists should look after in the explicating of difficult phaenomena, is not so much what the agent is or does, as, what changes are made in the patient, to bring it to exhibit the phaenomena, that are proposed; and by what means, and after what manner, those changes are effected. So that the mechanical philosopher being satisfied, that one part of matter can act upon another but by virtue of local motion, or the effects and consequences of local motion, he considers, that as if the proposed agent be not intelligible and physical, it can never physically explain the phaenomena, so, if it be intelligible and physical, it will be reducible to matter, and some or other of those only catholick affections of matter, already often mentioned. And the indefinite divisibility of matter, the wonderful efficacy of motion, and the almost infinite variety of coalitions and structures, that may be made of minute and insensible corpuscles, being duly weighed, I see not, why a philosopher should think it impossible, to make out, by their help, the mechanical possibility of any corporeal agent, how subtil, or diffused, or active soever it be, that can be solidly proved to be really existent in nature, by what name soever it be called or disguised.

. . .

. . . if we consider the thing itself, by a free examen of the pretended explanations, that the vulgar philosophers are wont, by recurring to nature, to give of the phaenomena of the universe; we shall not easily look on those accounts, as meriting the name of explications. For to explicate a phaenomenon, it is not enough to ascribe it to one general efficient, but we must intelligibly shew the particular manner, how that general cause produces the proposed effect. He must be a very dull inquirer, who, demanding an account of the phaenomena of a watch, shall rest satisfied with being told, that it is an engine made by a watch-maker; though nothing be thereby declared of the structure and co-aptation of the spring, wheels, balance, and other parts of the engine, and the manner, how they act on one another, so as to co-operate to make the needle point out the true hour of the day. And (to improve to my present purpose an example formerly touched upon) as he, that knows the structure and other mechanical affections of a watch, will be able by them to explicate the phaenomena of it, without supposing, that it has a soul or life to be the internal principle of its motions or operations; so he, that does not understand the mechanism of a watch, will never be enabled to give a rational account of the operations of it, by supposing, as those of *China* did, when the Jesuits first brought watches thither, that a watch is an European animal, or living body, and endowed with a soul. This comparison seems not ill to befit the

occasion of propounding it; but to second it by another, that is more
purely physical, when a person, unacquainted with the mathematics, admires to see, that the sun rises and sets in winter in some parts of the
horizon, and in summer in others, distant enough from them; that the
day, in the former season, is, by odds shorter, than in the latter, and sometimes (as some days before the middle of *March* and of *September*) the
days are equal to the night; that the moon is sometimes seen in conjunction with the sun, and sometimes in opposition to him; and, between those
two states, is every day variously illuminated; and that sometimes one of
those planets, and sometimes another, suffers an eclipse; this person, I say,
will be much assisted to understand, how these things are brought to pass,
if he be taught the clear mathematical elements of astronomy: but if he be
of a temper to reject these explications, as too defective, it is not like that
it will satisfy him, to tell him after *Aristotle* and the schoolmen, that the
orbs of the sun and moon, and other coelestial spheres, are moved by
angels or intelligences; since to refer him to such general and undeter-
mined causes, will little, or not at all, assist him to understand, how the
recited phaenomena are produced.

(Robert Boyle: *Origin of Forms and Qualities According
to the Corpuscular Philosophy,* 1666)

2. HARVEY: THE CIRCULATION OF THE BLOOD

*William Harvey (1578–1657) overthrew the theories of Galen
(130–201) that had subsisted for some fourteen centuries. According to Galen, the blood was the noble seat of the soul, and
the liver served as the reservoir of the blood. Harvey's theory of
blood circulation met with strong opposition in France where
the dean of the Faculty of Medicine denounced it as "paradoxi-
cal, useless for medicine, false, impossible, unintelligible, harmful to human life." For many more years French doctors continued the practice of purging and bloodletting on which
Molière heaped scorn and ridicule in his comedy,* The Imagi-
nary Invalid.

Were not the work indeed presented through you, my learned friends,
I should scarce hope that it could come out scatheless and complete; for
you have in general been the faithful witnesses of almost all the instances
from which I have either collected the truth or confuted error; you have
seen my dissections, and at my demonstrations of all that I maintain to be
objects of sense, you have been accustomed to stand by and bear me out

with your testimony. And as this book alone declares the blood to course and revolve by a new route, very different from the ancient and beaten pathway trodden for so many ages, and illustrated by such a host of learned and distinguished men, I was greatly afraid lest I might be charged with presumption did I lay my work before the public at home, or send it beyond seas for impression, unless I had first proposed its subject to you, had confirmed its conclusions by ocular demonstrations in your presence, had replied to your doubts and objections, and secured the assent and support of our distinguished President. For I was most intimately persuaded, that if I could make good my proposition before you and our College, illustrious by its numerous body of learned individuals, I had less to fear from others; I even ventured to hope that I should have the comfort of finding all that you had granted me in your sheer love of truth, conceded by others who were philosophers like yourselves. For true philosophers, who are only eager for truth and knowledge, never regard themselves as already so thoroughly informed, but that they welcome further information from whomsoever and from whencesoever it may come; nor are they so narrow-minded as to imagine any of the arts or sciences transmitted to us by the ancients, in such a state of forwardness or completeness, that nothing is left for the ingenuity and industry of others; very many, on the contrary, maintain that all we know is still infinitely less than all that still remains unknown; nor do philosophers pin their faith to others' precepts in such wise that they lose their liberty, and cease to give credence to the conclusions of their proper senses. Neither do they swear such fealty to their mistress Antiquity, that they openly, and in sight of all, deny and desert their friend Truth. . . .

My dear colleagues, I had no purpose to swell this treatise into a large volume by quoting the names and writings of anatomists, or to make a parade of the strength of my memory, the extent of my reading, and the amount of my pains; because I profess both to learn and to teach anatomy, not from books but from dissections; not from the positions of philosophers but from the fabric of nature. . . .

.   .   .

From these and other observations of the like kind, I am persuaded it will be found that the motion of the heart is as follows:

First of all, the auricle contracts, and in the course of its contraction throws the blood, (which it contains in ample quantity as the head of the veins, the store-house and cistern of the blood,) into the ventricle, which being filled, the heart raises itself straight way, makes all its fibres tense, contracts the ventricles, and performs a beat, by which beat it immediately sends the blood supplied to it by the auricle into the arteries; the right ventricle sending its charge into the lungs by the vessel which is called vena arteriosa, but which, in structure and function, and all things else, is an artery; the left ventricle sending its charge into the aorta, and through this by the arteries to the body at large.

These two motions, one of the ventricles, another of the auricles, take place consecutively, but in such a manner that there is a kind of harmony or rhythm preserved between them, the two concurring in such wise that but one motion is apparent, especially in the warmer blooded animals, in which the movements in question are rapid. Nor is this for any other reason than it is in a piece of machinery, in which, though one wheel gives motion to another, yet all the wheels seem to move simultaneously; or in that mechanical contrivance which is adapted to firearms, where the trigger being touched, down comes the flint, strikes against the steel, elicits a spark, which falling among the powder, it is ignited, upon which the flame extends, enters the barrel, causes the explosion, propels the ball, and the mark is attained — all of which incidents, by reason of the celerity with which they happen, seem to take place in the twinkling of an eye.

.   .   .

Thus far I have spoken of the passage of the blood from the veins into the arteries, and of the manner in which it is transmitted and distributed by the action of the heart; points to which some, moved either by the authority of Galen or Columbus, or the reasonings of others, will give in their adhesion. But what remains to be said upon the quantity and source of the blood which thus passes, is of so novel and unheard-of character, that I not only fear injury to myself from the envy of a few, but I tremble lest I have mankind at large for my enemies, so much doth wont and custom, that become as another nature, and doctrine once sown and that hath struck deep root, and respect for antiquity influence all men: Still the die is cast, and my trust is in my love of truth, and the candour that inheres in cultivated minds. And sooth to say, when I surveyed my mass of evidence, whether derived from vivisections, and my various reflections on them, or from the ventricles of the heart and the vessels that enter into and issue from them, the symmetry and size of these conduits, — for nature doing nothing in vain, would never have given them so large a relative size without a purpose, — or from the ar-

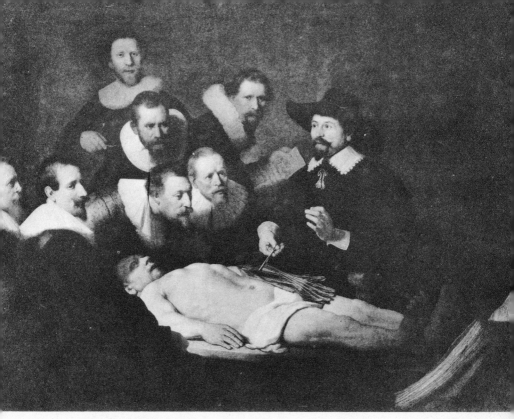

24. Rembrandt van Ryn, *The Anatomy Lesson*. Photo: Giraudon.

rangement and intimate structure of the valves in particular, and of the other parts of the heart in general, with many things besides, I frequently and seriously bethought me, and long revolved in my mind, what might be the quantity of blood which was transmitted, in how short a time its passage might be effected, and the like; and not finding it possible that this could be supplied by the juices of the ingested aliment without the veins on the one hand becoming drained, and the arteries on the other getting ruptured through the excessive charge of blood, unless the blood should somehow find its way from the arteries into the veins, and so return to the right side of the heart; I began to think whether there might not be A MOTION, AS IT WERE, IN A CIRCLE. Now this I afterwards found to be true; and I finally saw that the blood, forced by the action of the left ventricle into the arteries, was distributed to the body at large, and its several parts, in the same manner as it is sent through the lungs, impelled by the right ventricle into the pulmonary artery, and that it then passed through the veins and along the vena cava, and so round to the left ventricle in the manner already indicated. . . .

The heart, consequently, is the beginning of life; the sun of the microcosm, even as the sun in his turn might well be designated the heart of the world; for it is the heart by whose virtue and pulse the blood is moved, perfected, made apt to nourish, and is preserved from corruption and coagulation; it is the household divinity which, discharging its function, nourishes, cherishes, quickens the whole body, and is indeed the foundation of life, the source of all action.

(William Harvey: *De Motu Cordis et Sanguinis,* 1628)

PART

IV

The Ways of Reason

25. J. B. Martin, *View of the Chateau and the Gardens of Versailles.*
Photo: Giraudon.

The latter part of the seventeenth century is largely dominated by rationalism and all it implies: the subjection of emotions and passions to reason; the preference of what is universal (as reason itself) to that which is personal or quaint; the insistence on order and stability in society and political institutions; the demand that a reasonable measure, the golden mean, be observed in man's actions and thought and that nothing be done to excess.

While rationalism does not invade all the arts, literature and French architecture mirror many of its aspects: in the former, rational rules are introduced; as for the latter, a perfect ex-

26. Antoine Coysevox, *Louis XIV*. Photo: Giraudon.

*ample of order and symmetry can be found in the gardens of
the château of Versailles.*

*Rationalism is not necessarily synonymous with liberalism in
the sense we might be tempted to define it today, especially in
the following (not necessarily Lockian) chain of reasoning:
Reason leads to a belief in liberty; liberty means a preference
of democracy over authoritarian government; democracy is
political liberalism; hence reason leads to liberalism.*

*If we want to understand the seventeenth century, we must
first attempt to understand it on its own terms before applying
to it present-day standards of judgment. The century did not*

espouse the views concerning originality or even entertainment that are prevalent today — it is, in some ways, inconsistent. The social philosophers were not eager to establish a more equitable society; the political philosophers did not condemn royal authority the way they had attacked scholastic authority; still more paradoxically, far from renouncing Aristotle, the literary critics highly esteemed his Poetics *and took ancient literature as their model.*

In these fields then the seventeenth century was highly conservative, for rationalism can be employed to defend opposing causes. It may lead to the overthrow of authoritarian institutions and eventually to the French and American revolutions; it may also be used to defend the divine right of kings or authoritarian government. This is not so surprising as it may seem at first view; first, because, while reason is universally found in man, the rational method had to be universally learned and applied before man would be capable of ruling himself (and the lower classes were, of course, almost totally uneducated); secondly, many of the influential seventeenth-century thinkers and artists were members of the upper classes or had noble patrons and thus had little personal interest in destroying or overthrowing existing political and social institutions.

If reason does not necessarily lead to democracy and social justice, does it at least lead to happiness? The answer depends, of course, on what is meant by that. For the rationalist, Spinoza for example, happiness is possible only when reason dominates emotions and passions, that is to say: he desires (philosophical) peace of mind. But what is rational love like? or rational religion? These will be some of the questions we shall consider.

1

Literature and Literary Criticism

Nature, truth, reason: these are the keywords of seventeenth-century literary criticism. And as rational standards were being applied to the literary productions of the Middle Ages and of the Renaissance, most of them were found to be deficient. How could a rationalist accept the Arthurian romances, passion plays, the undisciplined theater of the sixteenth and early seventeenth century, or pastoral novels?

All these looked to rationalist critics like the disorderly products of too wild an imagination. Good models had to be found; rules had to be designed. The models were the authors of Greek and Latin classicism, the ancients; the rules, at least for the theater, could be devised by interpreting Aristotle's Poetics. *And soon there appeared the famous three unities of action, time, and place (one principal action to be limited to twenty-four hours and to one place).*

The seventeenth-century author lays no special claim to originality. He is content with the framework provided by the ancient writers; when he introduces changes of his own, he turns almost apologetic in justifying them. He is considerate of his audience whom he tries to please while conveying a moral lesson, and he writes humble dedications to kings and noblemen. The interesting question is how it was possible to produce masterpieces in the face of all these restrictions. Part of the answer is that they used the rules without being enslaved by them; besides, as Goethe remarked, restrictions help reveal a true master.

The role of literary critics was very important in the seventeenth century. Nicolas Boileau-Despréaux (1636–1711) was a close friend of Molière, Racine, and La Fontaine. His Satires *and* Art of Poetry *summarize the concepts of French literature during the age of Louis XIV. John Dryden (1631–1700) was not only the greatest English critic of the century but also the author of plays and satires. Jean de La Bruyère (1645–1696) is best known for his* Characters, *modeled after Theophrastus. Additional examples are drawn from the prefaces of various dramatic authors.*

The principal purpose of a literary work is to please.

Write what your Reader may be pleased to hear.
The public Censure for your Writings fear,
And to yourself be Critic most severe.

(Boileau: *The Art of Poetry,* Canto I; 1674)

I would be glad to know whether the grand rule of all rules is not to please; and whether a piece upon the stage that has gained its end, did not take a right way? Would you have it that the whole public is mistaken in these matters, and that every one should not be a judge of the pleasure he takes in 'em? . . . I say plainly the great art is to please, and that this comedy having pleased those it was made for, I think it sufficient for it, and that there is no reason to mind the rest.

(Molière: *The School for Wives Criticized*, 1663)

Every author who wishes to write clearly should put himself in the place of his readers, examine his own work as something new to him, which he reads for the first time, is not at all concerned in, and which has been submitted to his criticism; and then be convinced that no one will understand what is written merely because the author understands it himself, but because it is really intelligible.

(Jean de La Bruyère: "Of Works of the Mind," §56;
The Characters, 1669)

In order to please, the author must imitate "nature" and "truth." Since reason is the faculty that discerns the truth, the literary work must conform to reason.

What e'er you write or Pleasant or Sublime,
Always let sense accompany your Rhyme:
Love Reason then: and let what e're you Write
Borrow from her its Beauty, Force and Light.   (Canto I)

To study Nature be your only care:
Who e're knows man, and by a curious art
Discerns the hidden secrets of the heart. . . .
Nature in various Figures does abound;
And in each mind are diff'rent Humours found.
A glance, a touch, discovers to the wise. . . .
Your Action still should Reason's Rule obey,
Nor in an empty Scene may lose its way. . . .
And your Discourse Sententious be, and Wise:
The Passions must to Nature be confin'd.   (Canto III)

(Boileau: *The Art of Poetry*, 1674)

To imitate nature means not to choose unusual or bizarre exceptions but aspects that are common to all men, i.e. universal ideas.

Most Writers, mounted on a resty Muse,
Extravagant, and Senseless Objects chuse;
They think they erre, if in their Verse they fall
On any thought that's Plain, or Natural:
Fly this excess; . . .
Reason to go has often but one way.

(Boileau: *The Art of Poetry*, Canto I)

What is a new, brilliant, extraordinary thought? It is not, as ignorant people think, a thought that no one has ever had or can have had before; on the contrary, it is a thought that must have occurred to everybody and that someone happens to be the first to put into words. A clever saying is clever only insofar as it expresses something that everyone was thinking and that renders it in a lively, refined, and novel way.

(Boileau: Preface to his *Works*, 1701)

As far as the emotions are concerned, I have endeavored to follow Euripides closely. I admit that I am indebted to him for a number of features that have won the greatest approval in my tragedy; and I admit this all the more gladly because this approval has confirmed the esteem in which I have always held the works that remain of antiquity. I have noticed with pleasure by the effect obtained in our theater by all I have imitated from Homer or Euripides, that good sense and reason have been the same in all the centuries. Parisian taste has turned out to be in agreement with that of Athens; my spectators were moved by the same things which formerly brought tears to the eyes of the most learned people in Greece.

(Racine: Preface to *Iphigenia in Aulis*, 1674)

At the risk of sounding vain, I would nevertheless say this of my work: I am almost inclined to think that my portrayals must be depicting man in general, since they resemble so many individuals and since everybody thinks he recognizes in them such-and-such from his town or province. I have depicted, indeed, according to nature, but I have not always intended to portray this or that man in my book of *Manners*. I did not expose myself to the public in order to do portraits that would be only true and life-like for fear that sometimes they might not be believable or appear feigned or fictitious. Being more difficult, I went further: I have taken one trait here and one trait there, and of these various traits that could belong to one person I have made believable depictions, concerned less to

amuse my reader by the character or by satirizing someone, as my de-
tractors put it, than to expose to him defects to avoid and models to follow.

(Jean de La Bruyère: Preface to his *Discourse*
pronounced at the French Academy, 1694)

What then is originality?

After above 7,000 years, during which there have been men who have
thought, we have come too late to say anything that has not been said
already, the finest and most beautiful ideas on morals and manners have
been swept away before our times, and nothing is left for us but to glean
after the ancients and the ablest amongst the moderns. . . . "Horace or
Boileau have said such a thing before you." — "I take your word for it,
but I have used it as my own. May I not have the same thought after them,
as others may have after me?"

(Jean de La Bruyère: "Of Works of the Mind,"
§ 69, 1; *The Characters*)

I am taxed with stealing all my plays, and that by some who should be
the last men from whom I would steal any part of 'em. . . . 'Tis true that,
where ever I have liked any story in a romance, novel, or foreign play, I
have made no difficulty, nor ever shall, to take the foundation of it, to
build it up, and to make it proper for the English stage. . . . To witness
this, I need go no farther than this play: it was first Spanish and called
El astrólogo fingido [by Calderón]: then made French by the younger
Corneille;[1] and is now translated into English, and in print, under the
name of the *Feigned Astrologer*.[2] What I have performed in this will best
appear by comparing it with those: you will see that I have rejected some
adventures which I judged were not divertising; that I have heightened
those which I have chosen, and that I have added others which were
neither in the French nor Spanish. . . .

But these little critics do not well consider what is the work of a poet,
and what the graces of a poem. The story is the least part of either: I mean
the foundation of it, before it is modeled by the art of him who writes it;
who forms it with more care, by exposing only the beautiful parts of it to
view, than a skillful lapidary sets a jewel. On this foundation of the story
the characters are raised: and . . . it follows that it is to be altered and
enlarged with new persons, accidents, and designs, which will almost make
it new. When this is done, the forming it into acts and scenes, disposing of
actions and passions into their proper places, and beautifying both with

descriptions, similitudes, and propriety of language, is the principal employment of the poet; as being the largest field of fancy, which is the principle quality required of him. . . . Judgment, indeed, is necessary in him; but 'tis fancy that gives the life-touches, and the secret graces to it; especially in the serious plays, which depend not much on observation. . . .

But in general, the employment of a poet is like that of a curious gunsmith or watchmaker: the iron or silver is not his own; but they are the least part of that which gives the value: the price lies wholly in the workmanship.

(John Dryden: Preface to *An Evening's Love:*
or *The Mock Astrologer,* 1671)

The literary work must be useful: it must have a moral purpose.

> In prudent Lessons every where abound;
> With pleasant, join the useful, the sound:
> A Sober Reader, a vain Tale will slight;
> He seeks as well Instruction, as Delight. . . .
> To follow Virtue then be your desire.
> In vain your Art and Vigor are expressed;
> Th'obscene expression shows th'infected breast.

(Boileau: *The Art of Poetry,* Canto III)

> Fables are not what they at first appear,
> The simplest animals are teachers here.
> The naked moral soon the reader tires:
> Fiction the happy precept best inspires.
> To tell for telling's sake is childish play.
> Many great writers therefore of this kind,
> At once improve and animate the mind:
> They seek no ornament, nor labor'd length,
> And all their words are chosen for their strength.

(Jean de La Fontaine: "The Shepherd and the Lion,"
from *Fables,* Book VI; 1668)

I am sure of one thing: that I have not written a play in which virtue is more clearly exposed than in this one; the slightest faults are severely punished in it; the merest criminal thought is looked upon with as much horror as the crime itself . . . and vice is depicted everywhere in a way that makes its deformities known and hated. That is, properly speaking, the goal which every man who writes for the public must pursue, and that is what the first tragic poets had in mind in all they wrote. . . . It would be desirable that our works were as solid and filled with moral precepts as theirs. That would perhaps be one way of making tragedy acceptable to a number of persons renowned for their piety and doctrines who have recently condemned it. They would probably be more favorably disposed toward it if dramatic authors thought as much about educating their spectators as about entertaining them, which would enable them to observe the real purpose of tragedy.

(Jean Racine: Preface to *Phaedra*, 1677)

2

Politics and International Law

Most political thought in the seventeenth century was conservative by present-day standards; the only exceptions can be found in England, but other countries took care not to let such "subversive" ideas infiltrate them. Thus it was not until 1731 that the French were informed of English republican ideas through Voltaire. The idea of dethroning Louis XIV must have occurred to very few Frenchmen indeed. Besides, not all the English shared the same ideas: the civil wars that opposed King and Parliament for some twenty years did not inspire Hobbes with the same enthusiasm for regicide as Milton.

The political struggles usually opposed kings or princes and the nobility. The middle class, while rising in importance, was not yet strong enough to play a decisive role. As for the people, we need only read Richelieu's political testament to realize how insignificant they were.

The aim generally pursued by political philosophers was to maintain order and social stability. These require strong, central government by a king divinely appointed or by a sovereign chosen by necessity. Even Campanella's political utopia provides for a pyramid of power with final authority vested in one man. La Fontaine's fable at first seems to speak in favor of democracy; yet its moral lesson does not offer much hope.

And yet, grave questions are being raised and discussed: Can the social contract between sovereign and subjects be dissolved? Can the people judge the king? As long as the doctrine of the divine right of kings is accepted, the answer is obvious. But what matters is that these questions are raised. They will receive different answers in the following century.

A.   THE PEOPLE

The Frogs Who Demanded a King

The frogs grew tired of democratic laws,
  And giving up the cause,
  They made the air with clamors ring;
   The water-sops ran wild:
  At last Jove dropt them down a king,
  A humble prince, pacific, mild;
Yet fell his majesty with such a splash,
That threaten'd their destruction with a crash.
   The marshy folks, a timid race,
   Fled from their monarch's awful face,
   Down to the bulrushes and reeds,
   Each to his hole for safety speeds:
  Nor dared for days to take a look
At him they all for some dread giant took.
    Behold it was a log! . . .
With look so grave that frighten'd the first frog,
   Who had but just enough of soul
   To venture from his lurking hole.
   Trembling he came with cautious step;
Another follow'd and another yet:
   At last there came a swarm;
And grew familiar as they saw no harm;
Now on the royal shoulders jump'd at will,
The peaceful king permitted, and lay still.
   But Jove they now attack'd again,
   And almost split the monarch's brain:
   Give us a stirring king, they cried,
   We want some life, some bustling work.

> The king of gods in anger soon replied,
>   And sent them down a stork —
>   Who crack'd their bones, and gulped up
>   A mal-content at every sup.
> Horror! . . . The frogs now trembling and afraid
> Complain'd again — but Jove unto them said:
> What! must our will by your caprice be bound!
> You should have held the government ye had;
> Which having lost — the harmless king ye found,
> You should have cherish'd and been glad.
>
>   Be happy with your present curse,
>   For fear I send you still a worse.

> (Jean de La Fontaine: *Fables,* Book III)

Cardinal Richelieu (1585–1642) served as prime minister of Louis XIII. His threefold goal was to establish royal authority, check the French nobility's ambitions, and destroy the Protestants as a political force. All these objectives were achieved by Richelieu, who was also very deeply involved in the Thirty Years' War.

All political thinkers agree that, if the people were too much at ease, it would be impossible to maintain them within the bounds of their duty. The basis of this is that, having less knowledge than the other estates,[3] who are far more cultivated and educated, if they were not held in check by some necessity, they would only with difficulty remain within the bounds prescribed for them by reason and by the laws.

Reason does not permit exempting them from all burdens; for in thus losing the mark of their subjection, they would also lose the memory of their condition; and if they were freed of tributes to pay, they would think they were also freed of obedience. They must be compared to mules who, once accustomed to carrying burdens, are spoiled more by long rest than by work. But just as this work must be moderate and the burden of the animal proportionate to its strength, so it must be with the taxes imposed on the people; if not moderate, even if they were of public utility, they would still be unjust.

I know that when kings undertake public works, it is said truthfully that what the people gains by it is returned to them by payment of taxes; one can likewise maintain that what the kings collect from the people is returned to it and that it pays only in order to withdraw the money by the enjoyment of calm and its goods which can only be preserved if the people contributes to the subsistence of the state.

I know, moreover, that several princes have lost their states for failing to maintain the military strength necessary for their preservation, because they feared to burden the people too much; and that certain subjects have been subjected to servitude by their enemies for having wanted too much liberty under their natural sovereign. But there is a certain point beyond which one must not go. Common sense teaches us that there must be a proportion between the burden and the strength of those who have to bear it. This proportion must be so strictly observed that, just as a prince cannot be considered good if he takes more than he should from his subjects, so the best are not always those who never levy more than necessary.

Finally, as, when a man is injured, the heart weakened by the loss of blood draws for aid on the lower parts only after having exhausted the upper ones; so, in times of grave necessity, sovereigns should avail themselves of the abundance of the rich before bleeding the poor excessively.

(Richelieu [attributed to]: *Political Testament,*
published in Latin, 1643; in French, 1687)

B. THE DIVINE RIGHT OF KINGS

1. JAMES I: THE CASE FOR

James Stuart (James VI of Scotland, James I of Great Britain; 1566–1625) was the son of Mary, Queen of Scots, who had been forced to abdicate in 1567. After a period of regency, James acceded to the Scottish throne in 1583; until 1603 he struggled against the nobility of Scotland in his efforts to establish a strong central government. Invited upon Queen Elizabeth's death to succeed her, he was able to unite England and Scotland; however, he encountered much difficulty in attempting to introduce his political principles in England.

First I will set down the true grounds, whereupon I am to build, out of the Scriptures, since monarchy is the true pattern of divinity; next, from the law of nature, by diverse similitudes drawn out of the same; and will conclude by answering the most weighty and apparent incommodities that can be objected.

I. *The King's Duty to His Subjects*

A. DRAWN FROM THE SCRIPTURES

The Prince's duty to his subjects is so clearly set down in many places of the Scriptures, and so openly confessed by all good princes, as not needing to be long therein, I shall as shortly as I can run through it.

Kings are called gods by prophetical King David,[4] because they sit upon God his throne in the earth, and have the count of their administration to give unto him. Their office is "to minister justice and judgment to the people," as the same David saith; "to establish good laws to his people, and procure obedience to the same," as diverse good kings of Judah did; "to procure the peace of the people," as the same David saith; "to decide all controversies that arise among them," as Solomon did; "to be the minister of God for the weal of them that do well, and to take vengeance upon them that do evil," as Saint Paul saith; "to go out and in before his people, as a good pastor," as is said in first of Samuel; "that through the prince's prosperity, the people's peace may be procured," as Jeremiah saith. . . .

In short, to procure the weal and flourishing of the people, not only by maintaining and executing the old lowable laws of the country, by establishing new laws (as necessity and evil manners will require), but by all other means possible to foresee and prevent all dangers that are likely to fall upon them; and to maintain concord, wealth, and civility among them as a loving father and careful watchman, caring for them more than for himself, knowing himself to be ordained for them, and not they for him, accountable therefore to that great God, who placed him as his lieutenant over them, upon the peril of his soul to procure the weal of both souls and bodies, as far as in him lieth, of all them that are committed to his charge.

B. DRAWN FROM THE LAW OF NATURE

By the law of nature the king becomes a natural father to all his lieges at his coronation. As the father is bound to care for the nourishing, education, and virtuous government of his children, even so is the king bound to care for all his subjects. As all the toil and pain that the father can take for his children will be thought light and well bestowed by him, so the effect thereof redounds to their profit and weal; so ought the king do toward his people. As the kindly father ought to foresee all the inconveniences and dangers that may arise toward his children, and with the hazard of his own person to press to prevent the same; so ought the king toward his people. As the father's wrath and correction upon any of his children that offendeth ought, by fatherly chastisement to be seasoned with pity, as long as there is any hope of amendment in them; so ought the king toward any of his lieges that offend in that measure.

In short, as a father's chief joy ought to be in procuring his children's welfare, rejoicing at their weal, sorrowing and pitying at their woe, hazarding for their safety, traveling for their rest, waking for their sleep, thinking (in a word) that his earthly felicity and life standeth and lieth more in them than in himself; so ought a good prince to think of his people.

II. The Subjects' Duties to the King
A. DRAWN FROM THE SCRIPTURES

And will ye consider the very words of the text, as they are set down, it shall plainly declare the obedience that the people owe to their king in all respects.

Samuel declares unto them what points of justice and equity their king will break in his behaviour unto them; and . . . putteth them out of hope, that . . . they shall not have leave to shake off that yoke, which God through their importunity hath laid upon them. . . .

Now then, since the erection of this kingdom and monarchy among the Jews, and the law thereof may, and ought to be a pattern to all Christian and well-founded monarchies, as being founded by God himself, who by his oracle, and out of his own mouth gave the law thereof: what liberty can broiling spirits and rebellious minds claim justly against any Christian monarchy; since they can claim to no greater liberty on their part than the people of God might have done, and no greater tyranny was ever executed by any prince or tyrant, whom they can object, nor was here forewarned to the people of God, (and yet all rebellion countermanded unto them) if tyrannizing over man's persons, sons, daughters and servants . . . may be called a tyranny?

And that this proposition grounded upon the Scripture, may the more clearly appear to be true by the practice oft proved in the same book, we never read that ever the prophets persuaded the people to rebel against the prince, how wicked soever he was.

There was never a more monstrous persecutor and tyrant than *Ahab:* yet all the rebellion that *Elias* ever raised against him, was to fly to the wilderness, where for fault of sustenance he was fed with the corbies. And I think no man will doubt but *Samuel, David,* and *Elias* had as great power to persuade the people, if they had wanted to use their credit to rebellions against these wicked kings, as any of our seditious preachers in these days of whatsoever religion, either in this country or in France, had that busied themselves most to stir up rebellion under the cloak of religion. This far only the love of truth, I protest, without hatred at their persons, has moved me to be somewhat satirical.

To end then the ground of my propositions taken out of Scripture, let two special and notable examples, one from law, the other from Scripture, conclude this part of my argument. Under the law, *Jeremiah* threateneth the people of God with utter destruction for rebellion against *Nebuchadnezzar,* the king of Babel, who, although he was an idolatrous persecutor, a foreign king, a tyrant, and usurper of their liberties; yet in respect they had once received and acknowledged him for their king, he not only commandeth them to obey him, but even to pray for his prosperity, adding the reason to it: because in his prosperity stood their peace.[5]

And in the Scriptures, that king, whom *Paul* bids his *Romans* obey and serve for conscience's sake, was *Nero,* that bloody tyrant, an infamy to his age, and a monster to the world, being also an idolatrous persecutor, as the King of *Babel* was. If then idolatry and defection from God, tyranny over their people, and persecution of the saints, for their profession's sake, hindred not the Spirit of God to command his people under all highest pain to give them all due and hearty obedience for conscience's sake, giving to *Cesar* that which was *Cesar's,* and to God that which was God's, as Christ saith; and that this practice throughout the book of God agreeth with this law, which he made in the erection of that monarchy, what shameless presumption is it to any Christian people nowadays to claim that unlawful liberty which God refused to his own peculiar and chosen people? [6] Shortly then to sum up in two or three sentences, grounded upon all these arguments, from the law of God, the duty and allegiance of the people to their lawful king, their obedience, I say, ought to be to him as to God's lieutenant on earth, obeying his commands in all things, except directly against God, or the commands of God's minister, acknowledging him a judge set by God over them, having power to judge them, but to be judged only by God, to whom alone he must give account of his judgment; fearing him as their judge, loving him as their father, praying for him as their protector, for his continuance, if he be good; for his amendment, if he be wicked; following and obeying his lawful commands, eschewing and flying his fury in his unlawful, without resistance, but by sobs and tears to God. . . .

Not that I deny the old definition of a king, and of a law; which makes the king be a speaking law, and the law a dumb king: for certainly a king that governs not by his law can neither be accountable to God for his administration nor have a happy and established reign. For albeit it be true that I have at length proved that the king is above the law, as both the author and giver of strength thereto; yet a good king will not only delight his subjects by the law but even will conform himself in his own actions thereunto, always keeping that ground, that the health of the commonwealth be his chief law. As likewise, although I have said a good king will frame all his actions to be according to the law; yet is he not bound thereto but of his good will and for good example-giving to his subjects.

B. DRAWN FROM THE LAW OF NATURE

And the agreement of the law of nature in this ground with the laws and constitutions of God and man will by two similitudes easily appear. The king towards his people is rightly compared to a father of children, and to a head of a body composed of diverse members. For as fathers, the good princes and magistrates of the people of God acknowledged themselves to their subjects. And the proper office of a king towards his subjects agrees very well with the office of the head towards the body and all members thereof. For from the head, being the seat of judgment, proceedeth the care and foresight of guiding and preventing all evil that may come to the body or any part thereof. The head cares for the body — so doeth the king for his people. As the discourse and direction flows from the head, and the execution according thereunto belongs to the rest of the members, every one according to their office: so it is betwixt a wise prince and his people. As the judgment coming from the head may not only employ the members, every one in their own office, as long as they are able for it; but likewise in case any of them be affected with any infirmity must care and provide for their remedy, in case it be curable, and if otherwise, cut them off for fear of infecting the rest: even so it is betwixt the prince and his people.

And now first for the father's part, consider, I pray you, what duty his children owe to him, and whether upon any pretext whatsoever, it will not be thought monstrous and unnatural for his sons to rise up against him, to control him at their appetite, and, when they think good, to slay him, or cut him off, and to adopt for themselves any other they please in his place. Or can any pretence of wickedness or rigor on his part be just excuse for his children to put hand unto him? And although we see by the course of nature that love tends to descend more than to ascend, in case it were true that the father hated and wronged the children ever so much, will any man, endowed with the least spark of reason think it lawful for them

to meet him with the line? Yea, suppose the father were furiously following his sons with a drawn sword, is it lawful for them to turn and strike
back or make any resistance but by flight?

(James I of England: *The True Law of Free Monarchies,* 1598)

2. *MILTON: THE CASE AGAINST*

John Milton (1608–1674), best known for his heroic poem
Paradise Lost, *spoke up repeatedly in defence of liberty. In
1644 he had defended freedom of publication against censor-
ship; here he attacks the doctrine of the divine right of kings
in justifying the execution of Charles I.*

I shall here set down, from first beginning, the original of kings; how and
wherefore exalted to that dignity above their brethren; and from thence
shall prove, that turning to tyranny they may be as lawfully deposed and
punished, as they were at first elected: this I shall do by authorities and
reasons, not learnt in corners among schisms and heresies, as our doubling
divines are ready to calumniate, but fetched out of the midst of choicest
and most authentic learning, and no prohibited authors; nor many heathen, but Mosaical, Christian, orthodoxal, and, which must needs be more
convincing to our adversaries, presbyterial.

No man, who knows aught, can be so stupid to deny, that all men naturally were born free, being the image and resemblance of God himself, and
were, by privilege above all the creatures, born to command, and not to
obey: and that they lived so, till from the root of Adam's transgression
falling among themselves to do wrong and violence, and foreseeing that
such courses must needs tend to the destruction of them all, they agreed
by common league to bind each other from mutual injury, and jointly to
defend themselves against any that gave disturbance or opposition to such
agreement. Hence came cities, towns, and commonwealths. And because
no faith in all was found sufficiently binding, they saw it needful to ordain
some authority that might restrain by force and punishment what was
violated against peace and common right.

This authority and power of self-defence and preservation being originally and naturally in every one of them, and unitedly in them all; for
ease, for order, and lest each man should be his own partial judge, they
communicated and derived either to one, whom for the eminence of his
wisdom and integrity they chose above the rest, or to more than one,
whom they thought of equal deserving: the first was called a king; the
other, magistrates: not to be their lords and masters, (though afterward

those names in some places were given voluntarily to such as had been authors of inestimable good to the people,) but to be their deputies and commissioners, to execute, by virtue of their intrusted power, that justice, which else every man by the bond of nature and of covenant must have executed for himself, and for one another. And to him that shall consider well, why among free persons one man by civil right should bear authority and jurisdiction over another, no other end or reason can be imaginable.

These for a while governed well, and with much equity decided all things at their own arbitrement; till the temptation of such a power, left absolute in their hands, perverted them at length to injustice and partiality. Then did they, who now by trial had found the danger and inconveniences of committing arbitrary power to any, invent laws, either framed or consented to by all, that should confine and limit the authority of whom they chose to govern them: that so man, of whose failing they had proof, might no more rule over them, but law and reason, abstracted as much as might be from personal errors and frailties. "While, as the magistrate was set above the people, so the law was set above the magistrate." When this would not serve, but that the law was either not executed, or misapplied, they were constrained from that time, the only remedy left them, to put conditions and take oaths from all kings and magistrates at their first instalment, to do impartial justice by law: who, upon those terms and no other, received allegiance from the people, that is to say, bond or covenant to obey them in execution of those laws, which they, the people, had themselves made or assented to. And this ofttimes with express warning, that if the king or magistrate proved unfaithful to his trust, the people would be disengaged. They added also counsellors and parliaments, not to be only at his beck, but, with him or without him, at set times, or at all times, when any danger threatened, to have care of the public safety.... That this and the rest of what hath hitherto been spoken is most true, might be copiously made appear through all stories, heathen and Christian; even of those nations where kings and emperors have sought means to abolish all ancient memory of the people's right by their encroachments and usurpations. But I spare long insertions, appealing to the German, French, Italian, Arragonian, English, and not least the Scottish histories. . . .

It being thus manifest, that the power of kings and magistrates is nothing else but what is only derivative, transferred, and committed to them in trust from the people to the common good of them all, in whom the power yet remains fundamentally, and cannot be taken from them, without a violation of their natural birthright. . . .

Secondly, that to say, as is usual, the king hath as good right to his crown and dignity as any man to his inheritance, is to make the subject no better than the king's slave, his chattel, or his possession that may be bought and sold: and doubtless, if hereditary title were sufficiently inquired, the best foundation of it would be found but either in courtesy or convenience. But suppose it to be of right hereditary, what can be more just and legal, if a subject for certain crimes be to forfeit by law from himself and posterity all his inheritance to the king, than that a king, for crimes proportional, should forfeit all his title and inheritance to the people? Unless the people must be thought created all for him, he not for them, and they all in one body inferior to him single; which were a kind of treason against the dignity of mankind to affirm.

Thirdly, it follows, that to say kings are accountable to none but God, is the overturning of all law and government. For if they may refuse to give account, then all covenants made with them at coronation, all oaths are in vain, and mere mockeries; all laws which they swear to keep, made to no purpose: for if the king fear not God, (as how many of them do not,) we hold then our lives and estates by the tenure of his mere grace and mercy, as from a god, not a mortal magistrate; a position that none but court-parasites or men besotted would maintain! . . .

Therefore kingdom and magistracy, whether supreme or subordinate, is called "a human ordinance," (1 Pet ii. 13, &c.,) which we are there taught is the will of God we should submit to, so far as for the punishment of evil-doers, and the encouragement of them that do well. "Submit," saith he, "as free men." "But to any civil power unaccountable, unquestionable, and not to be resisted, no, not in wickedness, and violent actions, how can we submit as free men?" "There is no power but of God," saith Paul; (Rom. xiii.;) as much as to say, God put it into man's heart to find out that way at first for common peace and preservation, approving the exercise thereof; else it contradicts Peter, who calls the same authority an ordinance of man. . . . Therefore Saint Paul in the forecited chapter tells us, that such magistrates he means, as are not a terror to the good, but to the evil; such as bear not the sword in vain, but to punish offenders, and to encourage the good. . . .

(John Milton: *The Tenure of Kings and Magistrates,* 1648–1649)

C.   THE DEFENSE OF ABSOLUTISM

Thomas Hobbes (1588–1679), the son of a vicar, was educated at Oxford. He was engaged as a tutor by the Cavendish family to whom he remained attached until the end of his life. He traveled with them across Europe and met many scientists. When the civil wars began, Hobbes, always a cautious man, fled to Paris, where he wrote his Leviathan. *But his treatise got him into trouble with English émigré court circles in Paris; so he fled back to England where he made his submission to the Council of State. After the Restoration, Hobbes made his peace with Charles II and settled down to a quiet life.*

Hobbes is often quoted for his grim view of human nature. This, however, is inevitable, for advocates of authoritarian government must necessarily hold such or similar opinions in order to justify governmental controls; conversely, a belief in popular government implies the optimistic view that human beings are capable of governing themselves with a maximum of freedom, i.e. that basic human nature is good.

I. The Introduction

Nature (the Art whereby God hath made and governes the World) is by the *Art* of man, as in many other things, so in this also imitated, that it can make an Artificial Animal. For seeing life is but a motion of Limbs, the beginning whereof is in some principall part within; why may we not say, that all *Automata* (Engines that move themselves by springs and wheeles as doth a watch) have an artificiall life? For what is the *Heart,* but a *Spring;* and the *Nerves,* but so many *Strings;* and the *Joynts,* but so many *Wheeles,* giving motion to the whole Body, such as was intended by the Artificer? *Art* goes yet further, imitating that Rationall and most excellent worke of Nature, *Man.* For by Art is created that great LEVIATHAN called a COMMON-WEALTH, or STATE, (in latine CIVITAS) which is but an Artificiall Man; though of greater stature and strength than the Naturall, for whose protection and defence it was intended; and in which, the *Soveraignty* is an Artificiall *Soul,* as giving life and motion to the whole body; The *Magistrates,* and other *Officers* of Judicature and Execution, artificiall *Joynts; Reward* and *Punishment* (by which fastned to the seate of the Soveraignty, every joynt and member is moved to performe his duty) are the *Nerves,* that do the same in the Body Naturall; The *Wealth* and *Riches* of all the particular members, are the *Strength; Salus Populi* (the *peoples safety*) its *Businesse; Counsellors,* by whom all things needfull for it to know, are suggested unto it, are the *Memory; Equity* and *Lawes,* an artificiall *Reason* and *Will; Concord, Health; Sedition, Sicknesse;* and *Civill war, Death.* Lastly, the *Pacts* and *Covenants,* by which the parts of this Body Politique were at first made, set together, and united, resemble that *Fiat,* or the *Let us make man,* pronounced by God in the Creation.

.   .   .

II. *How and Why Men Establish the State Thereby Limiting Their Liberty*

Nature, hath made men so equall, in the faculties of body, and mind; as that though there bee found one man sometimes manifestly stronger in body, or of quicker mind then another; yet when all is reckoned together, the difference between man, and man, is not so considerable, as that one man can thereupon claim to himselfe any benefit, to which another may not pretend, as well as he. For as to the strength of body, the weakest has strength enough to kill the strongest, either by secret machination, or by confederacy with others, that are in the same danger with himselfe.

.   .   .

From this equality of ability, ariseth equality of hope in the attaining of our Ends. And therefore if any two men desire the same thing, which neverthelesse they cannot both enjoy, they become enemies; and in the way to their End, (which is principally their owne conservation, and sometimes their delectation only,) endeavour to destroy, or subdue one an other. And from hence it comes to passe, that where an invader hath no more to feare, than an other mans single power; if one plant, sow, build, or possesse a convenient Seat, others may probably be expected to come prepared with forces united, to dispossesse, and deprive him, not only of the fruit of his labour, but also of his life, or liberty. And the Invader again is in the like danger of another.

And from this diffidence of one another, there is no way for any man to secure himselfe, so reasonable, as Anticipation; that is, by force, or wiles, to master the persons of all men he can, so long, till he see no other power great enough to endanger him: And this is no more than his own conservation requireth, and is generally allowed. . . .

So that in the nature of man, we find three principall causes of quarrell. First, Competition; Secondly, Diffidence; Thirdly, Glory.

The first, maketh men invade for Gain; the second, for Safety; and the third, for Reputation. The first use Violence, to make themselves Masters of other mens persons, wives, children, and cattell; the second, to defend them; the third, for trifles, as a word, a smile, a different opinion, and any other signe of undervalue, either direct in their Persons, or by reflexion in their Kindred, their Friends, their Nation, their Profession, or their Name.

Hereby it is manifest, that during the time men live without a common Power to keep them all in awe, they are in that condition which is called Warre; and such a warre, as is of every man, against every man. For WARRE, consisteth not in Battell onely, or the act of fighting; but in a tract of time, wherein the Will to contend by Battell is sufficiently known: and therefore the notion of *Time*, is to be considered in the nature of Warre; as it is in the nature of Weather. For as the nature of Foule weather, lyeth not in a showre or two of rain; but in an inclination thereto of many dayes together: So the nature of War, consisteth not in actuall fighting; but in the known disposition thereto, during all the time there is no assurance to the contrary. All other time is PEACE.

Whatsoever therefore is consequent to a time of Warre, where every man is Enemy to every man; the same is consequent to the time, wherein men live without other security, than what their own strength, and their own invention shall furnish them withall. In such condition, there is no place for Industry; because the fruit thereof is uncertain: and consequently no Culture of the Earth; no Navigation, nor use of the commodities that may be imported by Sea; no commodious Building; no Instruments of moving, and removing such things as require much force; no Knowledge of the face of the Earth; no account of Time; no Arts; no Letters; no Society; and which is worst of all, continuall feare, and danger of violent death; And the life of man, solitary, poore, nasty, brutish, and short.

.   .   .

It may peradventure be thought, there was never such a time, nor condition of warre as this; and I believe it was never generally so, over all the world: but there are many places, where they live so now. For the savage people in many places of *America,* except the government of small Families, the concord whereof dependeth on naturall lust, have no government at all; and live at this day in that brutish manner, as I said before. Howsoever, it may be perceived what manner of life there would be, where there were no common Power to feare; by the manner of life, which men that have formerly lived under a peacefull government, use to degenerate into, in a civill Warre.

.   .   .

III. The Terms and Parties of the Contract

The finall Cause, End, or Designe of men, (who naturally love Liberty, and Dominion over others,) in the introduction of that restraint upon themselves, (in which wee see them live in Common-wealths,) is the foresight of their own preservation, and of a more contented life thereby; that is to say, of getting themselves out from that miserable condition of Warre, which is necessarily consequent (as hath been shewn) to the naturall Passions of men, when there is no visible Power to keep them in awe, and tye them by feare of punishment to the performance of their Covenants, and observation of those Lawes of Nature set down in the fourteenth and fifteenth Chapters.

For the Lawes of Nature (as *Justice, Equity, Modesty, Mercy,* and (in summe) *doing to others, as wee would be done to,*) of themselves, without the terrour of some Power, to cause them to be observed, are contrary to our naturall Passions, that carry us to Partiality, Pride, Revenge, and the like. And Covenants, without the Sword, are but Words, and of no strength to secure a man at all. Therefore notwithstanding the Lawes of Nature, (which every one hath then kept, when he has the will to keep them, when he can do it safely,) if there be no Power erected, or not great enough for our security; every man will, and may lawfully rely on his own strength and art, for caution against all other men . . .

The only way to erect such a Common Power, as may be able to defend them from the invasion of Forraigners, and the injuries of one another, and thereby to secure them in such sort, as that by their owne industrie, and by the fruites of the Earth, they may nourish themselves and live contentedly; is, to conferre all their power and strength upon one Man, or upon one Assembly of men, that may reduce all their Wills, by plurality of voices, unto one Will: which is as much as to say, to appoint one Man, or Assembly of men, to beare their Person; and every one to owne, and acknowledge himselfe to be Author of whatsoever he that so beareth their Person, shall Act, or cause to be Acted, in those things which concerne the Common Peace and Safetie; and therein to submit their Wills, every one to his Will, and their Judgements, to his Judgment. This is more than Consent, or Concord; it is a reall Unitie of them all, in one and the same Person, made by Covenant of every man with every man, in such manner as if every man should say to every man, *I Authorise and give up my Right of Governing my selfe, to this Man, or to this Assembly of men, on this condition, that thou give up thy Right to him, and Authorise all his Actions in like manner.* This done, the Multitude so united in one

Person, is called a COMMON-WEALTH, in latine CIVITAS. This is the Generation of that great LEVIATHAN, or rather (to speake more reverently) of that *Mortall God,* to which wee owe under the *Immortall God,* our peace and defence. For by this Authoritie, given him by every particular man in the Common-Wealth, he hath the use of so much Power and Strength conferred on him, that by terror thereof, he is inabled to forme the wills of them all, to Peace at home, and mutuall ayd against their enemies abroad. And in him consisteth the Essence of the Common-wealth; which (to define it,) is *One Person, of whose Acts a great Multitude, by mutuall Covenants one with another, have made themselves every one the Author, to the end he may use the strength and means of them all, as he shall think expedient, for their Peace and Common Defence.*

And he that carryeth this Person, is called SOVERAIGNE, and said to have *Soveraigne Power;* and every one besides, his SUBJECT.

The attaining to this Soveraigne Power, is by two wayes. One, by Naturall force; as when a man maketh his children, to submit themselves, and their children to his government, as being able to destroy them if they refuse; or by Warre subdueth his enemies to his will, giving them their lives on that condition. The other, is when men agree amongst themselves, to submit to some Man, or Assembly of men, voluntarily, on confidence to be protected by him against all others. This later, may be called a Politicall Common-wealth, or Common-wealth by *Institution;* and the former, a Common-wealth by *Acquisition.*

.　　.　　.

IV. Of the Rights of Soveraignes by Institution

A *Common-wealth* is said to be *Instituted,* when a *Multitude* of men do Agree, and *Covenant, every one, with every one,* that to whatsoever *Man,* or *Assembly of Men,* shall be given by the major part, the *Right* to *Present* the Person of them all, (that is to say, to be their *Representative;*) every one, as well he that *Voted for it,* as he that *Voted against it,* shall *Authorise* all the Actions and Judgements, of that Man, or Assembly of men, in the same manner, as if they were his own, to the end, to live peaceably amongst themselves, and be protected against other men.

From this Institution of a Common-wealth are derived all the *Rights,* and *Facultyes* of him, or them, on whom the Soveraigne Power is conferred by the consent of the People assembled.

First, because they Covenant, it is to be understood, they are not obliged by former Covenant to any thing repugnant hereunto. And Consequently they that have already Instituted a Common-wealth, being thereby bound by Covenant, to own the Actions, and Judgements of one, cannot lawfully make a new Covenant, amongst themselves, to be obedient to any other, in any thing whatsoever, without his permission. And therefore, they that are subjects to a Monarch, cannot without his leave cast off Monarchy, and return to the confusion of a disunited Multitude; nor transferre their Person from him that beareth it, to another Man, or other Assembly of men: for they are bound, every man to every man, to Own, and be reputed Author of all, that he that already is their Soveraigne, shall do, and judge fit to be done: so that any one man dissenting, all the rest should break their Covenant made to that man, which is injustice: and they have also every man given the Soveraignty to him that beareth their Person; and therefore if they depose him, they take from him that which is his own, and so again it is injustice. Besides, if he that attempteth to depose his Soveraign, be killed, or punished by him for such attempt, he is author of his own punishment, as being by the Institution, Author of all his Soveraign shall do: And because it is injustice for a man to do any thing, for which he may be punished by his own authority, he is also upon that title, unjust. . . .

Secondly, Because the Right of bearing the Person of them all, is given to him they make Soveraigne, by Covenant onely of one to another, and not of him to any of them; there can happen no breach of Covenant on the part of the Soveraigne; and consequently none of his Subjects, by any pretence of forfeiture, can be freed from his Subjection. That he which is made Soveraigne maketh no Covenant with his Subjects before-hand, is manifest; because either he must make it with the whole multitude, as one party to the Covenant; or he must make a severall Covenant with every man. With the whole, as one party, it is impossible; because as yet they are not one Person: and if he make so many severall Covenants as there be men, those Covenants after he hath the Soveraignty are voyd, because what act soever can be pretended by any one of them for breach thereof, is the act both of himselfe, and of all the rest, because done in the Person, and by the Right of every one of them in particular. Besides, if any one, or more of them, pretend a breach of the Covenant made by the Soveraigne at his Institution; and others, or one other of his Subjects, or himselfe alone, pretend there was no such breach, there is in this case, no Judge to decide the controversie: it returns therefore to the Sword again; and every man recovereth the right of Protecting himselfe by his own strength, contrary to the designe they had in the Institution.

Thirdly, because the major part hath by consenting voices declared a Soveraigne; he that dissented must now consent with the rest; that is, be contented to avow all the actions he shall do, or else justly be destroyed by the rest. For if he voluntarily entered into the Congregation of them that were assembled, he sufficiently declared thereby his will (and therefore tacitely covenanted) to stand to what the major part should ordayne: and therefore if he refuse to stand thereto, or make Protestation against any of their Decrees, he does contrary to his Covenant, and therfore unjustly. And whether he be of the Congregation, or not; and whether his consent be asked, or not, he must either submit to their decrees, or be left in the condition of warre he was in before; wherein he might without injustice be destroyed by any man whatsoever.

Fourthly, because every Subject is by this Institution Author of all the Actions, and Judgments of the Soveraigne Instituted; it followes, that whatsoever he doth, it can be no injury to any of his Subjects; nor ought he to be by any of them accused of Injustice. For he that doth any thing by authority from another, doth therein no injury to him by whose authority he acteth: But by this Institution of a Common-wealth, every particular man is Author of all the Soveraigne doth; and consequently he that complaineth of injury from his Soveraigne, complaineth of that whereof he himselfe is Author; and therefore ought not to accuse any man but himselfe; no nor himselfe of injury; because to do injury to ones selfe, is impossible. It is true that they that have Soveraigne power, may commit Iniquity; but not Injustice, or Injury in the proper signification.

Fiftly, and consequently to that which was sayd last, no man that hath Soveraigne power can justly be put to death, or otherwise in any manner by his Subjects punished. For seeing every Subject is Author of the actions of his Soveraigne; he punisheth another, for the actions committed by himselfe. . . .

.   .   .

Seventhly, is annexed to the Soveraigntie, the whole power of prescribing the Rules, whereby every man may know, what Goods he may enjoy, and what Actions he may doe, without being molested by any of his fellow Subjects: And this is it men call *Propriety*. For before constitution of Soveraign Power (as hath already been shewn) all men had right to all things; which necessarily causeth Warre: and therefore this Proprietie, being necessary to Peace, and depending on Soveraign Power, is the Act of that Power, in order to the publique peace.

.   .   .

Eightly, is annexed to the Soveraigntie, the Right of Judicature; that is to say, of hearing and deciding all Controversies, which may arise concerning Law, either Civill, or Naturall, or concerning Fact.

.   .   .

V. *Limits Imposed Upon the Power of the Soveraigne*

Liberty, or Freedome, signifieth (properly) the absence of Opposition; (by Opposition, I mean externall Impediments of motion;) and may be applyed no lesse to Irrationall, and Inanimate creatures, than to Rationall. For whatsoever is so tyed, or environed, as it cannot move, but within a certain space, which space is determined by the opposition of some externall body, we say it hath not Liberty to go further. And so of all living creatures, whilest they are imprisoned, or restrained, with walls, or chayns; and of the water whilest it is kept in by banks, or vessels, that otherwise would spread it selfe into a larger space, we use to say, they are not at Liberty, to move in such manner, as without those externall impediments they would. But when the impediment of motion, is in the constitution of the thing it selfe, we use not to say, it wants the Liberty; but the Power to move; as when a stone lyeth still, or a man is fastned to his bed by sicknesse.

And according to this proper, and generally received meaning of the word, *A* Free-Man, *is he, that in those things, which by his strength and wit he is able to do, is not hindred to doe what he has a will to.* But when the words *Free,* and *Liberty,* are applyed to any thing but *Bodies,* they are abused; for that which is not subject to Motion, is not subject to Impediment: And therefore, when 'tis said (for example) The way is Free, no Liberty of the way is signified, but of those that walk in it without stop. And when we say a Guift is Free, there is not meant any Liberty of the Guift, but of the Giver, that was not bound by any law, or Covenant to give it. So when we *speak Freely,* it is not the Liberty of voice, or pronunciation, but of the man, whom no law hath obliged to speak otherwise then he did. Lastly, from the use of the word *Free-will,* no Liberty can be inferred of the will, desire, or inclination, but the Liberty of the man; which consisteth in this, that he finds no stop, in doing what he has the will, desire, or inclination to doe.

.   .   .

Neverthelesse we are not to understand, that by such Liberty, the Soveraign Power of life, and death, is either abolished, or limited. For it has been already shewn, that nothing the Soveraign Representative can doe to a Subject, on what pretence soever, can properly be called Injustice, or Injury; because every Subject is Author of every act the Soveraign doth; so that he never wanteth Right to any thing, otherwise, than as he himself is the Subject of God, and bound thereby to observe the laws of Nature. And therefore it may, and doth often happen in Common-wealths, that a Subject may be put to death, by the command of the Soveraign Power; and yet neither doe the other wrong: As when *Jeptha* caused his daughter to be sacrificed: In which, and the like cases, he that so dieth, had Liberty to doe the action, for which he is neverthelesse, without Injury put to death. And the same holdeth also in a Soveraign Prince, that putteth to death an Innocent Subject.

.   .   .

First therefore, seeing Soveraignty by Institution, is by Covenant of every one to every one; and Soveraignty by Acquisition, by Covenants of the Vanquished to the Victor, or Child to the Parent; It is manifest, that every Subject has Liberty in all those things, the right whereof cannot by Covenant be transferred. . . .

If the Soveraign command a man (though justly condemned,) to kill, wound, or mayme himselfe; or not to resist those that assault him; or to abstain from the use of food, ayre, medicine, or any other thing, without which he cannot live; yet hath that man the Liberty to disobey.

If a man be interrogated by the Soveraign, or his Authority, concerning a crime done by himselfe, he is not bound (without assurance of Pardon) to confesse it; because no man (as I have shewn in the same Chapter) can be obliged by Covenant to accuse himselfe.

Again, the Consent of a Subject to Soveraign Power, is contained in these words, *I Authorise, or take upon me, all his actions;* in which there is no restriction at all, of his own former naturall Liberty: For by allowing him to *kill me,* I am not bound to kill my selfe when he commands me. 'Tis one thing to say, *Kill me, or my fellow, if you please;* another thing to say, *I will kill my selfe, or my fellow.* It followeth therefore, that

No man is bound by the words themselves, either to kill himselfe, or any other man; And consequently, that the Obligation a man may sometimes have, upon the Command of the Soveraign to execute any dangerous, or dishonourable Office, dependeth not on the Words of our Submission; but on the Intention; which is to be understood by the End thereof. When therefore our refusall to obey, frustrates the End for which the Soveraignty was ordained; then there is no Liberty to refuse: otherwise there is.

Upon this ground, a man that is commanded as a Souldier to fight against the enemy, though his Soveraign have Right enough to punish his refusall with death, may neverthelesse in many cases refuse, without Injustice; as when he substituteth a sufficient Souldier in his place: for in this case he deserteth not the service of the Common-wealth. And there is allowance to be made for naturall timorousnesse, not onely to women, (of whom no such dangerous duty is expected,) but also to men of feminine courage. When Armies fight, there is on one side, or both, a running away; yet when they do it not out of trechery, but fear, they are not esteemed to do it unjustly, but dishonourably. For the same reason, to avoyd battell, is not Injustice, but Cowardise. But he that inrowleth himselfe a Souldier, or taketh imprest mony, taketh away the excuse of a timorous nature; and is obliged, not onely to go to the battell, but also not to run from it, without his Captaines leave. And when the Defence of the Common-wealth, requireth at once the help of all that are able to bear Arms, every one is obliged; because otherwise the Institution of the Common-wealth, which they have not the purpose, or courage to preserve, was in vain.

. . .

As for other Lyberties, they depend on the Silence of the Law. In cases where the Soveraign has prescribed no rule, there the Subject hath the Liberty to do, or forbeare, according to his own discretion. And therefore such Liberty is in some places more, and in some lesse; and in some times more, in other times lesse, according as they that have the Soveraignty shall think most convenient. As for Example, there was a time, when in *England* a man might enter in to his own Land, (and dispossesse such as wrongfully possessed it,) by force. But in after-times, that Liberty of Forcible Entry, was taken away by a Statute made (by the King) in Parliament. And in some places of the world, men have the Liberty of many wives: in other places, such Liberty is not allowed.

(Thomas Hobbes: *Leviathan,* Introduction, Chaps. 13, 17, 18, 21; 1651)

D. THE UTOPIAN STATE

Tommaso Campanella (1568–1639) was a Dominican priest. In 1598 he became involved in a plot to free Naples from Spanish occupation. The plot failed and Campanella spent some twenty-eight years in prison during which time he showed unusual strength of character, since he resisted torture successfully. Released through papal intercession, he fled to France where he wrote his utopian work, The City of the Sun. *Campanella, who was deeply interested in astrology, presents a utopia that may well be called a forerunner of Huxley's* Brave New World *in many ways.*

1. The Government of the Solarians

Their supreme head is a priest whom they call in their language SOL (Sun) and whom we, in ours, would call the *Metaphysician.* He has absolute power over all matters, spiritual as well as temporal. His decisions are irrevocable and put an end to further discussion. He is assisted by three ministers, PON, SIN, and MOR, which names in our language are the equivalents of *Power, Wisdom, Love.*

The functions of POWER include declarations of war, the making of peace treaties, and everything concerning defence or attack. POWER possesses supreme authority with respect to war without, however, being above *Sun.*

WISDOM is charged with the direction of liberal and mechanical arts and all the sciences. He draws up the programs of the schools; all the learned men, all the professors are under his supervision; and for every science he has under him a special assistant, for example the astrologer, the cosmographer, the arithmetician, the geometrician, the historiographer, the poet, the physician, the physicist, etc.

The minister LOVE's principal function is to watch over everything connected with procreation and to arrange sexual unions in such a way as to result in the most beautiful race possible. . . . This minister has authority over the education of children, over medicine, drugs, agriculture . . . and the art of cooking; in a word, over everything concerning food, clothing, and sexual intercourse. He is assisted by various subordinates (men and women) who are in charge of these special functions.

2. Community Life

They decided to live a truly philosophical life as a community. Although the community of women does not exist among the other inhabitants of that region, the Solarians established one. Everything is owned in common and distributed by the ministers; however, everybody has such a large share in honors and in the enjoyments that no one would think of claiming for himself the exclusive possession of any property.

3. The Metaphysician

To rise to the supreme position of *Metaphysician,* one must know the history of all peoples, their religious ceremonies, their laws, and their various forms of government. He must know the general principles of all the mechanical arts and be conversant in the physical, mathematical, and astrological sciences. The knowledge of languages is less necessary, since there are several interpreters of each one in the Republic. What is required of him especially is that he be a profound metaphysician and theologian, that he have a perfect knowledge of the origin, the principles, and the proofs of all the arts and sciences; of the relationships of similarity or difference of things; of the necessity, the destiny, and the harmony of the world; of the power, wisdom, and love of beings and of God; of the hierarchy of creation; of the analogies existing among all the beings of heaven, earth, and the seas; and of the union of reality and ideal in God — at least as much as man can comprehend these matters. Besides, he must still know the books of the prophets. As so varied and extensive a knowledge is not commonly found, it is usually possible to predict who will rise to this supreme post. In order to obtain this exalted rank, one must be at least thirty-five years old. The tenure of office is for life, at least as long as another man of more profound knowledge and more worthy to rule is not found.

(To the objection that a man knowing so many things may not be qualified to govern, the following reply is made:) "We are far more certain of finding the science of government in a learned man than you who place at the head of your governments ignorant people whom you believe worthy of ruling solely because they happen to be born a prince or because a political faction has managed to place them there. But even if our metaphysician were completely incapable of governing the state, the vastness of his knowledge will prevent him from ever being wicked, cruel, or tyrannical. We claim that a man who has studied only one subject cannot master it perfectly, since no subject is entirely independent of the others, and that one who is skilled only in one field (from books, of course), has a mind lacking in flexibility and activity. Contrariwise, only an active and superior intelligence is capable of absorbing all sorts of subjects and to delve deeply into things, which necessarily is the case with our supreme head."

4. How Officials Are Changed

The will of the people suffices to change the officials, except for the four great ministers, unless these, after deliberation among themselves, resign in favor of another in whom they recognize superiority in knowledge, wisdom, and morality. They are so devoted and so disinterested that they submit themselves without difficulty to a man they believe to be superior to them; and they will not hesitate to follow his lessons. However, that can happen only rarely.

5. Justice

Every individual is judged by his particular superior. Thus, the work director has the power of judging the offender and of punishing him by exile, by the whip, by reprimand, by depriving him of the common table, by denying him religious observances or association with women. But when a citizen has been killed or wounded intentionally and with premeditation, the guilty one is punished by death; or else by application of the law of retaliation: an eye for an eye, a nose for a nose, a tooth for a tooth. If, on the contrary, the fight occurred accidentally and without premeditation, the sentence is milder. The right to reduce the severity of the law belongs not to the judge but to the three ministers. As a last resort, an appeal can be made to SUN, not to ask him to change the sentence but to sollicit his indulgence; for he alone has the right to pardon.

There are no prisons in the town of the Solarians, unless it be a tower where rebellious enemies are locked up. The judicial procedure is not a written one. The opposing parties and the witnesses appear before the judge and the minister POWER; the accusation is pronounced and the accused takes care of his own defence. The sentence of acquittal or punishment is pronounced immediately; if appeal to the minister is made, the new decision is rendered the next day. The following day the decision becomes definitive unless SUN uses his privilege to pardon the sentenced man. At any rate, the latter must make peace with his accuser and the witnesses, as if they were the doctors of his illness, and the reconciliation must be sealed by embraces.

For capital execution, the people themselves must put the sentenced man to death or stone him, but the first blows must always be struck by the accuser and the witnesses. This law was established because the Solarians do not want their town to be soiled by lictors or executioners. In some cases the condemned man may choose himself how he wants to die. In the presence of his fellow-citizens, who exhort him to die, he attaches powder sacks to himself which he sets on fire. The whole town in tears bewails the fact that they had to resort to casting out a gangrenous member and supplicate God to appease his anger. The citizens do their best to convince the condemned man of the necessity to expiate his crime and the sentence is not carried out until he himself is ready to ask for and desire death.

But if an attempt has been made on the Republic, the divine majesty, or the persons of the supreme leaders, the death penalty alone may be applied — the unfortunate man can hope for no pardon and is punished instantly. For religious reasons, the individual condemned to death is obliged to expose before the people any reasons why his life should be spared, to reveal conscientiously the crimes for which other citizens would have deserved the same penalty as he and to denounce the magistrate who, by similar misdeeds, would have deserved a still more terrible punishment. If his defence is convincing or his revelations turn out to be true, his punishment is commuted to exile. As for those who have been denounced by the accused, they are left in peace and get off with an admonition. For transgressions due to human frailty, the guilty person receives no more than a warning to adopt more moderate habits; as for those due to ignorance, he is forced to study the arts and sciences in which he has shown himself to be unskilled.

The Solarians are united amongst themselves like the members of one

28. Nicolas Ier
L'Armessin,
Tommaso Campanella.
Photo: Giraudon.

body and everybody is involved in everybody else's life. When a citizen accuses himself before his superior of a secret transgression, the punishment is much milder than if he had been discovered. Good care is taken to protect people against slander. Besides, the slanderer, according to the law of retaliation, is given the punishment the falsely accused would have received. Since the Solarians walk and work always in groups, five witnesses are required to convict a man; lacking which, he is freed on his own oath and advised to behave henceforth in a manner that will not lead to further accusations. If he fails to heed this advice, two or three witnesses suffice to convict him, and the punishment is doubled.

The laws of the City of the Sun are few in number and remarkably brief and clear. They are engraved on brass tablets and hung on the gates, I mean: on the pillars of the temple. There, traced on every column, inscriptions in a very concise, metaphysical style tell the citizens the meaning of God, the angels and the stars; of man, the world, destiny, virtue, etc. There, furthermore, are engraved the most precise definitions of all the virtues. The magistrate who represents each virtue has each his seat or rather: his tribunal at the foot of the very column containing the definition of the virtue he represents; and when one of them has to act as judge, he sits down at that place and says: "My son, you have sinned against the holy definition of charity, of generosity, etc., read." Then, after having heard the defence, he pronounces the sentence, if needed. These kinds of punishments are true and efficient remedies which are far more a token of affection than a retribution.

(Tommaso Campanella: *The City of the Sun*, 1637)

E. GROTIUS: INTERNATIONAL LAW

Hugo Grotius (1583–1645), a Dutchman, was one of the most learned men of his time. He wrote Latin verses at nine, was ripe for the university at twelve, and edited an encyclopedia at fifteen. In 1603, he was appointed historiographer by the States General. Sent to Utrecht to mediate a religious dispute, he was arrested and condemned to life imprisonment. His wife managed to free him by having him carried out of prison in a chest that supposedly contained books. He fled to France, and unable to return to Holland, he accepted a position as Swedish ambassador to France. He died during a trip when overtaken by a storm near Danzig.

Grotius' work on international law was the first to receive wide attention. In it he appeals to reason and to universal traits that would be binding on all men, an attitude typical of rationalism.

1. Prologue

Fully convinced that there is a common law among nations, which is valid alike for war and in war, I have had many and weighty reasons for undertaking to write upon this subject. Throughout the Christian world I observed a lack of restraint in relation to war, such as even barbarian races should be ashamed of; I observed that men rush to arms for slight causes, or no cause at all, and that when arms have once been taken up, there is no longer any respect for law, divine or human; it is as if, in accordance with a general decree, frenzy had openly been let loose for the committing of all crimes.

2. Lawful Wars

In the first principles of nature there is nothing which is opposed to war; rather all points are in its favour. The end and aim of war being the preservation of life and limb, and the keeping or acquiring of things useful to life, war is in perfect accord with those first principles of nature. If in order to achieve these ends it is necessary to use force, no inconsistency with the first principles of nature is involved, since nature has given to each animal strength sufficient for self-defence and self-assistance.

Right reason, moreover, and the nature of society, which must be studied in the second place and are of even greater importance, do not prohibit all use of force, but only that use of force which is in conflict with society, that is which attempts to take away the rights of others. For society has in view this object, that through community of resource and effort each individual be safeguarded in the possession of what belongs to him.

It is sufficiently well established therefore that not all wars are at variance with the law of nature; and this may also be said to be true of the law of nations.

That wars, moreover, are not condemned by the volitional law of nations, histories, and the laws and customs of all peoples fully teach us. [There] arises the distinction between a war which, according to the law of nations, is formally declared and is called legal, that is a complete war; and a war not formally declared, which nevertheless does not on that account cease to be a legal war, that is according to law. For as regards other wars, provided the cause be just, the law of nations does not indeed lend them support, but it does not oppose them. "It has been established by the law of nations," says Livy, "that arms are to be warded off by arms." And Florentinus declares that the law of nations authorizes us to ward off violence and injury in order to protect our body.

By authors of repute a war is often called lawful not from the cause from which it arises, nor from the importance of its exploits, but because of certain peculiar legal consequences. Of what sort a lawful war is, however, will best be perceived from the definition of enemies given by the Roman jurists.

"Enemies are those who in the name of the state declare war upon us, or upon whom we in the name of the state declare war; others are brigands and robbers," says Pomponius.

It needs only to be noted further that one may understand that any one who has the supreme authority in the state may take the place of the Roman people in our illustration. . . .

That a war may be lawful in the sense indicated, it is not enough that it be waged by sovereign powers on each side. It is also necessary that it should be publicly declared, and in fact proclaimed so publicly that the notification of this declaration be made by one of the parties to the other.

The reason why nations required a declaration for the kind of war which we have called lawful according to the law of nations was not that which some adduce, with the purpose that nothing should be done secretly or deceitfully, for this pertains to an exhibition of courage rather than to law. The purpose was, rather, that the fact might be established with certainty that war was being waged not by private initiative but by the will of each of the two peoples or of their heads.

From this consideration arise the peculiar effects which do not develop in a war against brigands, nor in a war which a king wages against his subjects. Thus Seneca distinguishes "wars declared upon neighbors, or waged with citizens."

Wars that are undertaken by public authority have, it is true, in some respects a legal effect, as do all judicial decisions; but they are not on that account more free from wrong if they are undertaken without cause. Thus Alexander, if he commenced war on the Persians and other peoples without cause was deservedly called a brigand by the Scythians, according to Curtius, as also by Seneca; likewise by Lucan he was styled a robber, and by the sages of India "a man given over to wickedness," while a pirate once put Alexander in the same class with himself.

Authorities generally assign to wars three justifiable causes: defence, recovery of property, and punishment.

If an attack by violence is made on one's person, endangering life, and no other way of escape is open, under such circumstances war is permissible, even though it involves the slaying of the assailant.

This right of self-defence has its origin directly, and chiefly, in the fact that nature commits to each his own protection, not in the injustice or crime of the aggressor. Wherefore, even if the assailant be blameless, as for instance, a soldier acting in good faith, or one who mistakes me for someone else, or one who is rendered irresponsible by madness or by sleeplessness — this, we read, has actually happened to some — the right of self-defence is not thereby taken away; it is enough that I am not under obligation to suffer what such an assailant attempts, any more than I should be if attacked by an animal belonging to another.

We may now come to injuries that are attempted upon property.

If we have in view expletive justice only, I shall not deny that in order to preserve property a robber can even be killed, in case of necessity. For the disparity between property and life is offset by the favourable position of the innocent party and the odious rôle of the robber. From this it follows, that if we have in view this right only, a thief fleeing with stolen property can be felled with a missile, if the property cannot otherwise be recovered.

If, furthermore, we leave divine and human law out of account, regard for others, viewed as a principle of conduct, interposes no hindrance to such action, unless the stolen property is of extremely slight value and consequently worthy of no consideration. . . .

A person is killed either intentionally or unintentionally. No one can be justly killed intentionally, except as a just penalty or in case we are able in no other way to protect our life and property; however, that punishment may be just, it is necessary that he who is killed shall himself have done wrong, and in a matter punishable with the penalty of death on a decision of a fair judge.

The counsel of Themistius, who warns us that we must distinguish between those who were responsible for war and those who followed the leadership of others, is supported by numerous historical examples. Herodotus relates that the Greeks exacted punishment from those who instigated the Thebans to desert to the Medes. So too, as Livy relates, the leaders of the revolt of Ardea were beheaded.

Furthermore, in considering those who are responsible for war, we must distinguish between the causes of their action; for there are some causes which are not indeed just, but still are such that they may deceive persons who are by no means wicked. The author of the *Ad Herennium* suggests this as a perfectly equitable reason for pardoning: when any one has done wrong not from hatred or cruelty, but moved by a sense of duty and righteous zeal. Seneca's wise man "will dismiss his enemies safe and sound, at times even with praise, if they have taken the field on honourable grounds, on behalf of loyalty, a treaty obligation, or liberty."

An enemy therefore who wishes to observe, not what the laws of men permit, but what his duty requires, what is right from the point of view of religion and morals, will spare the blood of his foes; and he will condemn no one to death, unless to save himself from death or some like evil, or because of personal crimes which have merited capital punishment. Furthermore, from humanitarian instincts, or on other grounds, he will either completely pardon, or free from the penalty of death those who have deserved such punishment.

3. *Unjustifiable Wars*

Quite untenable is the position, which has been maintained by some, that according to the law of nations it is right to take up arms in order to weaken a growing power which, if it becomes too great, may be a source of danger.

That this consideration does enter into deliberations regarding war, I admit, but only on grounds of expediency, not of justice. Thus if a war be justifiable for other reasons, for this reason also it might be deemed farsighted to undertake the war; that is the gist of the argument which the writers cited on this point present. But that the possibility of being attacked confers the right to attack is abhorrent to every principle of equity. Human life exists under such conditions that complete security is never guaranteed to us. For protection against uncertain fears we must rely on Divine Providence, and on a wariness free from reproach, not on force.

Not less unacceptable is the doctrine of those who hold that defence is justifiable on the part of those who have deserved that war be made upon them; the reason they allege is, that few are satisfied with exacting vengeance in proportion to the injury suffered. But fear of an uncertainty cannot confer the right to resort to force; hence a man charged with a crime, because he fears that his punishment may be greater than he deserves, does not, on that account, have the right to resist by force the representatives of public authority who desire to take him.

He who has done injury to another ought first to offer satisfaction to him whom he has injured, through the arbitrament of a fair-minded man; if such an offer of satisfaction is rejected, then his taking up of arms will be without reproach.

4. The Humanitarian Conduct of War

With respect to the destruction of those who are killed by accident and without intent, it is the bidding of mercy, if not of justice, that, except for reasons that are weighty and will affect the safety of many, no action should be attempted whereby innocent persons may be threatened with destruction.

With these principles recognized, the defining of provisions to cover the more special cases will not be difficult. "Let the child be excused by his age, the woman by her sex," says Seneca.

With regard to children we have the judgment of those people and ages over which moral right has exerted the greatest influence. "We have arms," says Camillus in Livy, "not against that age which is spared even when cities are taken, but against men in arms." He adds that this has a place among the laws of war, that is the national laws.

Again, that which is always the rule in respect to children who have not attained the use of reason is in most cases valid with regard to women. This holds good, that is, unless women have committed a crime which ought to be punished in a special manner, or unless they take the place of men. For they are, as Statius says, "a sex untrained and inexperienced in war."

The same principal is in general to be applied to men whose manner of life is opposed to war. In this class must be placed first, those who perform religious duties.

In the second place farmers should be spared. The canon adds merchants; and this provision is to be taken as applicable not only to those who make a temporary sojourn in hostile territory, but also to permanent subjects; for their life also is foreign to arms.

To come to those who have born arms, we have already mentioned the remark of Pyrrhus in Seneca, who says that a sense of shame, that is, respect for what is right, forbids us to deprive a prisoner of life.

The surrender of those who yield upon condition that their lives be spared ought not to be rejected. Thus Arrian says that the slaughter by the Thebans of persons who had surrendered was not in accordance with Greek custom, "not a Hellenic killing."

The same sense of justice bids that those be spared who yield themselves unconditionally to the victor, or who become suppliants. "To butcher those who have surrendered is savage" is the judgment of Tacitus.

Against these precepts of justice and the law of nature frequently exceptions are offered, which are by no means just; as, for example, if retaliation is required, if there is need of inspiring terror, if too determined a resistance has been offered. Yet he who recalls what has previously been said in regard to valid reasons for putting to death will easily perceive that such exceptions do not afford just grounds for an execution.

There is no danger from prisoners, those who have surrendered or desire to do so; therefore in order to warrant their execution, it is necessary that a crime shall have been previously committed, such a crime, moreover, as a just judge would hold punishable by death.

Nature does not sanction retaliation except against those who have done wrong. It is not sufficient that by a sort of fiction the enemy may be conceived as forming a single body. Plutarch accuses the Syracusians on this ground, that they slew the wives and children of Hicetas for the sole reason that Hicetas had killed the wife, sister, and son of Dion.

Even where the crimes are such that they may seem worthy of death, it will be part of mercy to give up something of one's full right because of the number of those involved. Such clemency, we see, began with God Himself; for He desired that the Canaanites and their neighbours, by far the most wicked people, should have the offer of peace, which would grant them their lives upon condition of payment of tribute. Here applies the saying of Seneca: "The severity of the general is directed against individuals, but pardon is necessary where the whole army has deserted. What takes away a wise man's anger? The crowd of wrongdoers."

29. Nicolas Poussin, *The Massacre of the Innocents*. Photo: Giraudon.

30. Nicolas Poussin, *The Abduction of the Sabine Women*. Photo: Anderson-Giraudon.

What decision according to the law of nature should be rendered in regard to hostages may be gathered from what we have said already. In former times it was commonly believed that each person had over his own life the same right which he had over other things that come under ownership, and that this right, by tacit or expressed consent, passed from individuals to the state. It is, then, not to be wondered at if we read that hostages who were personally guiltless were put to death for a wrong done by their state, either as though done by their individual consent, or by the public consent in which their own was included. But now that a truer knowledge has taught us that lordship over life is reserved for God, it follows that no one by his individual consent can give another a right over life, either his own life, or that of a fellow-citizen. . . .

You may read in many places that the raping of women in time of war is permissible, and in many others that it is not permissible. Those who sanction rape have taken into account only the injury done to the person of another, and have judged that it is not inconsistent with the law of war that anything which belongs to the enemy should be at the disposition of the victor. A better conclusion has been rendered by others who have taken into consideration not only the injury but the unrestrained lust of the act; also, the fact that such acts do not contribute to safety or to punishment, and should consequently not go unpunished in war any more than in peace.

The latter view is the law not of all nations, but of the better ones. Thus Marcellus, before capturing Syracuse, is said to have taken pains for the protection of chastity, even in the case of the enemy. In Livy, Scipio says that it is a matter of concern for himself and for the Roman people "that they should not violate what is anywhere held sacred." "Anywhere," that is to say, among the more advanced people. Aelian, having related that the chastity of the women and girls of Pellene was violated by the victorious Sicyonians, exclaimed: "These are most brutal acts, ye gods of Greece, and not held honourable even among barbarians, so far as my memory serves."

Among Christians it is right that the view just presented shall be enforced, not only as a part of military discipline, but also as a part of the law of nations; that is, whoever forcibly violates chastity, even in war, should everywhere be subject to punishment.

(Hugo Grotius: *De Jure Belli ac Pacis,* 1625)

3

Education

The seventeenth-century ideas on education strike us as very modern. No wonder; it was a period when, as in ours, science was held in great esteem. One of the demands therefore was for a more practical approach to learning. Milton's small college campus, Locke's suggestion of reasoning with children; the insistence by both that languages should no longer be the principal subjects and that they be taught more quickly and simply — all this carries the familiar earmarks of "progressive education." It is, however, evident that both writers strongly insist on the moral and humanistic aspects of education.

The end then of learning is to repair the ruins of our first parents by regaining to know God aright, and out of that knowledge to love him, to imitate him, to be like him, as we may the nearest by possessing our souls of true virtue, which, being united to the heavenly grace of faith, makes up the highest perfection. But because our understanding cannot in this body found itself but on sensible things, nor arrive so clearly to the knowledge of God and things invisible as by orderly conning over the visible and inferior creature, the same method is necessarily to be followed in all discreet teaching. And seeing every nation affords not experience and tradition enough for all kind of learning, therefore we are chiefly taught the languages of those people who have at any time been most industrious after wisdom; so that language is but the instrument conveying to us things useful to be known. And though a linguist should pride himself to have all the tongues that Babel cleft the world into, yet if he have not studied the solid things in them as well as the words and lexicons, he were nothing so much to be esteemed a learned man as any yeoman or tradesman competently wise in his mother dialect only.

Hence appear the many mistakes which have made learning generally so unpleasing and so unsuccessful. First, we do amiss to spend seven or eight years merely in scraping together so much miserable Latin and Greek as might be learned otherwise easily and delightfully in one year. And that which casts our proficiency therein so much behind, is our time lost partly in too oft idle vacancies given both to schools and universities; partly in a preposterous exaction, forcing the empty wits of children to compose themes, verses, and orations, which are the acts of ripest judgment, and the final work of a head filled, by long reading and observing, with elegant maxims and copious invention. These are not matters to be wrung from poor striplings, like blood out of the nose, or the plucking of untimely fruit; besides the ill habit which they get of wretched barbarizing against the Latin and Greek idiom with their untutored Anglicisms, odious to be read, yet not to be avoided without a well-continued and judicious conversing among pure authors digested, which they scarce taste. Whereas, if after some preparatory grounds of speech by their certain forms got into memory, they were led to the praxis thereof in some chosen short book lessoned thoroughly to them, they might then forthwith proceed to learn the substance of good things, and arts in due order, which would bring the whole language quickly into their power. This I take to be the most rational and most profitable way of learning languages, and whereby we may best hope to give account to God of our youth spent herein.

And for the usual method of teaching arts, I deem it to be an old error of universities not yet well recovered from the scholastic grossness of barbarous ages, that instead of beginning with arts most easy (and those be such as are most obvious to the sense), they present their young unmatriculated novices, at first coming, with the most intellective abstractions of logic and metaphysics; so that they, having but newly left those grammatic flats and shallows where they stuck unreasonably to learn a few words with lamentable construction, and now on the sudden transported under another climate to be tossed and turmoiled with their unballasted wits in fathomless and unquiet deeps of controversy, do for the most part grow into hatred and contempt of learning, mocked and deluded all this while with ragged notions and babblements, while they expected worthy and delightful knowledge; till poverty or youthful years call them importunately their several ways, and hasten them, with the sway of friends, either to an ambitious and mercenary or ignorantly zealous divinity: some allured to the trade of law, grounding their purposes, not on the prudent and heavenly contemplation of justice and equity, which was never taught them, but on the promising and pleasing thoughts of litigious terms, fat contentions, and flowing fees; others betake them to state affairs, with souls so unprincipled in virtue and true generous breeding that flattery and court-shifts and tyrannous aphorisms appear to them the highest points of wisdom, instilling their barren hearts with a conscientious slavery, if, as I rather think, it be not feigned. Others, lastly, of a more delicious and airy spirit, retire themselves — knowing no better — to the enjoyments of ease and luxury, living out their days in feast and jollity; which indeed is the wisest and the safest course of all these, unless they were with more integrity undertaken. And these are the errors, and these are the fruits, of misspending our prime youth at the schools and universities as we do, either in learning mere words, or such things chiefly as were better unlearnt.

I shall detain you now no longer in the demonstration of what we should not do, but straight conduct ye to a hillside where I will point ye out the right path of a virtuous and noble education; laborious indeed at the first ascent, but else so smooth, so green, so full of goodly prospect and melodious sounds on every side, that the harp of Orpheus was not more charming. I doubt not but ye shall have more ado to drive our dullest and laziest youth, our stocks and stubs, from the infinite desire of such a happy nurture, than we have now to hale and drag our choicest and hopefullest wits to that asinine feast of sow-thistles and brambles which is commonly set before them as all the food and entertainment of their tenderest and most docible age. I call therefore a complete and generous education that which fits a man to perform justly, skilfully, and magnanimously all the offices, both private and public, of peace and war. And how all this may be done between twelve and one and twenty, less time than is now bestowed in pure trifling at grammar and sophistry, is to be thus ordered.

First, to find out a spacious house and ground about it fit for an academy, and big enough to lodge a hundred and fifty persons, whereof twenty or thereabout may be attendants, all under the government of one, who shall be thought of desert sufficient, and ability either to do all or wisely to direct and oversee it done. This place should be at once both school and university, not needing a remove to any other house of scholarship, except it be some peculiar college of law or physic, where they mean to be practitioners; but as for those general studies which take up all our time from Lily to the commencing, as they term it, Master of Art, it should be absolute. After this pattern, as many edifices may be converted to this use as shall be needful in every city throughout this land, which would tend much to the increase of learning and civility everywhere. This number, less or more thus collected, to the convenience of a foot company, or interchangeably two troops of cavalry, should divide their day's work into three parts as it lies orderly: their studies, their exercise, and their diet.

For their studies: first, they should begin with the chief and necessary rules of some good grammar, either that now used or any better; and while this is doing, their speech is to be fashioned to a distinct and clear pronunciation, as near as may be to the Italian, especially in the vowels. For we Englishmen, being far northerly, do not open our mouths in the cold air wide enough to grace a southern tongue, but are observed by all other nations to speak exceeding close and inward, so that to smatter Latin with an English mouth is as ill a hearing as law French. Next, to make them expert in the usefullest points of grammar, and withal to season them and win them early to the love of virtue and true labour, ere any flattering seducement or vain principle seize them wandering, some easy and delightful book of education would be read to them, whereof the Greeks have store, as Cebes, Plutarch, and other Socratic discourses. But in Latin we have none of classic authority extant, except the two or three first books of Quintilian and some select pieces elsewhere.

But here the main skill and groundwork will be to temper them such lectures and explanations, upon every opportunity, as may lead and draw them in willing obedience, inflamed with the study of learning and the admiration of virtue, stirred up with high hopes of living to be brave men and worthy patriots, dear to God and famous to all ages; that they may despise and scorn all their childish and ill-taught qualities to delight in manly and liberal exercises, which he who hath the art and proper eloquence to catch them with, what with mild and effectual persuasions and what with the intimation of some fear, if need be, but chiefly by his own example, might in a short space gain them to an incredible diligence and courage, infusing into their young breasts such an ingenuous and noble ardour as would not fail to make many of them renowned and matchless men. At the same time, some other hour of the day, might be taught them the rules of arithmetic; and soon after the elements of geometry, even playing, as the old manner was. After evening repast, till bedtime, their thoughts will be best taken up in the easy grounds of religion and the story of Scripture. . . .

The course of study hitherto briefly described is, what I can guess by reading, likest to those ancient and famous schools of Pythagoras, Plato, Isocrates, Aristotle, and such others, out of which were bred up such a number of renowned philosophers, orators, historians, poets, and princes all over Greece, Italy, and Asia, beside the flourishing studies of Cyrene and Alexandria. But herein it shall exceed them and supply a defect as great as that which Plato noted in the commonwealth of Sparta; whereas that city trained up their youth most for war, and these in their academies and Lyceum all for the gown, this institution of breeding which I here delineate shall be equally good both for peace and war. Therefore about an hour and a half ere they eat at noon should be allowed them for exer-

31. Abraham Bosse, *The Schoolmaster.*

cise and due rest afterwards, but the time for this may be enlarged at
pleasure, according as their rising in the morning shall be early.

(John Milton: *Of Education*, 1644)

I myself have been consulted of late by so many who profess themselves
at a loss how to breed their children, and the early corruption of youth
is now become so general a complaint that he cannot be thought wholly
impertinent who brings the consideration of this matter on the stage, and
offers something, if it be but to excite others, or afford matter of correction: for errors in education should be less indulged than any. These,
like faults in the first concoction, that are never mended in the second or
third, carry their afterwards incorrigible taint with them through all the
parts and stations of life.

I imagine the minds of children as easily turned this or that way as
water itself:

That which every gentleman (that takes any care of his education) desires for his son, besides the estate he leaves him, is contained, I suppose, in these four things, *virtue, wisdom, breeding* and *learning*. I will not trouble myself whether these names do not some of them sometimes stand for the same thing, or really include one another. It serves my turn here to follow the popular use of these words, which, I presume, is clear enough to make me be understood, and I hope there will be no difficulty to comprehend my meaning.

I placed *virtue* as the first and most necessary of those endowments that belong to a man or a gentleman; as absolutely requisite to make him valued and beloved by others, acceptable or tolerable to himself. Without that, I think, he will be happy neither in this nor the other world.

As the foundation of this, there ought very early to be imprinted on his mind a true notion of God, as of the independent Supreme Being, Author and Maker of all things, from Whom we receive all our good, Who loves us, and gives us all things. And consequent to this, instill into him a love and reverence of this Supreme Being. This is enough to begin with, without going to explain this matter any farther; for fear lest by talking too early to him of spirits, and being unseasonably forward to make him understand the incomprehensible nature of that Infinite Being, his head be either filled with false or perplexed with unintelligible notions of Him. Let him only be told upon occasion, that God made and governs all things, hears and sees everything, and does all manner of good to those that love and obey Him; you will find, that being told of such a God, other thoughts will be apt to rise up fast enough in his mind about Him; which, as you observe them to have any mistakes, you must set right. . . .

Having laid the foundations of virtue in a true notion of a God, such as the creed wisely teaches, as far as his age is capable, and by accustoming him to pray to Him, the next thing to be taken care of is to keep him exactly to speaking of truth, and by all the ways imaginable inclining him to be good-natured. Let him know that twenty faults are sooner to be forgiven than the straining of truth to cover anyone by an excuse. And to teach him betimes to love and be good-natured to others is to lay early the true foundation of an honest man; all injustice generally springing from too great love of ourselves and too little of others.

This is all I shall say of this matter in general, and is enough for laying the first foundations of virtue in a child. As he grows up, the tendency of his natural inclination must be observed; which, as it inclines him more than is convenient on one or t'other side from the right path of virtue, ought to have proper remedies applied. For few of Adam's children are so happy, as not to be born with some bias in their natural temper, which it is the business of education either to take off or counterbalance. But to enter into particulars of this would be beyond the design of this short treatise of education. I intend not a discourse of all the virtues and vices, how each virtue is to be attained, and every particular vice by its peculiar remedies cured, though I have mentioned some of the most ordinary faults, and the ways to be used in correcting them.

Wisdom I take in the popular acceptation, for a man's managing his business ably and with foresight in this world. This is the product of a good natural temper, application of mind, and experience together, and so above the reach of children. The greatest thing that in them can be done towards it is to hinder them, as much as may be, from being cunning; which, being the ape of wisdom, is the most distant from it that can be: and as an ape for the likeness it has to a man, wanting what really should make him so, is by so much the uglier; cunning is only the want of under-standing, which, because it cannot compass its ends by direct ways, would do it by a trick and circumvention; and the mischief of it is, a cunning trick helps but once, but hinders ever after. No cover was ever made so big or so fine as to hide itself: nobody was ever so cunning as to conceal their being so; and when they are once discovered, everybody is shy, everybody distrustful of crafty men; and all the world forwardly join to oppose and defeat them; whilst the open, fair, wise man has everybody to make way for him, and goes directly to his business. To accustom a child to have true notions of things, and not to be satisfied till he has them, to raise his mind to great and worthy thoughts, and to keep him at a distance from falsehood and cunning, which has always a broad mix-ture of falsehood in it, is the fittest preparation of a child for wisdom. The rest, which is to be learned from time, experience, and observation, and an acquaintance with men, their tempers, and designs, is not to be expected in the ignorance and inadvertency of childhood, or the incon-siderate heat and unweariness of youth. All that can be done towards it, during this unripe age, is, as I have said, to accustom them to truth and sincerity, to a submission to reason, and as much as may be to reflection on their own actions.

The next good quality belonging to a gentleman is *good breeding*. There are two sorts of ill breeding: the one a sheepish bashfulness, and the other a misbecoming negligence and disrespect in our carriage; both which are avoided by duly observing this one rule, *not to think meanly of ourselves, and not to think meanly of others.*

Keep them from vice and vicious dispositions, and such a kind of behaviour in general will come with every degree of their age, as is suitable to that age and the company they ordinarily converse with; and as they grow in years, they will grow in attention and application. But that your words may always carry weight and authority with them, if it shall happen upon any occasion that you bid him leave off the doing of any even childish things, you must be sure to carry the point, and not let him have the mastery. But yet, I say, I would have the father seldom interpose his authority and command in these cases, or in any other, but such as have a tendency to vicious habits. I think there are better ways of prevailing with them: and a gentle persuasion in reasoning, when the first point of submission to your will is got, will most times do much better.

It will perhaps be wondered that I mention *reasoning* with children; and yet I cannot but think that the true way of dealing with them. They understand it as early as they do language; and, if I misobserve not, they love to be treated as rational creatures sooner than is imagined. 'Tis a pride should be cherished in them, and, as much as can be, made the greatest instrument to turn them by.

But when I talk of reasoning, I do not intend any other but such as is suited to the child's capacity and apprehension. Nobody can think a boy of three or seven years old should be argued with as a grown man. Long discourses and philosophical reasonings, at best, amaze and confound but do not instruct children. When I say, therefore, that they must be *treated as rational creatures,* I mean that you should make them sensible, by the mildness of your carriage, and the composure even in your correction of them, that what you do is reasonable in you, and useful and necessary for them; and that it is not out of *caprichio,* passion, or fancy that you command or forbid them anything. This they are capable of understanding; and there is no virtue they should be excited to nor fault they should be kept from which I do not think they may be convinced of; but it must be by such reasons as their age and understandings are capable of, and those proposed always in very few and plain words.

You will wonder, perhaps, that I put *learning* last, especially if I tell you I think it the least part. This may seem strange in the mouth of a bookish man; and this making usually the chief, if not only bustle and stir about children, this being almost that alone which is thought on, when people talk of education, makes it the greater paradox. When I consider what ado is made about a little Latin and Greek, how many years are spent in it, and what a noise and business it makes to no purpose, I can hardly forbear thinking that the parents of children still live in fear of the schoolmaster's rod, which they look on as the only instrument of education; as a language or two to be its whole business. How else is it possible that a child should be chained to the oar seven, eight, or ten of the best years of his life, to get a language or two, which, I think, might be had at a great deal cheaper rate of pains and time, and be learned almost in playing?

(John Locke: *Some Thoughts Concerning Education,* 1693)

4
Society

*We have already seen that, for the time being, the social struc-
ture is not subject to rational criticism, since order and stability
seem more desirable goals than social justice.*

*Rational scrutiny, however, is being applied to manners,
social customs and behavior. If reason commands us to be
virtuous, why are people wicked? If sincerity is a virtue, why
do people behave hypocritically?*

*In a highly sophisticated court society where favors and
advancement are sought in devious ways, where exaggerated
courtesies and blown-up compliments are expected — in such a
society, how can a man be virtuous, how can he be sincere?*

*These are grave and fundamental questions of the sort that
only an outsider can ask. To such a man only two solutions are
possible: either he forces society to reform itself, or else he
adapts himself to society by compromising his ideas or sur-
rendering completely. Even if he is a strong man, the struggle
is an uneven one, and he is likely to turn into a hater of mankind who may eventually retire into solitude.*

A. A POLITICAL MISANTHROPE

Sir William Temple (1628–1699) was educated at Cambridge. After traveling on the Continent, he became a member of the Irish parliament, but moved to England in 1663. Attached to the foreign office, he was appointed minister resident to the Spanish court at Brussels. In 1668, he negotiated the Triple Alliance between England, the United Netherlands, and Sweden. He was named ambassador to the Hague and negotiated a treaty with the Dutch in 1671. Although a member of the Privy Council, he fell into disfavor and was struck off the council in 1681. Below, he writes of the reasons for his retirement.

Besides all these public circumstances, I considered myself in my own humour, temper, and disposition, which a man may disguise to others, though very hardly, but cannot to himself. I had learned by living long in courts and public affairs, that I was fit to live no longer in either. I found the arts of a court were contrary to the frankness and openness of my nature; and the constraints of public business too great for the liberty of my humour and my life. The common and proper ends of both are the advancement of men's fortunes; and that I have never minded, having as much as I needed, and, which is more, as I desired. The talent of gaining riches I ever despised, as observing it to belong to the most despicable men in other kinds: and I had the occasions of it so often in my way, if I would have made use of them, that I grew to disdain them, as a man does meat that he has always before him. Therefore, I could never go to service for nothing but wages, nor endure to be fettered in business when I thought it was to no purpose. I knew very well the arts of a court are, to talk the present language, to serve the present turn, and to follow the present humour of the prince, whatever it is: of all these I found myself so incapable, that I could not talk a language I did not mean, nor serve a turn I did not like, nor follow any man's humour wholly against my own. Besides, I have had, in twenty years experience, enough of the uncertainty of princes, the caprices of fortune, the corruption of ministers, the violence of factions, the unsteadiness of counsels, the infidelity of friends; nor do I think the rest of my life enough to make any new experiments.

(Sir William Temple: *Memoirs*, published 1720)

B. A SOCIAL MISANTHROPE

Molière (1622–1673), who had already satirized social manners in The Romantic Ladies, *tackled a far more difficult subject when, instead of dealing with provincial damsels, he took on sophisticated court society.*

Molière's portrayal of this society must have been faithful, for it aroused no criticism. The same cannot be said of the principal character Alceste, the misanthrope. In various comedies Molière had attacked vices, especially hyprocrisy (in Tartuffe). *Now, sincerity being a virtue, one would be justified in assuming that Molière is using Alceste as his spokesman; and yet there are a number of scenes in which Alceste is depicted as ridiculous.*

A great deal has been written on this problem ever since Jean-Jacques Rousseau identified himself with Alceste and accused Molière of having ridiculed virtue. Once more we must try not to judge the seventeenth century through the eyes of later periods. There is another major theme that runs, in true classical fashion, through most of Molière's comedies: the insistence on the golden mean, the warning against obsessions and extremes. Can one then go to excess in demanding sincerity of men? In his answer Philinte sounds like a typical rational man:

> *Good sense views all extremes with detestation,*
> *And bids us to be noble in moderation. (Act I, Scene 1)*

Critics have argued whether Alceste or Philinte is Molière's spokesman. It may be neither one, for one can admire Alceste's principles and find his application of them rigid, literal-minded, and excessive. One can approve of Philinte's reasonable attitude, yet find his philosophical, disabused acceptance of people as they are pessimistic, lackadaisical, and even cynical. The attraction of the play, which has constantly increased as successive interpretations were made of it, lies exactly in the tension caused by this ambivalence.

A word about how to read seventeenth-century literature, and Molière in particular, may be in order at this point. As

32. Nicolas Mignard,
Molière.
Photo: Giraudon.

*Dryden pointed out, it is not the subject that matters so much
as the treatment of it by the author. This does not mean that
the author is excused from conducting the plot in a manner
such as to maintain our interest in it; rather, what it implies is
that we must read with an attitude different from the way we
may have been conditioned by reading much of nineteenth- and
twentieth-century literature. Our attention must be centered
less on anticipation, suspense, on desiring to know how it will
all end than on enjoying the present moment, admiring a brilliant scene, savoring a particularly fitting remark. In other
words, we must read with a particular rhythm.*

*As for Molière, he frequently concluded his comedies with
an artificial ending; in* The Misanthrope, *however, the ending
is a natural one, entirely brought on by the characters of those*

*involved. Another problem is the word "comedy," which the
play is called. The reader may not find it very funny; in fact,
at times it may strike him as downright tragic. The best thing
to do is not to worry about this. Let us simply assume that* The
Misanthrope *is a play in the modern sense of the term. Laugh
when you feel like it, smile if you prefer, cry if you are moved.
Molière himself gave us this precept in* The School for Wives
Criticized *(Scene 7): "Let us therefore . . . never consult anything in a play but the effect it has on us. Let us heartily follow
the things that take our fancy, and never hunt for reasons to
prevent our having pleasure."*

ACT I
Scene 1
PHILINTE, ALCESTE

PHILINTE. Now, what's got into you?

ALCESTE, *seated.* Kindly leave me alone.

PHILINTE. Come, come, what is it? This lugubrious tone . . .

ALCESTE. Leave me, I said; you spoil my solitude.

PHILINTE. Oh, listen to me, now, and don't be rude.

ALCESTE. I choose to be rude, Sir, and to be hard of hearing.

PHILINTE. These ugly moods of yours are not endearing;
Friends though we are, I really must insist . . .

ALCESTE, *abruptly rising.* Friends? Friends, you say? Well, cross me off
your list.
I've been your friend till now, as you well know;
But after what I saw a moment ago
I tell you flatly that our ways must part.
I wish no place in a dishonest heart.

PHILINTE. Why, what have I done, Alceste? Is this quite just?

ALCESTE. My God, you ought to die of self-disgust.
I call your conduct inexcusable, Sir,
And every man of honor will concur.
I see you almost hug a man to death,
Exclaim for joy until you're out of breath,
And supplement these loving demonstrations

With endless offers, vows, and protestations;
Then when I ask you "Who was that?" I find
That you can barely bring his name to mind!
Once the man's back is turned, you cease to love him,
And speak with absolute indifference of him!
By God, I say it's base and scandalous
To falsify the heart's affections thus;
If I caught myself behaving in such a way,
I'd hang myself for shame, without delay.

PHILINTE. It hardly seems a hanging matter to me;
    I hope that you will take it graciously
    If I extend myself a slight reprieve,
    And live a little longer, by your leave.

ALCESTE. How dare you joke about a crime so grave?

PHILINTE. What crime? How else are people to behave?

ALCESTE. I'd have them be sincere, and never part
    With any word that isn't from the heart.

PHILINTE. When someone greets us with a show of pleasure,
    It's but polite to give him equal measure,
    Return his love the best that we know how,
    And trade him offer for offer, vow for vow.

ALCESTE. No, no, this formula you'd have me follow,
    However fashionable, is false and hollow,
    And I despise the frenzied operations
    Of all these barterers of protestations,
    These lavishers of meaningless embraces,
    These utterers of obliging commonplaces,
    Who court and flatter everyone on earth
    And praise the fool no less than the man of worth.
    Should you rejoice that someone fondles you,
    Offers his love and service, swears to be true,
    And fills your ears with praises of your name,
    When to the first damned fop he'll say the same?
    No, no: no self-respecting heart would dream
    Of prizing so promiscuous an esteem;
    However high the praise, there's nothing worse
    Than sharing honors with the universe.
    Esteem is founded on comparison:

To honor all men is to honor none.
Since you embrace this indiscriminate vice,
Your friendship comes at far too cheap a price;
I spurn the easy tribute of a heart
Which will not set the worthy man apart:
I choose, Sir, to be chosen; and in fine,
The friend of mankind is no friend of mine.

PHILINTE. But in polite society, custom decrees
That we show certain outward courtesies. . . .

ALCESTE. Ah, no! we should condemn with all our force
Such false and artificial intercourse.
Let men behave like men; let them display
Their inmost hearts in everything they say;
Let the heart speak, and let our sentiments
Not mask themselves in silly compliments.

PHILINTE. In certain cases it would be uncouth
And most absurd to speak the naked truth;
With all respect for your exalted notions,
It's often best to veil one's true emotions.
Wouldn't the social fabric come undone
If we were wholly frank with everyone?
Suppose you met with someone you couldn't bear;
Would you inform him of it then and there?

ALCESTE. Yes.

PHILINTE.   Then you'd tell old Emilie it's pathetic
The way she daubs her features with cosmetic
And plays the gay coquette at sixty-four?

ALCESTE. I would.

PHILINTE.   And you'd call Dorilas a bore,
And tell him every ear at court is lame
From hearing him brag about his noble name?

ALCESTE. Precisely.

PHILINTE.   Ah, you're joking.

ALCESTE.   *Au contraire:*
In this regard there's none I'd choose to spare.
All are corrupt; there's nothing to be seen
In court or town but aggravates my spleen.

I fall into deep gloom and melancholy
When I survey the scene of human folly,
Finding on every hand base flattery,
Injustice, fraud, self-interest, treachery. . . .
Ah, it's too much; mankind has grown so base,
I mean to break with the whole human race.

PHILINTE. This philosophic rage is a bit extreme;
You've no idea how comical you seem;
Indeed, we're like those brothers in the play
Called *School for Husbands,* one of whom was prey . . .

ALCESTE. Enough, now! None of your stupid similes.

PHILINTE. Then let's have no more tirades, if you please.
The world won't change, whatever you say or do;
And since plain speaking means so much to you,
I'll tell you plainly that by being frank
You've earned the reputation of a crank,
And that you're thought ridiculous when you rage
And rant against the manners of the age.

ALCESTE. So much the better; just what I wish to hear.
No news could be more grateful to my ear.
All men are so detestable in my eyes,
I should be sorry if they thought me wise.

PHILINTE. Your hatred's very sweeping, is it not?

ALCESTE. Quite right: I hate the whole degraded lot.

PHILINTE. Must all poor human creatures be embraced,
Without distinction, by your vast distaste?
Even in these bad times, there are surely a few . . .

ALCESTE. No, I include all men in one dim view:
Some men I hate for being rogues; the others
I hate because they treat the rogues like brothers,
And, lacking a virtuous scorn for what is vile,
Receive the villain with a complaisant smile.
Notice how tolerant people choose to be
Toward that bold rascal who's at law with me.
His social polish can't conceal his nature;
One sees at once that he's a treacherous creature;
No one could possibly be taken in

By those soft speeches and that sugary grin.
The whole world knows the shady means by which
The low-brow's grown so powerful and rich,
And risen to a rank so bright and high
That virtue can but blush, and merit sigh.
Whenever his name comes up in conversation,
None will defend his wretched reputation;
Call him knave, liar, scoundrel, and all the rest,
Each head will nod, and no one will protest.
And yet his smirk is seen in every house,
He's greeted everywhere with smiles and bows,
And when there's any honor that can be got
By pulling strings, he'll get it, like as not.
My God! It chills my heart to see the ways
Men come to terms with evil nowadays;
Sometimes, I swear, I'm moved to flee and find
Some desert land unfouled by humankind.

PHILINTE. Come, let's forget the follies of the times
And pardon mankind for its petty crimes;
Let's have an end of rantings and of railings,
And show some leniency toward human failings.
This world requires a pliant rectitude;
Too stern a virtue makes one stiff and rude;
Good sense views all extremes with detestation,
And bids us to be noble in moderation.
The rigid virtues of the ancient days
Are not for us; they jar with all our ways
And ask of us too lofty a perfection.
Wise men accept their times without objection,
And there's no greater folly, if you ask me,
Than trying to reform society.
Like you, I see each day a hundred and one
Unhandsome deeds that might be better done,
But still, for all the faults that meet my view,
I'm never known to storm and rave like you.
I take men as they are, or let them be,
And teach my soul to bear their frailty;
And whether in court or town, whatever the scene,
My phlegm's as philosophic as your spleen.

ALCESTE. This phlegm which you so eloquently commend,

Does nothing ever rile it up, my friend?
Suppose some man you trust should treacherously
Conspire to rob you of your property,
And do his best to wreck your reputation?
Wouldn't you feel a certain indignation?

PHILINTE. Why, no. These faults of which you so complain
Are part of human nature, I maintain,
And it's no more a matter for disgust
That men are knavish, selfish and unjust,
Than that the vulture dines upon the dead,
And wolves are furious, and apes ill-bred.

ALCESTE. Shall I see myself betrayed, robbed, torn to bits,
And not . . . Oh, let's be still and rest our wits.
Enough of reasoning, now. I've had my fill.

PHILINTE. Indeed, you would do well, Sir, to be still.
Rage less at your opponent, and give some thought
To how you'll win this lawsuit that he's brought.

ALCESTE. I assure you I'll do nothing of the sort.

PHILINTE. Then who will plead your case before the court?

ALCESTE. Reason and right and justice will plead for me.

PHILINTE. Oh, Lord. What judges do you plan to see?

ALCESTE. Why, none. The justice of my cause is clear.

PHILINTE. Of course, man; but there's politics to fear. . . .

ALCESTE. No, I refuse to lift a hand. That's flat.
I'm either right, or wrong.

PHILINTE.   Don't count on that.

ALCESTE. No, I'll do nothing.

PHILINTE.   Your enemy's influence
Is great, you know . . .

ALCESTE.   That makes no difference.

PHILINTE. It will; you'll see.

ALCESTE.   Must honor bow to guile?
If so, I shall be proud to lose the trial.

PHILINTE. Oh, really . . .

ALCESTE.   I'll discover by this case

Whether or not men are sufficiently base
And impudent and villainous and perverse
To do me wrong before the universe.

PHILINTE. What a man!

ALCESTE.   Oh, I could wish, whatever the cost,
Just for the beauty of it, that my trial were lost.

PHILINTE. If people heard you talking so, Alceste,
They'd split their sides. Your name would be a jest.

ALCESTE. So much the worse for jesters.

PHILINTE.   May I enquire
Whether this rectitude you so admire,
And these hard virtues you're enamored of
Are qualities of the lady whom you love?
It much surprises me that you, who seem
To view mankind with furious disesteem,
Have yet found something to enchant your eyes
Amidst a species which you so despise.
And what is more amazing, I'm afraid,
Is the most curious choice your heart has made.
The honest Éliante is fond of you,
Arsinoé, the prude, admires you too;
And yet your spirit's been perversely led
To choose the flighty Célimène instead,
Whose brittle malice and coquettish ways ·
So typify the manners of our days.
How is it that the traits you most abhor
Are bearable in this lady you adore?
Are you so blind with love that you can't find them?
Or do you contrive, in her case, not to mind them?

ALCESTE. My love for that young widow's not the kind
That can't perceive defects; no, I'm not blind.
I see her faults, despite my ardent love,
And all I see I fervently reprove.
And yet I'm weak; for all her falsity,
That woman knows the art of pleasing me,
And though I never cease complaining of her,
I swear I cannot manage not to love her.
Her charm outweighs her faults; I can but aim

To cleanse her spirit in my love's pure flame.

PHILINTE. That's no small task; I wish you all success.
You think then that she loves you?

ALCESTE.   Heavens, yes!
I wouldn't love her did she not love me.

PHILINTE. Well, if her taste for you is plain to see,
Why do these rivals cause you such despair?

ALCESTE. True love, Sir, is possessive, and cannot bear
To share with all the world. I'm here today
To tell her she must send that mob away.

PHILINTE. If I were you, and had your choice to make,
Éliante, her cousin, would be the one I'd take;
That honest heart, which cares for you alone,
Would harmonize far better with your own.

ALCESTE. True, true: each day my reason tells me so;
But reason doesn't rule in love, you know.

PHILINTE. I fear some bitter sorrow is in store;
This love . . .

Scene 2
ORONTE, ALCESTE, PHILINTE

ORONTE, *to* ALCESTE. The servants told me at the door
That Éliante and Célimène were out,
But when I heard, dear Sir, that you were about,
I came to say, without exaggeration,
That I hold you in the vastest admiration,
And that it's always been my dearest desire
To be the friend of one I so admire.
I hope to see my love of merit requited,
And you and I in friendship's bond united.
I'm sure you won't refuse — if I may be frank —
A friend of my devotedness — and rank.

During this speech of ORONTE'S, ALCESTE *is abstracted, and seems unaware that he is being spoken to. He only breaks off his reverie when* ORONTE *says:*

It was for you, if you please, that my words were intended.

ALCESTE. For me, Sir?

ORONTE.   Yes, for you. You're not offended?

ALCESTE. By no means. But this much surprises me. . . .
    The honor comes most unexpectedly. . . .

ORONTE. My high regard should not astonish you;
    The whole world feels the same. It is your due.

ALCESTE. Sir . . .

ORONTE.   Why, in all the State there isn't one
    Can match your merits; they shine, Sir, like the sun.

ALCESTE. Sir . . .

ORONTE.   You are higher in my estimation
    Than all that's most illustrious in the nation.

ALCESTE. Sir . . .

ORONTE.   If I lie, may heaven strike me dead!
    To show you that I mean what I have said,
    Permit me, Sir, to embrace you most sincerely,
    And swear that I will prize our friendship dearly.
    Give me your hand. And now, Sir, if you choose,
    We'll make our vows.

ALCESTE.   Sir . . .

ORONTE.   What! You refuse?

ALCESTE. Sir, it's a very great honor you extend:
    But friendship is a sacred thing, my friend;
    It would be profanation to bestow
    The name of friend on one you hardly know.
    All parts are better played when well-rehearsed;
    Let's put off friendship, and get acquainted first.
    We may discover it would be unwise
    To try to make our natures harmonize.

ORONTE. By heaven! You're sagacious to the core;
    This speech has made me admire you even more.
    Let time, then, bring us closer day by day;
    Meanwhile, I shall be yours in every way.
    If, for example, there should be anything
    You wish at court, I'll mention it to the King.
    I have his ear, of course; it's quite well known
    That I am much in favor with the throne.
    In short, I am your servant. And now, dear friend,

Since you have such fine judgment, I intend
To please you, if I can, with a small sonnet
I wrote not long ago. Please comment on it,
And tell me whether I ought to publish it.

ALCESTE. You must excuse me, Sir; I'm hardly fit
To judge such matters.

ORONTE.   Why not?

ALCESTE.   I am, I fear,
Inclined to be unfashionably sincere.

ORONTE. Just what I ask; I'd take no satisfaction
In anything but your sincere reaction.
I beg you not to dream of being kind.

ALCESTE. Since you desire it, Sir, I'll speak my mind.

ORONTE. *Sonnet*. It's a sonnet. . . . *Hope* . . . The poem's addressed
To a lady who wakened hopes within my breast.
Hope . . . this is not the pompous sort of thing,
Just modest little verses, with a tender ring.

ALCESTE. Well, we shall see.

ORONTE.   *Hope* . . . I'm anxious to hear
Whether the style seems properly smooth and clear,
And whether the choice of words is good or bad.

ALCESTE. We'll see, we'll see.

ORONTE.   Perhaps I ought to add
That it took me only a quarter-hour to write it.

ALCESTE. The time's irrelevant, Sir: kindly recite it.

ORONTE, *reading*.
            Hope comforts us awhile, 'tis true,
            Lulling our cares with careless laughter,
            And yet such joy is full of rue,
            My Phyllis, if nothing follows after.

PHILINTE. I'm charmed by this already; the style's delightful.

ALCESTE, *sotto voce, to* PHILINTE. How can you say that? Why, the thing
is frightful.

ORONTE. *Your fair face smiled on me awhile,*
            But was it kindness so to enchant me?

> *'Twould have been fairer not to smile,*
> *If hope was all you meant to grant me.*

PHILINTE. What a clever thought! How handsomely you phrase it!

ALCESTE, *sotto voce, to* PHILINTE. You know the thing is trash.
    How dare you praise it?

ORONTE. *If it's to be my passion's fate*
    Thus everlastingly to wait,
    Then death will come to set me free:
    For death is fairer than the fair;
    Phyllis, to hope is to despair
    When one must hope eternally.

PHILINTE. The close is exquisite — full of feeling and grace.

ALCESTE, *sotto voce, aside.* Oh, blast the close; you'd better close your face
    Before you send your lying soul to hell.

PHILINTE. I can't remember a poem I've liked so well.

ALCESTE, *sotto voce, aside.* Good Lord!

ORONTE, *to* PHILINTE.   I fear you're flattering me a bit.

PHILINTE. Oh, no!

ALCESTE, *sotto voce, aside.*
                    What else d'you call it, you hypocrite?

ORONTE, *to* ALCESTE. But you, Sir, keep your promise now: don't shrink
    From telling me sincerely what you think.

ALCESTE. Sir, these are delicate matters; we all desire
    To be told that we've the true poetic fire.
    But once, to one whose name I shall not mention,
    I said, regarding some verse of his invention,
    That gentlemen should rigorously control
    That itch to write which often afflicts the soul;
    That one should curb the heady inclination
    To publicize one's little avocation;
    And that in showing off one's works of art
    One often plays a very clownish part.

ORONTE. Are you suggesting in a devious way
    That I ought not . . .

ALCESTE.   Oh, that I do not say.
    Further, I told him that no fault is worse

Than that of writing frigid, lifeless verse,
And that the merest whisper of such a shame
Suffices to destroy a man's good name.

ORONTE. D'you mean to say my sonnet's dull and trite?

ALCESTE. I don't say that. But I went on to cite
Numerous cases of once-respected men
Who came to grief by taking up the pen.

ORONTE. And am I like them? Do I write so poorly?

ALCESTE. I don't say that. But I told this person, "Surely
You're under no necessity to compose;
Why you should wish to publish, heaven knows.
There's no excuse for printing tedious rot
Unless one writes for bread, as you do not.
Resist temptation, then, I beg of you;
Conceal your pastimes from the public view;
And don't give up, on any provocation,
Your present high and courtly reputation,
To purchase at a greedy printer's shop
The name of silly author and scribbling fop."
These were the points I tried to make him see.

ORONTE. I sense that they are also aimed at me;
But now — about my sonnet — I'd like to be told . . .

ALCESTE. Frankly, that sonnet should be pigeonholed.
You've chosen the worst models to imitate.
The style's unnatural. Let me illustrate:

For example, *Your fair face smiled on me awhile,*
Followed by, *'Twould have been fairer not to smile!*
Or this: *such joy is full of rue;*
Or this: *For death is fairer than the fair;*
Or, *Phyllis, to hope is to despair*
When one must hope eternally!

This artificial style, that's all the fashion,
Has neither taste, nor honesty, nor passion;
It's nothing but a sort of wordy play,
And nature never spoke in such a way.
What, in this shallow age, is not debased?
Our fathers, though less refined, had better taste;

I'd barter all that men admire today
For one old love song I shall try to say:

If the King had given me for my own
Paris, his citadel,
And I for that must leave alone
Her whom I love so well,
I'd say then to the Crown,
Take back your glittering town;
My darling is more fair, I swear,
My darling is more fair.

The rhyme's not rich, the style is rough and old,
But don't you see that it's the purest gold
Beside the tinsel nonsense now preferred,
And that there's passion in its every word?

If the King had given me for my own
Paris, his citadel,
And I for that must leave alone
Her whom I love so well,
I'd say then to the Crown,
Take back your glittering town;
My darling is more fair, I swear,
My darling is more fair.

There speaks a loving heart. (*To* PHILINTE) You're laughing, eh?
Laugh on, my precious wit. Whatever you say,
I hold that song's worth all the bibelots
That people hail today with ah's and oh's.

ORONTE. And I maintain my sonnet's very good.

ALCESTE. It's not at all surprising that you should.
    You have your reasons; permit me to have mine
    For thinking that you cannot write a line.

ORONTE. Others have praised my sonnet to the skies.

ALCESTE. I lack their art of telling pleasant lies.

ORONTE. You seem to think you've got no end of wit.

ALCESTE. To praise your verse, I'd need still more of it.

ORONTE. I'm not in need of your approval, Sir.

ALCESTE. That's good; you couldn't have it if you were.

ORONTE. Come now, I'll lend you the subject of my sonnet;

    I'd like to see you try to improve upon it.

ALCESTE. I might, by chance, write something just as shoddy;
    But then I wouldn't show it to everybody.

ORONTE. You're most opinionated and conceited.

ALCESTE. Go find your flatterers, and be better treated.

ORONTE. Look here, my little fellow, pray watch your tone.

ALCESTE. My great big fellow, you'd better watch your own.

PHILINTE, *stepping between them.* Oh, please, please, gentlemen! This will
    never do.

ORONTE. The fault is mine, and I leave the field to you.
    I am your servant, Sir, in every way.

ALCESTE. And I, Sir, am your most abject valet.

Scene 3
PHILINTE, ALCESTE

PHILINTE. Well, as you see, sincerity in excess
    Can get you into a very pretty mess;
    Oronte was hungry for appreciation. . . .

ALCESTE. Don't speak to me.

PHILINTE.   What?

ALCESTE.   No more conversation.

PHILINTE. Really, now . . .

ALCESTE.   Leave me alone.

PHILINTE.   If I . . .

ALCESTE.   Out of my sight!

PHILINTE. But what . . .

ALCESTE.   I won't listen.

PHILINTE.   But . . .

ALCESTE.   Silence!

PHILINTE.   Now, is it polite . . .

ALCESTE. By heaven, I've had enough. Don't follow me.

PHILINTE. Ah, you're just joking. I'll keep you company.

ACT IV
Scene 3
CÉLIMÈNE, ALCESTE

ALCESTE, *aside*. Sweet heaven, help me to control my passion.

CÉLIMÈNE, *aside*. Oh, Lord.
> *To* ALCESTE.

> Why stand there staring in that fashion?
> And what d'you mean by those dramatic sighs,
> And that malignant glitter in your eyes?

ALCESTE. I mean that sins which cause the blood to freeze
> Look innocent beside your treacheries;
> That nothing Hell's or Heaven's wrath could do
> Ever produced so bad a thing as you.

CÉLIMÈNE. Your compliments were always sweet and pretty.

ALCESTE. Madam, it's not the moment to be witty.
> No, blush and hang your head; you've ample reason,
> Since I've the fullest evidence of your treason.
> Ah, this is what my sad heart prophesied;
> Now all my anxious fears are verified;
> My dark suspicion and my gloomy doubt
> Divined the truth, and now the truth is out.
> For all your trickery, I was not deceived;
> It was my bitter stars that I believed.
> But don't imagine that you'll go scot-free;
> You shan't misuse me with impunity.
> I know that love's irrational and blind;
> I know the heart's not subject to the mind,
> And can't be reasoned into beating faster;
> I know each soul is free to choose its master;
> Therefore had you but spoken from the heart,
> Rejecting my attentions from the start,
> I'd have no grievance, or at any rate
> I could complain of nothing but my fate.
> Ah, but so falsely to encourage me —
> That was a treason and a treachery
> For which you cannot suffer too severely,
> And you shall pay for that behavior dearly.

Yes, now I have no pity, not a shred;
My temper's out of hand; I've lost my head;
Shocked by the knowledge of your double-dealings,
My reason can't restrain my savage feelings;
A righteous wrath deprives me of my senses,
And I won't answer for the consequences.

CÉLIMÈNE. What does this outburst mean? Will you please explain?
Have you, by any chance, gone quite insane?

ALCESTE. Yes, yes, I went insane the day I fell
A victim to your black and fatal spell,
Thinking to meet with some sincerity
Among the treacherous charms that beckoned me.

CÉLIMÈNE. Pooh. Of what treachery can you complain?

ALCESTE. How sly you are, how cleverly you feign!
But you'll not victimize me any more.
Look: here's a document you've seen before.
This evidence, which I acquired today,
Leaves you, I think, without a thing to say.

CÉLIMÈNE. Is this what sent you into such a fit?

ALCESTE. You should be blushing at the sight of it.

CÉLIMÈNE. Ought I to blush? I truly don't see why.

ALCESTE. Ah, now you're being bold as well as sly;
Since there's no signature, perhaps you'll claim . . .

CÉLIMÈNE. I wrote it, whether or not it bears my name.

ALCESTE. And you can view with equanimity
This proof of your disloyalty to me!

CÉLIMÈNE. Oh, don't be so outrageous and extreme.

ALCESTE. You take this matter lightly, it would seem.
Was it no wrong to me, no shame to you,
That you should send Oronte this billet-doux?

CÉLIMÈNE. Oronte! Who said it was for him?

ALCESTE.   Why, those
Who brought me this example of your prose.
But what's the difference? If you wrote the letter
To someone else, it pleases me no better.
My grievance and your guilt remain the same.

CÉLIMÈNE. But need you rage, and need I blush for shame,
  If this was written to a *woman* friend?

ALCESTE. Ah! Most ingenious. I'm impressed no end;
  And after that incredible evasion
  Your guilt is clear. I need no more persuasion.
  How dare you try so clumsy a deception?
  D'you think I'm wholly wanting in perception?
  Come, come, let's see how brazenly you'll try
  To bolster up so palpable a lie:
  Kindly construe this ardent closing section
  As nothing more than sisterly affection!
  Here, let me read it. Tell me, if you dare to,
  That this is for a woman . . .

CÉLIMÈNE.   I don't care to.
  What right have you to badger and berate me,
  And so highhandedly interrogate me?

ALCESTE. Now, don't be angry; all I ask of you
  Is that you justify a phrase or two . . .

CÉLIMÈNE. No, I shall not. I utterly refuse,
  And you may take those phrases as you choose.

ALCESTE. Just show me how this letter could be meant
  For a woman's eyes, and I shall be content.

CÉLIMÈNE. No, no, it's for Oronte; you're perfectly right.
  I welcome his attentions with delight,
  I prize his character and his intellect,
  And everything is just as you suspect.
  Come, do your worst now; give your rage free rein;
  But kindly cease to bicker and complain.

ALCESTE, *aside.* Good God! Could anything be more inhuman?
  Was ever a heart so mangled by a woman?
  When I complain of how she has betrayed me,
  She bridles, and commences to upbraid me!
  She tries my tortured patience to the limit;
  She won't deny her guilt; she glories in it!
  And yet my heart's too faint and cowardly
  To break these chains of passion, and be free,
  To scorn her as it should, and rise above
  This unrewarded, mad, and bitter love.

To Célimène.
Ah, traitress, in how confident a fashion
You take advantage of my helpless passion,
And use my weakness for your faithless charms
To make me once again throw down my arms!
But do at least deny this black transgression;
Take back that mocking and perverse confession;
Defend this letter and your innocence,
And I, poor fool, will aid in your defense.
Pretend, pretend, that you are just and true,
And I shall make myself believe in you.

Célimène. Oh, stop it. Don't be such a jealous dunce,
Or I shall leave off loving you at once.
Just why should I *pretend?* What could impel me
To stoop so low as that? And kindly tell me
Why, if I loved another, I shouldn't merely
Inform you of it, simply and sincerely!
I've told you where you stand, and that admission
Should altogether clear me of suspicion;
After so generous a guarantee,
What right have you to harbor doubts of me?
Since women are (from natural reticence)
Reluctant to declare their sentiments,
And since the honor of our sex requires
That we conceal our amorous desires,
Ought any man for whom such laws are broken
To question what the oracle has spoken?
Should he not rather feel an obligation
To trust that most obliging declaration?
Enough, now. Your suspicions quite disgust me;
Why should I love a man who doesn't trust me?
I cannot understand why I continue,
Fool that I am, to take an interest in you.
I ought to choose a man less prone to doubt,
And give you something to be vexed about.

Alceste. Ah, what a poor enchanted fool I am;
These gentle words, no doubt, were all a sham;
But destiny requires me to entrust
My happiness to you, and so I must.

I'll love you to the bitter end, and see
How false and treacherous you dare to be.

CÉLIMÈNE. No, you don't really love me as you ought.

ALCESTE. I love you more than can be said or thought;
Indeed, I wish you were in such distress
That I might show my deep devotedness.

(Molière: *The Misanthrope,* 1666)

5

A Rational Psychology

The seventeenth-century philosophers, in their writings on psychology, use, of course, terms different from present-day psychologists and psychiatrists, but their aim is the same: to help people overcome the harmful effects of emotions in order to live a sane and virtuous life. In an age of reason and science, it was their task to teach that emotions can be overcome by the proper use of reason, and to avail themselves of the latest findings of science (especially physiology) for this purpose.

To the extent that these findings were incomplete or that they arrived at false conclusions, their theories are necessarily obsolete, but they do not therefore lose in interest since they are often extremely brilliant errors. And if we are not led astray by the simple vocabulary employed (soul, mind, emotions, passions), we may be surprised to discover that these weighty philosophers, far from being naïve, knew a great deal about the complexities of human psychology.

Since Descartes had maintained that body and soul are completely distinct, the great problem was to determine how the soul, being immaterial, could act on the body. It is on this point that these philosophers disagree most profoundly. What is remarkable is that each of them develops his views of psychology in close harmony with his over-all philosophical system.

A. DESCARTES: PHYSICAL PSYCHOLOGY

Even though Descartes came up with an erroneous hypothesis by assigning to the pineal gland the role of bond between soul and body, his treatise on The Passions of the Soul *constitutes a landmark in the history of psychology. Descartes insists that the passions are not simply limited to the heart and the blood, but that the mind through the will is capable of changing their nature. He presents two principles that will continue to be accepted and developed until the late nineteenth century: first, that ideas and feelings tend to be associated; and, secondly, that there is a purely physical aspect to certain emotions. Descartes' "well-adjusted" man is the "generous" man, a model that may still be proposed in our times.*

ARTICLE II.

That in order to understand the passions of the soul, its functions must be distinguished from those of the body.

We do not observe the existence of any subject which more immediately acts upon our soul than the body to which it is joined, and that we must consequently consider that what in our soul is a passion is in the body, commonly speaking, an action; so that there is no better means of arriving at a knowledge of our passions than to examine the difference which exists between soul and body in order to know to which of the two we must attribute each one of the functions which are within us.

ARTICLE III.

What rule we must follow to bring about this result.

As to this we should not find much difficulty if we realise that all that we experience as being in us, and that to observation may exist in wholly inanimate bodies, must be attributed to our body alone; and, on the other hand, that all that which is in us and which we cannot in any way conceive as possibly pertaining to a body, must be attributed to our soul.

ARTICLE X.

How the animal spirits are produced in the brain.

But what is here most worthy of remark is that all the most animated and subtler portions of the blood which the heat has rarefied in the heart, enter ceaselessly in large quantities into the cavities of the brain. And the reason which causes them to go there rather than elsewhere, is that all the blood which issues from the heart by the great artery takes its course in a straight line towards that place, and not being able to enter it in its entirety, because there are only very narrow passages there, those of its parts which are the most agitated and the most subtle alone pass through, while the rest spreads abroad in all the other portions of the body. But these very subtle parts of the blood form the animal spirits; and for this end they have no need to experience any other change in the brain, unless it be that they are separated from the other less subtle portions of the blood; for what I here name spirits are nothing but material bodies and their one peculiarity is that they are bodies of extreme minuteness and that they move very quickly like the particles of the flame which issues from a torch. Thus it is that they never remain at rest in any spot, and just as some of them enter into the cavities of the brain, others issue forth by the pores which are in its substance, which pores conduct them into the nerves, and from these into the muscles, by means of which they move the body in all the different ways in which it can be moved.

ARTICLE XXVII.

The definition of the passions of the soul.

After having considered in what the passions of the soul differ from all its other thoughts, it seems to me that we may define them generally as the perceptions, feelings, or emotions of the soul which we relate specially to it, and which are caused, maintained, and fortified by some movement of the spirits.

ARTICLE XXXIV.

How the soul and the body act on one another.

Let us then conceive here that the soul has its principal seat in the little gland which exists in the middle of the brain, from whence it radiates forth through all the remainder of the body by means of the animal spirits, nerves, and even the blood, which, participating in the impressions of the spirits, can carry them by the arteries into all the members. And recollecting what has been said above about the machine of our body, i.e. that the little filaments of our nerves are so distributed in all its parts, that on the occasion of the diverse movements which are there excited by sensible objects, they open in diverse ways the pores of the brain, which causes the animal spirits contained in these cavities to enter in diverse ways into the muscles, by which means they can move the members in all the different ways in which they are capable of being moved; and also that all the other causes which are capable of moving the spirits in diverse ways suffice to conduct them into diverse muscles; let us here add that the small gland which is the main seat of the soul is so suspended between the cavities which contain the spirits that it can be moved by them in as many different ways as there are sensible diversities in the object, but that it may also be moved in diverse ways by the soul, whose nature is such that it receives in itself as many diverse impressions, that is to say, that it possesses as many diverse perceptions as there are diverse movements in this gland. Reciprocally, likewise the machine of the body is so formed that from the simple fact that this gland is diversely moved by the soul, or by such other cause, whatever it is, it thrusts the spirits which surround it towards the pores of the brain, which conduct them by the nerves into the muscles, by which means it causes them to move the limbs.

ARTICLE XLI.

The power of the soul in regard to the body.

But the will is so free in its nature, that it can never be constrained; and of the two sorts of thoughts which I have distinguished in the soul (of which the first are its actions, i.e. its desires, the others its passions, taking this word in its most general significance, which comprises all kinds of perceptions), the former are absolutely in its power, and can only be indirectly changed by the body, while on the other hand the latter depend absolutely on the actions which govern and direct them, and they can only indirectly be altered by the soul, excepting when it is itself their cause. And the whole action of the soul consists in this, that solely because it desires something, it causes the little gland to which it is closely united to move in the way requisite to produce the effect which relates to this desire.

ARTICLE LXIX.

That there are only six primitive passions.

But the number of those which are simple and primitive is not very large. For, in making a review of all those which I have enumerated, we may easily notice that there are but six which are such, i.e. wonder, love, hatred, desire, joy and sadness; and that all the others are composed of some of these six, or are species of them.

ARTICLE LXXIX.

The definition of love and hate.

Love is an emotion of the soul caused by the movement of the spirits which incites it to join itself willingly to objects which appear to it to be agreeable. And hatred is an emotion caused by the spirits which incite the soul to desire to be separated from the objects which present themselves to it as hurtful. I say that these emotions are caused by the spirits in order to distinguish love and hate, which are passions and depend on the body, both from the judgments which also induce the soul by its free will to unite itself with the things which it esteems to be good, and to separate itself from those it holds to be evil, and from the emotions which these judgments excite of themselves in the soul.

ARTICLE CVII.

What is the cause of the movements of the blood and the spirits in Love.

And I deduce the reasons for all this from what has been said above, that there is a connection between our soul and our body such that when we have once joined some corporeal action with some thought, the one of the two never presents itself to us without the other presenting itself at the same time. We see in the case of those who have in illness taken some concoction with great aversion, that they can neither drink nor eat afterwards anything approaching it in taste without the same aversion coming back to them; and similarly they cannot think of the aversion in which the medicines are held, without the same taste coming back to them in thought. For it seems to me that the earliest passions that our soul had when first it was joined to our body must be due to the fact that sometimes the blood or other juice which entered into the heart was a more suitable nutriment than usual for the maintenance there of heat, which is the principle of life, and that was the cause of the soul uniting itself to this nutriment of its own free will, that is to say, liking it, and at the same time the animal spirits flowed from the brain to the muscles which might press or agitate the parts from which it had come to the heart, in order to cause them to send it yet more; and these parts were the stomach and the intestines the agitation of which increases our appetite, or else the liver and lung likewise, which the muscles of the diaphragm may compress. That is why this same movement of animal spirits has always since accompanied the passion of love.

ARTICLE CXLVIII.

That the exercise of virtue is a sovereign remedy against the passions.

And, inasmuch as these inward emotions touch us most nearly, and in consequence have much more power over us than the passions from which they differ, and which are met with in conjunction with them, it is certain that, provided our soul is always possessed of something to content itself with inwardly, none of the troubles that come from elsewhere have any

33. François Girardon, *Sorrow*.
Photo: Giraudon.

34. Abraham Bosse,
Feed Those Who Are Hungry.

power to harm it, but rather serve to increase its joy, inasmuch as, seeing that it cannot be harmed by them, it is made sensible of its perfection. And in order that our soul may thus have something with which to be content, it has no need but to follow exactly after virtue. For whoever has lived in such a way that his conscience cannot reproach him for ever having failed to perform those things which he has judged to be the best (which is what I here call following after virtue) receives from this a satisfaction which is so powerful in rendering him happy that the most violent efforts of the passions never have sufficient power to disturb the tranquillity of his soul.

ARTICLE CLII.

For what reasons we may esteem ourselves.

And because one of the principal parts of wisdom is to know in what way and for what cause each person ought to esteem or despise himself, I shall here try to place on record my opinion on the matter. I only remark in us one thing which might give us good reason to esteem ourselves, to wit, the use of our free will, and the empire which we possess over our wishes. Because it is for those actions alone which depend on this free will that we may with reason be praised or blamed; and this in a certain measure renders us like God in making us masters of ourselves, provided that we do not through remissness lose the rights which He gives us.

ARTICLE CLIII.

In what Generosity consists.

Thus I think that true generosity which causes a man to esteem himself as highly as he legitimately can, consists alone partly in the fact that he knows that there is nothing that truly pertains to him but this free disposition of his will, and that there is no reason why he should be praised or blamed unless it is because he uses it well or ill; and partly in the fact that he is sensible in himself of a firm and constant resolution to use it well, that is to say, never to fail of his own will to undertake and execute all the things which he judges to be the best — which is to follow perfectly after virtue.

ARTICLE CLXI.

How Generosity may be acquired.

And it must be observed that what we commonly name virtues are habitudes in the soul, which dispose it to certain thoughts in such a way that they are different from these thoughts, but can produce them, and reciprocally can be produced by them. It must also be observed that these thoughts may be produced by the soul alone, but that it often happens that some movement of the spirits fortifies them, and that then they are actions of virtue, and at the same time passions of the soul. Thus, while there is no virtue to which it appears as though good native qualities contribute so much as to that which causes us only to esteem ourselves at a just value, and as it is easy to believe that all the souls that God places in human bodies are not equally noble and strong (which is the reason for my having called this virtue generosity, following the usage of our language, rather than magnanimity, following the usage of the Schools where it is not much known) it is yet certain that good instruction serves much in correcting the faults of birth, and that, if we frequently occupy ourselves in the consideration of what free-will is, and how great are the advantages which proceed from a firm resolution to make a good use of it, as also, on the other hand, how vain and useless are all the cares which exercise the ambitions, we may excite in ourselves the passion, and then acquire the virtue of generosity, which, being so to speak the key of all other virtues, and a general remedy for all the disorders of the passions, it appears to me that this consideration is well worthy of notice.

ARTICLE CCXI.

A general remedy against the Passions.

And now that we are acquainted with them all, we have much less reason to fear them than we formerly had. For we see that they are all good in their nature and that we have nothing to avoid but their evil uses or their excesses, against which the remedies which I explained might suffice, if each one of us took sufficient heed to practise them. But because I have placed amongst these remedies the forethought and diligence whereby we can correct our natural faults in exercising ourselves in separating within us the movements of the blood and spirits from the thoughts to which they are usually united. I confess that there are few people who are sufficiently prepared in this way to meet all the accidents of life, and that these movements excited in the blood by the objects of the passions follow so promptly from these single impressions that are made in the brain and from the disposition of the organs, although the soul contributes in no wise to them, that there is no human wisdom capable of resisting them when sufficient preparation is not made for doing so. . . . But what we can always do on such occasions, and what I think I can here put forward as the most general remedy and that most easy to practise against all excesses of the passions, is that, when we feel our blood to be thus agitated, we should be warned of the fact, and recollect that all that presents itself before the imagination tends to delude the soul and causes the reasons which serve to urge it to accomplish the object of its passion to appear much stronger than they are, and those which serve to dissuade it to be much weaker. And when the passions urge us only towards things the execution of which necessitates some delay, we ought to abstain from pronouncing any judgment on the spot, and to divert ourselves by other thoughts until time and rest shall have entirely calmed the emotion which is in the blood. And finally, when it incites us to actions regarding which it is requisite that an immediate resolution should be taken, the will must make it its main business to consider and follow up the reasons which are contrary to those set up by the passions, although they appear to be less strong; just as when we are suddenly attacked by some enemy, the occasion does not permit of our taking time to deliberate. But it seems to me that what those who are accustomed to reflect on their actions can always do when they feel themselves to be seized with fear, is to try to turn their thoughts away from the consideration of danger by representing to themselves the reasons which prove that there is much more certainty and honour in resistance than in flight. And on the other hand, when they feel that the desire of vengeance and anger incites them to run thoughtlessly towards those who attack them, they will recollect that it is imprudence to lose their lives when they can without dishonour save themselves, and that, if the match is very unequal, it is better to beat an honourable retreat or ask quarter, than to expose oneself doggedly to certain death.

ARTICLE CCXII.

That it is on them alone that all the good and evil of this life depends.

For the rest, the soul may have pleasures of its own, but as to those which are common to it and the body, they depend entirely on the passions, so that the men whom they can most move are capable of partaking most of enjoyment in this life. It is true that such men may also find most bitterness when they do not know how to employ them well, or fortune is contrary to them. But the principal use of prudence or self-control is that it teaches us to be masters of our passions, and to so control and guide them that the evils which they cause are quite bearable, and that we even derive joy from them all.

(René Descartes: *The Passions of the Soul*, 1649)

B. HENRY MORE: ANOTHER THEORY OF THE UNION OF BODY AND SOUL

Henry More (1614–1687) was a member of the Cambridge Platonists, a group that attempted to reconcile religion and philosophy. More, who was mystically inclined, at first admired Descartes greatly, but soon found himself dissatisfied with the Frenchman's theory of the soul as having no attributes except to think. To combat this abstraction, More attempts to prove that the soul occupies space, i.e. that it is material.

The greatest difficulty is to fancy how this *Spirit,* being so *incorporeal,* can be able to move the *Matter,* though it be in it. For it seems so subtle, that it will pass through, leaving no more footsteps of its being there than the lightning does in the scabbard, though it may haply melt the sword, because it there finds resistance. But a *Spirit* can find no resistance anywhere, the closest matter being easily penetrable and pervious to an *incorporeal* substance. The ground of this difficulty is founded upon the unconceivableness of any union that can be betwixt the *Matter,* and a substance that can so *easily pass through it.* For if we could but once imagine an *union* betwixt *Matter* and a *Spirit,* the activity then of the *Spirit* would certainly have influence upon *Matter,* either for *begetting,* or *increasing,* or *directing* the motion thereof.

But notwithstanding the *penetrability* and easy passage of a *Spirit* through *Matter,* there is yet for all that a capacity of a strong union betwixt them, and every whit as conceivable as betwixt the parts of *Matter* themselves. For what glue or cement holds the parts of hard matter in stones and metal together, or, if you will, of what is absolutely hard, that has no pores or particles, but is one continued and perfectly homogeneous body, not only to sense, but according to the exact *idea* of reason? What cement holds together the parts of such a body as this? Certainly nothing but *immediate union and rest.* Now for *union,* there is no comparison betwixt that of *Matter* with *Matter,* and this of *Spirit* with *Matter.* For the first is only superficial; in this latter the very inward parts are united, point to point throughout. Nor is there any fear it will not take hold, because it has a capacity of passing through. For in this absolutely solid, hard body, which let be A, in which let us conceive some inward superficies, suppose EAC, this superficies is so smooth as nothing can be conceived smoother: Why does not therefore the upper EDC slide upon the neather

part EFC upon the least motion imaginable, especially EFC being supposed to be held fast whilst the other is thrust against? This facility therefore of one body passing upon another without any sticking, seeming as
necessary to our fancy as a *Spirit's* passing through all bodies without taking hold of them . . . a firm union of *Spirit* and *Matter* is very possible,
though we cannot conceive the manner thereof.

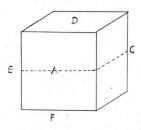

And as for *rest,* it is compatible to this conjunction of *Matter* with
Spirit, as well as of *Matter* with *Matter.* For suppose the whole body A
moved with like swiftness in every part, the parts A then are according to
that sense of *rest,* by which they would explain the adherence of the parts
of *Matter* one with another, truly quiescent. So say I that in the *union* of
Matter and *Spirit,* the parts of the *Matter* receiving from the *Spirit* just
such a velocity of motion as the *Spirit* exerts, and no more, they both rest
in firm *union* one with another. That what comes to pass even then when
there is far less immediate *union* than we speak of. For if we do but lay a
book on our hand, provided our hand be not moved with a swifter motion
than it communicates to the book, nor the book be pushed on faster than
the swiftness of the hand; the book and our hand will most certainly retain
their union and go together. So natural and easy is it to conceive how a
Spirit may move a *body* without any more perplexity or contradiction
than is found in the *union* and *motion* of the parts of *Matter* itself.

(Henry More: *The Immortality of the Soul,* Book I, Chap. 7; 1675)

C.   THE THEORIES CRITICIZED

He [Descartes] held, finally, that although each motion of this gland seems
to be connected by nature to a certain one of our thoughts at the beginning of our lives, yet it could be joined through habit to others: this he
endeavours to prove in the *Passions de l'Ame,* Part I., Art. 50. Hereby he
concludes that there is no mind so weak that it cannot, if well directed,
acquire absolute power of its passions. For these as defined by him are per-

ceptions or feelings or disturbances of the mind which have reference to it as species, and which are produced, preserved, and strengthened by some movement of the spirits (see Descartes' *Passions de l'Ame,* Part I., Art. 27). But since we can join each motion of the gland, and consequently of the spirits, to any will, the determination of the will depends on our power alone. If, therefore, we determine our will by certain fixed decisions according to which we wish to direct the actions of our life, and unite the movements of the passions which we wish to have to these decisions, we shall acquire absolute dominion over our passions. This is the opinion of that illustrious man (as I gather it from his own words), which I would scarcely have believed to have been put forward by so great a man, were it less acute. I cannot sufficiently wonder that a philosophic man, who clearly stated that he would deduce nothing save from self-evident bases of argument, and that he would assert nothing save what he perceived clearly and distinctly — one, moreover, who so many times reproved the Schoolmen for wishing to explain obscure things by means of occult qualities, should take an hypothesis far more occult than all the occult qualities. What does he understand, I ask, by the union of mind and body? What clear and distinct conception, I say, has he of thought closely united with a certain particle of quantity or extension? Truly I should like him to explain this union through its proximate cause. But he conceived the mind so distinct from the body that he could not assign a cause for this union nor for the mind itself, but he had perforce to recur to the cause of the whole universe, that is, to God. Again, I should like to know what degree of motion can the mind impart to this pineal gland, and with what force can it hold it suspended? For I know not whether this gland can be acted upon more quickly or slowly by the mind than by the animal spirits, and whether the movements of the passions which we unite securely to certain firm decisions cannot be disjoined from them by causes appertaining to the body: from which it would follow that although the mind fixedly proposed to go out against dangers and had joined to this decision the motions of daring, yet at the sight of the peril the gland would be so suspended that the mind would only be able to think of flight. And clearly as there is no relation between will and motion, so also there can be no comparison between the power or strength of the mind and body; and consequently the strength of one cannot be determined by the strength of the other. Add to this that this gland is not found thus situated in the middle of the brain, which has such easy action all around and in such a number of ways, and that the nerves are not all extended to the cavities of the brain.

(Baruch Spinoza: *Ethics,* Part V, Preface; 1677)

D. EMPIRICAL PSYCHOLOGY

In psychology Hobbes uses his theory of motion to define endeavor as infinitely small motion, thus making use of the findings of physical scientists. This theory enabled Hobbes to explain psychological effects in terms of materialism. Thus movements coming from without pass through the body and eventually produce observable movements of desire and aversion. The different reactions depend upon the effect of these exterior movements on the vital motions (the motions of the blood). This theory then attempted to propose that human actions could be as mechanically explained in terms of antecedent motions as the movements of projectiles.

There be in Animals, two sorts of *Motions* peculiar to them: One called *Vitall;* begun in generation, and continued without interruption through their whole life; such as are the *course* of the *Bloud,* the *Pulse,* the *Breathing,* the *Concoction, Nutrition, Excretion,* &c.; to which Motions there needs no help of Imagination: The other is *Animall motion,* otherwise called *Voluntary motion;* as to *go,* to *speak,* to *move* any of our limbes, in such manner as is first fancied in our minds. That Sense, is Motion in the organs and interiour parts of mans body, caused by the action of the things we See, Heare, &c; And that Fancy is but the Reliques of the same Motion, remaining after Sense, has been already sayd in the first and second Chapters. And because *going, speaking,* and the like Voluntary motions, depend alwayes upon a precedent thought of *whither, which way,* and *what;* it is evident, that the Imagination is the first internall beginning of all Voluntary Motion. And although unstudied men, doe not conceive any motion at all to be there, where the thing moved is invisible; or the space it is moved in, is (for the shortnesse of it) insensible; yet that doth not hinder, but that such Motions are. For let a space be never so little, that which is moved over a greater space, whereof that little one is part, must first be moved over that. These small beginnings of Motion, within the body of Man, before they appear in walking, speaking, striking, and other visible actions, are commonly called ENDEAVOUR.

This Endeavour, when it is toward something which causes it, is called APPETITE, or DESIRE; the later, being the generall name; and the other, often-times restrayned to signifie the Desire of Food, namely *Hunger* and *Thirst.* And when the Endeavour is fromward something, it is generally called AVERSION. These words *Appetite,* and *Aversion* we have from the *Latines;* and they both of them signifie the motions, one of approaching, the other of retiring. So also do the Greek words for the same, which are ὁρμὴ, and ἀφορμὴ. For Nature it selfe does often presse upon men those truths, which afterwards, when they look for somewhat beyond Nature, they stumble at. For the Schooles find in meere Appetite to go, or move, no actuall Motion at all: but because some Motion they must acknowledge, they call it Metaphoricall Motion; which is but an absurd speech: for though Words may be called metaphoricall; Bodies, and Motions cannot.

That which men Desire, they are also sayd to LOVE: and to HATE those things, for which they have Aversion. So that Desire, and Love, are the same thing; save that by Desire, we alwayes signifie the Absence of the Object; by Love, most commonly the Presence of the same. So also by Aversion, we signifie the Absence; and by Hate, the Presence of the Object.

.   .   .

And because the constitution of a mans Body, is in continuall mutation; it is impossible that all the same things should alwayes cause in him the same Appetites, and Aversions: much lesse can all men consent, in the Desire of almost any one and the same Object.

But whatsoever is the object of any mans Appetite or Desire; that is it, which he for his part calleth *Good:* And the object of his Hate, and Aversion, *Evill;* And of his Contempt, *Vile* and *Inconsiderable.* For these words of Good, Evill, and Contemptible, are ever used with relation to the person that useth them: There being nothing simply and absolutely so; nor any common Rule of Good and Evill, to be taken from the nature of the objects themselves; but from the Person of the man (where there is no Common-wealth;) or, (in a Common-wealth,) from the Person that representeth it; or from an Arbitrator or Judge, whom men disagreeing shall by consent set up, and make his sentence the Rule thereof.

.   .   .

Pleasure therefore, (or *Delight*,) is the apparence, or sense of Good; and *Molestation* or *Displeasure,* the apparence, or sense of Evill. And consequently all Appetite, Desire, and Love, is accompanied with some Delight more or lesse; and all Hatred, and Aversion, with more or lesse Displeasure and Offence.

Of Pleasures, or Delights, some arise from the sense of an object Present; And those may be called *Pleasures of Sense,* (The word *sensuall,* as it is used by those onely that condemn them, having no place till there be

Lawes.) Of this kind are all Onerations and Exonerations of the body; as also all that is pleasant, in the *Sight, Hearing, Smell, Tast,* or *Touch;* Others arise from the Expectation, that proceeds from foresight of the End, or Consequence of things; whether those things in the Sense Please or Displease: And these are *Pleasures of the Mind* of him that draweth those consequences; and are generally called JOY. In the like manner, Displeasures, are some in the Sense, and called PAYNE; others, in the Expectation of consequences, and are called GRIEFE.

These simple Passions called *Appetite, Desire, Love, Aversion, Hate, Joy,* and *Griefe,* have their names for divers considerations diversified. As first, when they one succeed another, they are diversly called from the opinion men have of the likelihood of attaining what they desire. Secondly, from the object loved or hated. Thirdly, from the consideration of many of them together. Fourthly, from the Alteration or succession it selfe.

.   .   .

And because in Deliberation, the Appetites, and Aversions are raised by foresight of the good and evill consequences, and sequels of the action whereof we Deliberate; the good or evill effect thereof dependeth on the foresight of a long chain of consequences, of which very seldome any man is able to see to the end. But for so farre as a man seeth, if the Good in those consequences, be greater than the Evill, the whole chaine is that which Writers call *Apparent,* or *Seeming Good.* And contrarily, when the Evill exceedeth the Good, the whole is *Apparent* or *Seeming Evill:* so that he who hath by Experience, or Reason, the greatest and surest prospect of Consequences, Deliberates best himselfe; and is able when he will, to give the best counsell unto others.

Continuall successe in obtaining those things which a man from time to time desireth, that is to say, continuall prospering, is that men call FELICITY; I mean the Felicity of this life. For there is no such thing as perpetuall Tranquillity of mind, while we live here; because Life it selfe is but Motion, and can never be without Desire, nor without Feare, no more than without Sense. What kind of Felicity God hath ordained to them that devoutly honour him, a man shall no sooner know, than enjoy; being joyes, that now are as incomprehensible, as the word of Schoole-men *Beatificall Vision* is unintelligible.

.   .   .

Vertue generally, in all sorts of subjects, is somewhat that is valued for eminence; and consisteth in comparison. For if all things were equally in all men, nothing would be prized. And by *Vertues* INTELLECTUALL, are alwayes understood such abilityes of the mind, as men praise, value, and desire should be in themselves; and go commonly under the name of a *good wit;* though the same word WIT, be used also, to distinguish one certain ability from the rest.

These *Vertues* are of two sorts; *Naturall,* and *Acquired.* By Naturall, I mean not, that which a man hath from his Birth: for that is nothing else but Sense; wherein men differ so little one from another, and from brute Beasts, as it is not to be reckoned amongst Vertues. But I mean, that *Wit,* which is gotten by Use onely, and Experience; without Method, Culture, or Instruction. This NATURALL WIT, consisteth principally in two things; *Celerity of Imagining,* (that is, swift succession of one thought to another;) and *steddy direction* to some approved end. On the Contrary a slow Imagination, maketh that Defect, or fault of the mind, which is commonly called DULNESSE, *Stupidity,* and sometimes by other names that signifie slownesse of motion, or difficulty to be moved.

And this difference of quicknesse, is caused by the difference of mens passions; that love and dislike, some one thing, some another: and therefore some mens thoughts run one way, some another; and are held to, and observe differently the things that passe through their imagination. . . .

As for *acquired Wit,* (I mean acquired by method and instruction,) there is none but Reason; which is grounded on the right use of Speech; and produceth the Sciences. . . .

The causes of this difference of Witts, are in the Passions: and the difference of Passions, proceedeth partly from the different Constitution of the body, and partly from different Education. For if the difference proceeded from the temper of the brain, and the organs of Sense, either exterior or interior, there would be no lesse difference of men in their Sight, Hearing, or other Senses, than in their Fancies, and Discretions. It proceeds therefore from the Passions; which are different, not onely from the difference of mens complexions; but also from their difference of customes, and education.

The Passions that most of all cause the differences of Wit, are principally, the more or lesse Desire of Power, of Riches, of Knowledge, and of Honour. All which may be reduced to the first, that is Desire of Power. For Riches, Knowledge and Honour are but severall sorts of Power.

And therefore, a man who has no great Passion for any of these things; but is as men terme it indifferent; though he may be so farre a good man, as to be free from giving offence; yet he cannot possibly have either a great Fancy, or much Judgement. For the Thoughts, are to the Desires, as

Scouts, and Spies, to range abroad, and find the way to the things Desired: All Stedinesse of the minds motion, and all quicknesse of the same, proceeding from thence. For as to have no Desire, is to be Dead: so to have weak Passions, is Dulnesse; and to have Passions indifferently for every thing, GIDDINESSE, and *Distraction;* and to have stronger, and more vehement Passions for any thing, than is ordinarily seen in others, is that which men call MADNESSE.

Whereof there be almost as many kinds, as of the Passions themselves. Sometimes the extraordinary and extravagant Passion, proceedeth from the evill constitution of the organs of the Body, or harme done them; and sometimes the hurt, and indisposition of the Organs, is caused by the vehemence, or long continuance of the Passion. But in both cases the Madnesse is of one and the same nature.

The Passion, whose violence, or continuance maketh Madnesse, is either great *vaine-Glory;* which is commonly called *Pride,* and *selfe-conceipt;* or great *Dejection* of mind.

Pride, subjecteth a man to Anger, the excesse whereof, is the Madnesse called RAGE, and FURY. And thus it comes to passe that excessive desire of Revenge, when it becomes habituall, hurteth the organs, and becomes Rage: That excessive love, with jealousie, becomes also Rage: Excessive opinion of a mans own selfe, for divine inspiration, for wisdome, learning, forme, and the like, becomes Distraction, and Giddinesse: The same, joyned with Envy, Rage: Vehement opinion of the truth of any thing, contradicted by others, Rage.

Dejection, subjects a man to causelesse fears; which is a Madnesse commonly called MELANCHOLY, apparent also in divers manners; as in haunting of solitudes, and graves; in superstitious behaviour; and in fearing some one, some another particular thing. In summe, all Passions that produce strange and unusuall behaviour, are called by the generall name of Madnesse. But of the severall kinds of Madnesse, he that would take the paines, might enrowle a legion. And if the Excesses be madnesse, there is no doubt but the Passions themselves, when they tend to Evill, are degrees of the same.

(Thomas Hobbes: *Leviathan,* Chaps. 6 and 8; 1651)

E. THE PSYCHOLOGY OF ORGANIC UNITY

For Spinoza body and soul are parallel manifestations of a fundamental unity. Hence, since physical and psychological actions occur jointly, emotions are states at once of the body and the soul. Spinoza's ideal man is the truly rational and intellectual philosopher.

Most who have written on the emotions, the manner of human life, seem to have dealt not with natural things which follow the general laws of nature, but with things which are outside the sphere of nature: they seem to have conceived man in nature as a kingdom within a kingdom. For they believe that man disturbs rather than follows the course of nature, and that he has absolute power in his actions, and is not determined in them by anything else than himself. They attribute the cause of human weakness and inconstancy not to the ordinary power of nature, but to some defect or other in human nature, wherefore they deplore, ridicule, despise, or, what is most common of all, abuse it: and he that can carp in the most eloquent or acute manner at the weakness of the human mind is held by his fellows as almost divine. Yet excellent men have not been wanting (to whose labour and industry I feel myself much indebted) who have written excellently in great quantity on the right manner of life, and left to men counsels full of wisdom: yet no one has yet determined, as far as I know, the nature and force of the emotions and what the mind can do in opposition to them for their constraint. I know that the most illustrious Descartes, although he also believed that the human mind had absolute power in its actions, endeavoured to explain the human emotions through their first causes, and to show at the same time the way in which the mind could have complete control over the emotions: but, in my opinion, he showed nothing but the greatness and ingenuity of his intellect, as I shall show in its proper place. For I wish to revert to those who prefer rather to abuse and ridicule the emotions and actions of men than to understand them. It will doubtless seem most strange to these that I should attempt to treat on the vices and failings of men in a geometrical manner, and should wish to demonstrate with accurate reasoning those things which they cry out against as opposed to reason, as vain, absurd, and disgusting. This, however, is my plan. Nothing happens in nature which can be attributed to a defect of it: for nature is always the same and one everywhere, and its ability and power of acting, that is, the laws and rules of nature according to which all things are made and changed from one form into another, are everywhere and always the same, and therefore one and the same manner must there be of understanding the nature of all things, that is, by means of the universal laws and rules of nature. For such emotions as hate, wrath, envy, etc., considered in themselves, follow from the same necessity

and ability of nature as other individual things: and therefore they acknowledge certain causes through which they are understood, and have certain properties equally worthy of our knowledge as the properties of any other thing, the contemplation alone of which delights us. And so I shall treat of the nature and force of the emotions, and the power of the mind over them, in the same manner as I treated of God and the mind in the previous parts, and I shall regard human actions and desires exactly as if I were dealing with lines, planes, and bodies.

VI. Love (*amor*) is pleasure accompanied by the idea of an external cause.

Explanation. — This definition sufficiently explains the essence of love. That one given by authors who define that love is the wish of the lover to unite himself to the object loved, does not explain the essence of love, but a property thereof: and as the essence of love has not been perceived sufficiently by the authors in question, they accordingly have neither a clear conception of its property, and accordingly their definition is considered by all to be exceedingly obscure. But let it be remarked that when I say

36. Anonymous,
Portrait of Spinoza.
Photo: Giraudon.

Baugin, *Still Life*
h Chessboard.
oto: Giraudon.

that it is a property of the essence of love that the lover wishes to be united
to the object of his love, I do not understand by will or wish, consent, deliberation, or free decision . . . nor even the wish of the lover to be united
with the object of his love when it is absent, nor of continuing in its presence when it is present (for love can be conceived without either of these
desires); but by wish I understand the satisfaction which is in the love by
reason of the presence of the object loved, by which the pleasure of the
lover is maintained, or at least cherished.

PROP. XLI. Pleasure clearly is not evil but good; but pain, on the contrary, is clearly evil.

Proof. — Pleasure is an emotion by which the power of acting of the
body is increased or aided; but pain contrariwise is an emotion whereby
the body's power of acting is diminished or hindered; and therefore pleasure is certainly good, etc.

PROP. XLIV. Love and desire can be excessive.

Proof. — Love is pleasure accompanied by the idea of an external cause.
Therefore titillation accompanied by the idea of an external cause is love;

and therefore love can be excessive. Again, desire is the greater according as the emotion from which it arose is greater. Wherefore, as an emotion can surpass all the other actions of man, so also can desire which arises from that emotion surpass other desires, and so it can have the same excess as we proved in the previous proposition titillation to have.

Note. — Merriment, which we said to be good, can be more easily conceived than observed. For the emotions by which we are daily assailed have reference rather to some part of the body which is affected beyond the others, and so the emotions as a rule are in excess, and so detain the mind in the contemplation of one object that it cannot think of others; and although men are liable to many emotions, and therefore few are found who are always assailed by one and the same emotion, yet there are not wanting those to whom one and the same emotion adheres with great pertinacity. We see that men are sometimes so affected by one object that, although it is not present, yet they believe it to be present with them; when this happens to a man who is not asleep, we say that he is delirious or insane; nor are they thought less mad who are fired with love, and who spend night and day in dreaming of their ladylove or mistress, for they cause laughter. But when a miser thinks of nothing save money and coins, or an ambitious man of nothing save honour, these are not thought to be insane, for they are harmful, and are thought worthy of hatred. But in truth, avarice, ambition, lust, etc., are nothing but species of madness, although they are not enumerated among diseases.

PROP. III. An emotion which is a passion ceases to be a passion as soon as we form a clear and distinct idea of it.

Proof. — An emotion which is a passion is a confused idea. If, therefore, we form a clear and distinct idea of this emotion, this idea will be distinguished from the emotion in so far as it has reference to the mind alone by reason alone: and therefore the emotion will cease to be a passion.

Corollary. — Therefore the more an emotion becomes known to us, the more it is within our power and the less the mind is passive to it.

. . . we perceive many things and form universal notions, first, from individual things represented to our intellect mutilated, confused, and without order, and therefore we are wont to call such perceptions knowledge from vague or casual experience; second, from signs, *e.g.,* from the fact that we remember certain things through having read or heard certain words and form certain ideas of them similar to those through which we imagine things. Both of these ways of regarding things I shall call hereafter knowledge of the first kind, opinion, or imagination. Third, from the fact that we have common notions and adequate ideas of the properties of things. And I shall call this reason and knowledge of the second kind. Besides these two kinds of knowledge there is a third, as I shall show in what follows, which we shall call intuition. Now this kind of knowing proceeds from an adequate idea of the formal essence of certain attributes of God to the adequate knowledge of the essence of things. I shall illustrate these three by one example. Let three numbers be given to find the fourth, which is in the same proportion to the third as the second is to the first. Tradesmen without hesitation multiply the second by the third and divide the product by the first: either because they have not forgotten the rule which they received from the school-master without any proof, or because they have often tried it with very small numbers, or by conviction of the proof of Prop. 19, Book VII., of Euclid's elements, namely, the common property of proportionals. But in very small numbers there is no need of this, for when the numbers 1, 2, 3, are given, who is there who could not see that the fourth proportional is 6? and this is much clearer because we conclude the fourth number from the same ratio which intuitively we see the first bears to the second.

PROP. XXXVIII. The more the mind understands things by the second and third kinds of knowledge, the less it will be passive to emotions which are evil, and the less it will fear death.

Proof. — The essence of the mind consists of knowledge. The more things then the mind understands by the second and third kinds of knowledge, the greater will be that part of it that remains, and consequently the greater will be the part of it that is not touched by emotions which are contrary to our nature, that is, which are evil. The more then the mind understands things by the second and third kinds of knowledge, the greater will be that part of it which remains unhurt, and consequently it will be less subject to emotions, etc.

PROP. XLII. Blessedness is not the reward of virtue, but virtue itself: nor should we rejoice in it for that we restrain our lusts, but, on the contrary, because we rejoice therein we can restrain our lusts.

Proof. — Blessedness consists of love towards God, and this love arises from the third kind of knowledge. And therefore this love must be referred to the mind in so far as it is active, and therefore it is virtue itself: which is the first point. Again, the more the mind rejoices in this divine love or blessedness, the more it understands, that is, the more power it has over the emotions, and the less passive it is to emotions which are evil. And therefore, by the very fact that the mind rejoices in this divine love or blessedness, it has the power of restraining lusts, inasmuch as human power to restrain lusts consists of intellect alone. Therefore no one rejoices in blessedness because he restrained lusts, but, on the contrary, the power of restraining lusts arises from blessedness itself.

Note. — Thus I have completed all I wished to show concerning the power of the mind over emotions or the freedom of the mind. From which it is clear how much a wise man is in front of and how stronger he is than an ignorant one, who is guided by lust alone. For an ignorant man, besides being agitated in many ways by external causes, never enjoys one true satisfaction of the mind: he lives, moreover, almost unconscious of himself, God, and things, and as soon as he ceases to be passive, ceases to be. On the contrary, the wise man, in so far as he is considered as such, is scarcely moved in spirit: he is conscious of himself, of God, and things by a certain eternal necessity, he never ceases to be, and always enjoys satisfaction of mind. If the road I have shown to lead to this is very difficult, it can yet be discovered. And clearly it must be very hard when it is so seldom found. For how could it be that it is neglected practically by all, if salvation were close at hand and could be found without difficulty? But all excellent things are as difficult as they are rare.

(Baruch Spinoza: *Ethics,* Parts III, IV, II, V; 1677)

6

Love

Reason was an excellent tool for scientific investigations, for establishing rules of politics, of law, of literature, of education. But could it be applied to an emotion such as love? Subsequent centuries (the nineteenth especially) have accustomed us to think of love as something irrational, almost mystical. Even Molière's misanthrope states that "reason doesn't rule in love," but then Alceste is scarcely a typical rationalist.

What then is rational love? It is one in which the heart is ruled by the head, the passions by the will. One finds among the rationalists a definite effort not to be carried away by emotions. Descartes and Spinoza both make reason the supreme arbiter, and lovers usually follow their advice.

Love is not only rational but also virtuous; and its most perfect form, marital love, is hailed by Milton. The "precious"

Madeleine de Scudéry systematizes love, showing the roads one can choose, the various stages of amorous development, as if they were stops on a road map. Campanella, in his utopia, reduces love to scientifically arranged sexual unions; and Congreve presents us with a love relation from which all emotions seem to have been distilled. But Mme de La Fayette points out the ever present and destructive force of passions that are threatening to invade this rational world and which we shall encounter later on in the plays of Racine.

A. MARITAL LOVE

John Milton (1608–1674) succeeded in a type of literature that, during the seventeenth century, enjoyed the greatest esteem of all: the epic or heroic poem. The reason it occupied such a high rank was that the masterworks of the ancients had been of this kind. Since then Dante, Ariosto, and Tasso had successfully imitated them. The great accomplishment of Milton was to have done the same for English literature by choosing for his subject the Fall of Man.

> This said unanimous, and other rites
> Observing none but adoration pure,
> Which God likes best, into their inmost bower
> Handed they went; and, eased the putting-off
> These troublesome disguises which we wear,
> Straight side by side were laid; nor turned, I ween,
> Adam from his fair spouse, nor Eve the rites
> Mysterious of connubial love refused:
> Whatever hypocrites austerely talk
> Of purity, and place, and innocence,
> Defaming as impure what God declares
> Pure, and commands to some, leaves free to all.
> Our maker bids increase; who bids abstain
> But our destroyer, foe to God and Man?
> Hail, wedded Love, mysterious law, true source
> Of human offspring, sole propriety
> In Paradise of all things common else!
> By thee adulterous lust was driven from men
> Among the bestial herds to range; by thee,

Founded in reason, loyal, just, and pure,
Relations dear, and all the charities
Of father, son, and brother, first were known.
Far be it that I should write thee sin or blame,
Or think thee unbefitting holiest place,
Perpetual fountain of domestic sweets,
Whose bed is undefiled and chaste pronounced,
Present or past, as saints and patriarchs used.
Here Love his golden shafts employs, here lights
His constant lamp, and waves his purple wings,
Reigns here and revels: not in the bought smile
Of harlots, loveless, joyless, unendeared,
Casual fruition; nor in court-amours
Mixed dance, or wanton mask, or midnight ball,
Or serenate, which the starved lover sings
To his proud fair, best quitted with disdain.
These, lulled by nightingales, embracing slept,
And on their naked limbs the flowery roof
Showered roses, which the morn repaired.

(John Milton: Paradise Lost, IV, 736–773; 1667)

B. PRECIOUS LOVE

Madeleine de Scudéry (1607–1701), as previously noted, was one of the foremost members of the French "precious" group. Precious love, in which the lover was kept waiting in a state of hope and servitude as long as possible, has been called an art without a heart. In her ten-volume novel Clélie, *the author explains graphically the roads a woman may choose on the Map of Loveland. It is to be noted that the roads to the left (where the heart is located) are less safe than those on the right.*

You remember that Clélie had been asked by which road one can go from New Friendship to Tender. As you see, one has to set out from that first town, which is on the bottom of this map, to go to the others; for, in order to understand Clélie's drawing better, you will see that she imagined that one can feel tenderness for three different reasons: through great esteem, through gratefulness, or through inclination. And this obliged her to establish three towns of Tender on three rivers that carry these three names and to trace three routes to get there. So that, as one says Cumae on

the Ionic Sea and Cumae on the Tyrrhenian Sea, she speaks of Tender on Inclination, Tender on Esteem, and Tender on Gratitude. However, as she has assumed that the tenderness born of inclination needs nothing else to be what it is, Clélie has not placed a single village along the banks of that river which flows so swiftly that one needs no lodgings along its shores in order to go from New Friendship to Tenderness.

But, in order to go to Tender on Esteem, the same does not hold true, for Clélie has very cleverly placed along the road as many villages as there are little and great matters that can contribute to arouse through esteem this tenderness she intends to illustrate. Indeed, you see that from New Friendship one first passes by a place called Noble Mind, because that is how esteem usually begins; then you see the pleasant villages of Pretty Verse, Fond Epistle, Love Letter, which are the usual procedures of a noble mind at the beginning of a friendship. Now, to progress along this road, you see Sincerity, Noble Heart, Uprightness, Generosity, Respect, Punctuality, and Kindness, which is close up against Tender, so as to indicate that there can be no true esteem without kindness and that one can-

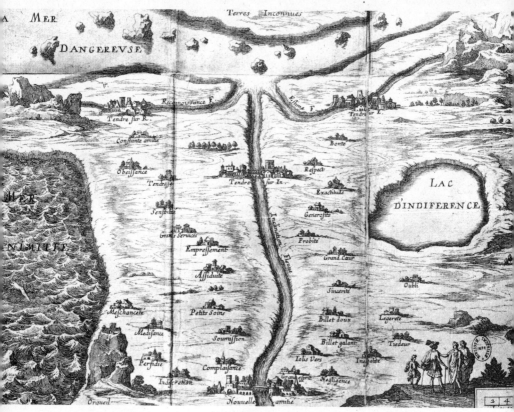

38. Illustration from *Clélie, The Map of Loveland.* Photo: Giraudon.

not reach that side of Tender unless one possesses this precious quality.

Now let us return to New Friendship and see by which route one goes from there to Tender on Gratitude. You see that first one must go from New Friendship to Obligingness, then to that little village called Submission which touches another very pleasant one called Delicate Attentions. From there one passes through Assiduity to indicate that it is not enough to display for a few days all those obliging delicate attentions that call forth so much gratitude, if one does not display them assiduously. Then you see the road passes through another village called Promptness, for one should not behave like some calm people who never hurry for a moment, no matter how much one begs it of them and who are incapable of that promptness which sometimes is so gratifying. After that you see that one has to pass through Important Services and that in order to note that few people render them, this village is smaller than the others. Then one has to continue to Sensibility to point out that one must feel even the smallest pains of the beloved; then, in order to arrive at Tender, one must pass through Tenderness, for friendship attracts friendship. Next, one must continue to Obedience, since there is almost nothing that engages the heart of those one obeys more than to do so blindly; and to arrive at where one wants to go, one has to continue to Constant Friendship, which is no doubt the surest road to get to Tender on Gratitude.

But, as there is no road where one cannot get lost, Clélie has arranged the map in such a way that if those who are at New Friendship go a little too far to the right or to the left, they likewise can get lost. For if upon leaving Noble Mind, one goes on to Negligence, which you see close by on the map; if then, continuing on this wrong road, one goes to Fickleness, from there to Tepidity, on to Inconsiderateness and to Forgetting; one ends up in the Lake of Indifference, which you see marked on this map and which, by its calm waters, certainly illustrates the thing it is called after. On the other side, if, upon leaving New Friendship, one goes a little too far to the left, to Indiscretion, Unfaithfulness, Pride, Slander, or Wickedness; instead of being at Tender on Gratitude, one ends up in the Sea of Enmity, where all boats come to shipwreck and which, by its agitated waves, very appropriately expresses this impetuous passion Clélie wants to represent.

Thus she shows by these different routes that one must have a thousand good qualities to induce her to have a relationship of tender friendship, and that those with bad qualities can expect from her only hatred or indifference. Furthermore, this nice girl, to reveal on the map that she has never been in love and that she would never feel more than tenderness in her heart, has the Inclination River flow into a sea she calls Dangerous Sea, because it is rather dangerous for a woman to go even a little bit beyond the limits of friendship; and beyond this sea she has placed what we call Unknown Lands, for we do not know what there is and we do not think that any one has gone further than Hercules. In this way she has managed to create a pleasant moral lesson about friendship by a simple imaginative game and to allude in a very intimate manner to the fact that she has never been in love and never will be.

(Madeleine de Scudéry: *Clélie*, Vol. I; 1654)

C. LOVE IN UTOPIA

In Tommaso Campanella's utopia love is rigidly controlled; in fact, love is essentially reduced to "scientific" procreation.

The age required for sexual intercourse, for the purpose of propagating the race, is 19 years for women and 21 years for men. For lymphatic temperaments the age limit is raised; on the other hand, certain individuals receive permission to have relations with women before the required age but only with those who are pregnant or certified as sterile, and with the provision that they will not engage in relations contrary to nature.

One inflexible rule is to couple women who are remarkable for their constitution or their beauty with tall and vigorous men, individuals who are plump with those who are not so in order to perfect the race.

The individuals selected for the reproductive process may commence the act only after they have digested their food and offered their prayers to God. . . . The procreators remain in separate cells until the appointed hour for their union and at that exact moment a matron opens the two doors. The propitious hour is determined by the astrologer and the physician. Before engaging again in sexual intercourse, the procreator is required to have abstained from it for three days, to have committed no bad act or to have reconciled himself with God. As for those, who for reasons of health or because of an excessively fiery temperament, have relations with women that are pregnant, sterile or *base*, they are not restricted to these formalities. The magistrates (who are all priests) and the men who devote themselves exclusively to scientific studies, may engage in the procreative act only after having undergone a longer period of abstinence and some rules especially made for them. For their continuous intellectual work and the incessant brain tension affect their nervous rhythm, weakens their virility, and deprives them of any vital energy to be transmitted. They would therefore produce only weakly children, and pains are taken to prevent this. Therefore they are coupled only with fiery, lively, and cheerful women of great beauty. As for men who distinguish themselves by their activity, their energy and a passionate temperament, they are coupled with women of oily complexion and gentle manners.

The Solarians say that all virtues are the result of a good organization and that education cannot make up for a bad one. They maintain that, once the fear of the laws or of God which serve as a check on people of perverse nature, have ceased to be effective, these people will corrupt the Republic by their open or secret actions. That is why in unions designed to reproduce the species they think that only natural qualities must be taken into account and no thought be given to the dowry of women and the very doubtful nobility of birth.

If upon a first attempt a woman has not become pregnant, she is successively coupled with other procreators; when it is finally ascertained that she is sterile, she is declared common; but then she is deprived of the honors due mothers in the temple and at the common table. This is done to avoid that the love of pleasure might induce some women to become sterile voluntarily.

What happens if someone falls madly in love with a woman and the woman returns his affection? They may talk together, play together, and express their passion by writing verses or offering wreaths of flowers to the beloved. But if this couple does not fulfill the requirements for sexual intercourse, they are strictly forbidden to engage in sexual relations unless the woman has been certified as sterile or is already pregnant by another man, an event which the lover awaits impatiently. Besides, the affection of two such lovers is rarely the result of carnal lust, but is rather born of nobler and more elevated sentiments.

(Tommaso Campanella: The City of the Sun, 1637)

D. MUNDANE LOVE

William Congreve (1670–1729) was one of the foremost writers of English Restoration comedy. In the frivolous society he describes, financial and social advantages so completely dominate sentimental considerations that a marriage proposal resembles far more a business deal than a declaration of love.

MIRABELL: "Like Daphne she, as lovely and as coy." Do you lock yourself up from me, to make my search more curious? Or is this pretty artifice contrived to signify that here the chase must end, and my pursuits be crowned? For you can fly no further.

MILLAMANT: Vanity! no — I'll fly, .and be followed to the last moment. Though I am upon the very verge of matrimony, I expect you should solicit me as much as if I were wavering at the grate of a monastery, with one foot over the threshold. I'll be solicited to the very last, nay, and afterwards.

MIRABELL: What, after the last?

MILLAMANT: Oh, I should think I was poor and had nothing to bestow, if I were reduced to an inglorious ease, and freed from the agreeable fatigues of solicitations.

MIRABELL: But do not you know, that when favours are conferred upon instant and tedious solicitation, that they diminish in their value, and that both the giver loses the grace, and the receiver lessens his pleasure?

39. Abraham Bosse, *Allegory of Spring.*

MILLAMANT: It may be in things of common application; but never sure
in love. Oh, I hate a lover that can dare to think he draws a moment's
air, independent of the bounty of his mistress. There is not so impudent a thing in nature, as the saucy look of an assured man, confident
of success. The pedantic arrogance of a very husband has not so prag-
matical an air. Ah! I'll never marry, unless I am first made sure of my
will and pleasure.

MIRABELL: Would you have 'em both before marriage? Or will you be contented with the first now, and stay for the other till after grace?

MILLAMANT: Ah! don't be impertinent. My dear liberty, shall I leave thee?
My faithful solitude, my darling contemplation, must I bid you then
adieu? Ay-h adieu — my morning thoughts, agreeable wakings, indo-
lent slumbers, ye *douceurs,* ye *sommeils du matin,* adieu? — I can't
do't, 'tis more than impossible — positively, Mirabell, I'll lie abed in a
morning as long as I please.

MIRABELL: Then I'll get up in a morning as early as I please.

MILLAMANT: Ah! idle creature, get up when you will — and d'ye hear, I

40. Jacques Callot, *Masked Lady.*

won't be called names after I'm married; positively I won't be called names.

MIRABELL: Names!

MILLAMANT: Ay, as wife, spouse, my dear, joy, jewel, love, sweetheart, and the rest of that nauseous cant, in which men and their wives are so fulsomely familiar — I shall never bear that — good Mirabell, don't let us be familiar or fond, nor kiss before folks, like my Lady Fadler and Sir Francis: nor go to Hyde-park together the first Sunday in a new chariot, to provoke eyes and whispers, and then never to be seen there together again; as if we were proud of one another the first week, and ashamed of one another ever after. Let us never visit together, nor go to a play together; but let us be very strange and well bred: let us be as strange as if we had been married a great while; and as well bred as if we were not married at all.

MIRABELL: Have you any more conditions to offer? Hitherto your demands are pretty reasonable.

MILLAMANT: Trifles! As liberty to pay and receive visits to and from whom I please; to write and receive letters, without interrogatories or wry faces on your part; to wear what I please; and choose conversation with regard only to my own taste; to have no obligation upon me to converse with wits that I don't like, because they are your acquaintance; or to be intimate with fools, because they may be your relations. Come to dinner when I please; dine in my dressing-room when I'm out of humour, without giving a reason. To have my closet inviolate; to be sole empress of my tea-table, which you must never presume to approach without first asking leave. And lastly, wherever I am, you shall always knock at the door before you come in. These articles subscribed, if I continue to endure you a little longer, I may by degrees dwindle into a wife.

MIRABELL: Your bill of fare is something advanced in this latter account. — Well, have I liberty to offer conditions — that when you are dwindled into a wife, I may not be beyond measure enlarged into a husband?

MILLAMANT: You have free leave; propose your utmost, speak and spare not.

MIRABELL: I thank you. — *Imprimis* then. I covenant, that your acquaintance be general; that you admit no sworn confidant, or intimate of your own sex; no she friend to screen her affairs under your countenance, and tempt you to make trial of a mutual secrecy. No decoy duck to wheedle you a fop — scrambling to the play in a mask — then bring you home in a pretended fright, when you think you shall be found out — and rail at me for missing the play, and disappointing the frolic which you had to pick me up, and prove my constancy.

MILLAMANT: Detestable *imprimis!* I go to the play in a mask!

MIRABELL: *Item,* I article, that you contique to like your own face, as long as I shall: and while it passes current with me, that you endeavour not to newcoin it, to which end, together with all vizards for the day, I prohibit all masks for the night, made of oiled-skins, and I know not what — hog's bones, hares' gall, pig-water, and the marrow of a roasted cat. In short, I forbid all commerce with the gentlewoman in what d'ye call it court. *Item,* I shut my doors against all bawds with baskets, and penny-worths of muslin, china, fans, atlasses, etc. — *Item,* when you shall be breeding —

MILLAMANT: Ah! name it not.

MIRABELL: Which may be presumed with a blessing on our endeavours.

MILLAMANT: Odious endeavours!

MIRABELL: I denounce against all strait lacing, squeezing for a shape, till you mould my boy's head like a sugar-loaf, and instead of a man child, make me father to a crooked billet. Lastly, to the dominion of the tea-table I submit — but with a proviso, that you exceed not in your province; but restrain yourself to native and simple tea-table drinks, as tea, chocolate, and coffee: as likewise to genuine and authorized tea-table talk — such as mending and fashions, spoiling reputations, railing at absent friends, and so forth — but that on no account you encroach upon the men's prerogative, and presume to drink healths or toast fellows; for prevention of which I banish all foreign forces, all auxiliaries to the tea-table, as orange brandy, all aniseed, cinnamon, citron and Barbadoes waters, together with ratafia, and the most noble spirits of clary — but for cowslip, wine, poppy water, and all dormitives, those I allow. — These provisos admitted, in other things I may prove a tractable and complying husband.

MILLAMANT: Oh horrid provisos! filthy strong-waters! I toast fellows! odious men! I hate your odious provisos!

MIRABELL: Then we are agreed! Shall I kiss your hand upon the contract?

(William Congreve: *The Way of the World,* 1700)

E.   THE DANGERS OF PASSIONATE LOVE

Marie Madeleine de La Fayette (1634–1693), married to a provincial nobleman, spent most of her time in Paris where her home was frequented by a small group of intellectuals, among whom were Mme de Sévigné and the Duc de La Rochefoucauld, the author of the well-known Maxims. *Being a close friend of Henrietta of England, Louis XIV's sister-in-law, she eventually gained access to the court which she describes in* La Princesse de Clèves *under the disguise of the court of Henri II (about 1560). This work, the first modern French novel, depicts the dilemma of the heroine, married to a man she respects, but dangerously attracted to the Duc de Nemours, a handsome ladies' man who has sincerely fallen in love with her.*

The first excerpt describes the scene in which the Princess, at the end of her strength, confides in her husband that she is in danger of being overcome by her passion. This avowal, overheard by Nemours, contributes to her husband's death. The sec-

*ond excerpt deals with the confrontation of the two lovers after
M. de Clèves' death. The way seems to be clear for their happiness, yet the Princess refuses Nemours' offer of marriage, because, exhausted by the turmoil of passion, she prefers peace of
mind to the uncertainty of passionate love.*

He heard Monsieur de Clèves say to his wife: "But why don't you wish to
return to Paris? Whoever is keeping you in the country? You have recently had a taste for solitude that surprises me, and that pains me because it keeps us apart. I find you in lower spirits even than usual, and I
am afraid something is worrying you."

"I have nothing on my mind," she replied, with some embarrassment;
"but the bustle of the Court is so great and there are always so many people at our house that it is impossible for mind and body. not to tire and to
seek rest."

"Rest," he answered, "is scarcely suited to a person of your age. Your
position at home and at Court is such that you are spared fatigue, and I
am rather inclined to fear that you are glad to be away from me."

"You would do me great injustice if you thought that," she replied,
with increasing embarrassment; "but I beg you to leave me here. If you
could stay too, I should be delighted, provided that you would stay alone,
and would consent not to have with you the throng of people who scarcely
ever leave you."

"Ah, Madame," exclaimed Monsieur de Clèves, "your looks and your
words show me that you have reasons unknown to me for wishing to be
alone, and I beg you to tell me of them."

For some time he urged her to tell him — but without success; and, after
she had resisted his pleadings in a way that increased still further her husband's curiosity, she remained silent, with eyes cast down: then, suddenly,
raising her eyes to his, she burst forth: "Do not force me," said she, "to
confess something I have not strength to confess, although I have several
times intended to do so. Only remember that it is contrary to prudence for
a woman of my age, mistress of her actions, to be exposed to the dangers
of the Court."

"What do you suggest to my mind, Madame?" cried Monsieur de Clèves.
"I do not dare say it for fear of offending you."

Madame de Clèves did not reply, and her silence confirmed what her
husband had in mind.

"You do not reply," he continued, "and that means I am not mistaken."

"Then, sir," she answered, falling at his feet, "I am going to make a confession such as was never made to a husband; but the innocence of my

actions and of my intentions gives me the necessary strength. It is true that I have reasons for keeping away from Court, and that I wish to avoid the perils that sometimes beset women of my age. I have never given the least sign of weakness, and I should not fear that I might do so, if you allowed me to withdraw from Court or if I still had Madame de Chartres to help me and guide me. However dangerous may be the course I am now taking, I am taking it gladly to keep me worthy of you. I beg you earnestly to pardon me if I have feelings that grieve you; at any rate, I shall never grieve you by my actions. Remember that to do what I am doing requires more affection and more esteem for a husband than anyone has ever had. Guide me, pity me, and love me still — if you can."

Monsieur de Clèves had remained during the whole of this confession with his head buried in his hands, beside himself, not thinking even of bidding his wife to rise.

When she ceased speaking, when his eyes fell on her and he saw her at his feet, her face wet with tears and bewitching in its beauty, he thought he should die of grief. Kissing her, and helping her to her feet, he said:

"Madame, have pity on me also. I deserve it, and forgive me if, in the first moments of a grief as poignant as mine, I do not respond as I ought to what you have just done. You appear to me more worthy of esteem and admiration than any woman who ever lived, but yet I regard myself as the unhappiest man that ever was. You awoke love in me the first time I saw you. Neither your early indifference nor marital relations have been able to cool this love. It still endures. But I have never been able to awaken love in you, and I see that you fear you love another. And who, Madame, is the happy man who gives rise to this fear? How long has he attracted you? How did he attract you? How did he find the way to your heart? I consoled myself to some extent for not having touched it by the thought that it could not be moved. Meanwhile another has done what I could not do. I have at once the jealousy of a husband and of a lover, but it is impossible to entertain that of a husband after what you have just done. That is too noble not to bring complete peace of mind. It consoles me even as your lover. The confidence and the sincerity that you have shown me are above all price. You esteem me enough to believe that I shall not take an unfair advantage of this confession. You are right, Madame: I shall not do so, and I shall love you no less because of it. You destroy my happiness by the greatest proof of fidelity that a woman ever gave her husband; but, Madame, go on and tell me who it is you wish to avoid."

"I entreat you not to ask me that," she replied; "I am determined not to tell you, and I think that prudence requires me not to do so."

"Have no fear, Madame," said Monsieur de Clèves; "I know too much of life to be ignorant of the fact that appreciation of the husband does not prevent a man from falling in love with the wife. He ought to hate those who do so, but not complain. So once more, Madame, I beg of you to tell me what I want to know."

"You would insist in vain," she replied. "I have strength enough to keep secret what I think I ought not to divulge. My confession to you was not the result of weakness; and it needs more courage to confess such things than to undertake to hide them."

.   .   .

Monsieur de Clèves, however, was doing his best to find it out; and, after he had insisted in vain, his wife said: "It seems to me that you ought to be satisfied with my candour; do not ask me anything more, and do not give me cause to regret what I have just done. Content yourself with the further assurance I give you that no action of mine has betrayed my feelings, and that not a word has been said to me at which I could take offence."

"Oh, Madame," Monsieur de Clèves suddenly exclaimed, "I cannot believe you. I remember your embarrassment the day your portrait was lost. You gave it away, Madame — you gave away the portrait that was so dear to me, and that was so rightly mine. You could not hide your feelings — you love — and your lover knows it — your virtue has so far preserved you from anything more."

"Is it possible," cried the Princess, "that you can imagine there is any deception in a confession like mine, which I was not obliged to make? Believe what I say. I am paying dearly for the confidence that I ask of you. Believe, I implore you, that I did not give away my portrait — it is true that I saw it taken, but I did not wish to appear to see it for fear of exposing myself to hearing things that he has not yet dared to say."

"How, then, did he show you that he loved you?" asked Monsieur de Clèves; "and what indication of love did he give you?"

"Spare me the ordeal," she replied, "of relating details that I am ashamed to have noticed, and that convinced me only too completely of my weakness."

"You are right, Madame," he said. "I am unjust. Refuse to answer whenever I ask you such questions; yet do not be angry if I ask them."

.   .   .

After several months, she passed from this state of violent grief to one of sadness and languor. Madame de Martigues paid a visit to Paris and called on her assiduously during her stay there. She chatted about the Court and all that was going on, and, although Madame de Clèves seemed to take no interest, Madame de Martigues went on talking about these things to occupy her mind.

She gave her news of the Vidame, of Monsieur de Guise, and of all the others who were distinguished in looks or in deeds. "As for Monsieur de Nemours," she said, "I do not know whether affairs have taken the place of gallantry in his mind, but he is much less cheerful than he used to be; he seems to shun feminine society; he comes up to Paris frequently, and I think he is here now."

Mention of Monsieur de Nemours surprised Madame de Clèves, and caused her to blush; she changed the subject, and Madame de Martigues did not notice her confusion.

Next day, the Princess, who sought occupations in keeping with her condition, went to see a man near her home who worked in silk in a particular way, and went there with the intention of having similar work done for her. When she had been shown some, she saw the door of a room where she thought there was more, and asked to have it opened. The proprietor replied that he had not the key, and that it was occupied by a man who came sometimes during the day to draw the fine houses and gardens to be seen from the windows. "He is the most comely man in the world," he went on; "he scarcely looks as though he were forced to earn a living. Every time he comes here, I see him always gazing at the houses and the gardens, but I never see him work."

Madame de Clèves listened to this with close attention; what Madame de Martigues had said about Monsieur de Nemours' being in Paris connected itself in her mind with this comely man who frequented a house near hers, and it brought up the picture of Monsieur de Nemours, and of Monsieur de Nemours trying to see her. This caused her a confused emotion of which she did not know the cause. She went towards the windows to see on what they looked; she found herself looking over all her garden and the front of her apartment. When she was in her room, she easily distinguished the same window to which she had been told this man came. The thought that it was Monsieur de Nemours entirely changed the state of her mind: she was no longer in a certain sorrowful calm that she was beginning to appreciate; she felt uneasy and agitated; in short, she wanted to get away from herself; and she left the house and went for air into a garden beyond the suburbs where she thought she would be alone. She thought when she arrived that this was the case; she saw no sign of anyone, and walked there for some time.

After going through a grove, she noticed, at the end of a path in the most secluded part of the garden, a kind of shelter open on all sides, to which she directed her steps. When she was near it, she saw a man lying on one of the seats, apparently plunged in deep thought, and she recognized Monsieur de Nemours. At the sight of him, she stopped short; but her servants, who were following her, made a noise that aroused Monsieur de Nemours from his day-dreams. Without noticing who had caused the noise he had heard, he got up to avoid the people coming towards him, and turned down another path, after bowing so low that he could not even see whom he was saluting.

Had he known what he was avoiding, with what ardour would he have retraced his steps! But he went on following the path, and Madame de Clèves saw him leave by a back gate, where his carriage was waiting for him. What an effect this fleeting glimpse had on Madame de Clèves' heart! What latent love rekindled in her heart, and with what violence! She sat down in the very place Monsieur de Nemours had just left; and there she remained as if overwhelmed. The Duke came to her mind, lovable above all in the world, loving her with a passion full of respect and constancy, neglecting all for her, respecting even her grief, thinking of seeing her without thinking of being seen; leaving the Court, where he charmed every one, in order to go and gaze upon the walls that sheltered her, to come and muse in places where he had no hope of meeting her; in short, a man worthy of being loved for his faithfulness alone, to whom she was so violently attracted that she would have loved him even if he had not loved her; but, in addition, a man of high rank and suited to her own. Neither duty nor virtue stood any longer in the way of her feelings: all obstacles were removed, and there remained of their past condition only the love of Monsieur de Nemours for her and her love for him.

All these thoughts were new to the Princess. Her grief at Monsieur de Clèves' death had so occupied her that she had been prevented from realizing the situation. The presence of Monsieur de Nemours brought them crowding to her mind; but when she had marshalled them all, and recalled also that the very man she considered might marry her was the one whom she had loved while her husband was alive and who was the cause of his death, and that even on his death-bed her husband had expressed the fear that she should marry him, her strict virtue was so shocked by the idea that she found it scarcely less a crime to marry Monsieur de Nemours than she had found it to love him during her husband's life-time. She gave herself up to reflections so opposed to her happiness; she fortified them further with several reasons that had to do with her tranquillity and the troubles she foresaw if she married the Duke. At length, after two hours spent in that place, she returned home, convinced that she ought to avoid the sight of him as something completely opposed to her duty.

But this conviction, which was a product of her reason and her virtue, did not carry with it her heart. That remained true to Monsieur de Nemours with an ardour that reduced her to a state worthy of compassion, and that left her no more peace. She passed one of the most cruel nights she had ever passed. Next morning her first impulse was to look whether there was anyone at the window that overlooked her house. She did so — and saw Monsieur de Nemours. The sight of him surprised her, and she withdrew so quickly that the Duke inferred he had been recognized. He had often wished to be so, since his love had led him to discover this way of seeing Madame de Clèves, and, when he could not hope for this pleasure, he would go and dream in the garden where she had found him.

Weary at last of a state so unhappy and so uncertain, he decided to find some way of learning his fate. "What am I waiting for?" he said. "I have known for some time that she loves me; she is free; she can no longer plead duty. Why restrict myself to seeing her without being seen, and without speaking to her? Is it possible that love has so completely deprived me of sense and boldness, and that it has made me so different from what I was in former affairs? I had to respect Madame de Clèves' grief; but I am respecting it too long, and I am giving her time to stifle the love she has for me."

Thereupon he considered the means he must use to see her. He believed there was now nothing that obliged him to hide his love from the Vidame de Chartres: he decided to tell him about it and to speak to him of his intentions concerning his niece.

The Vidame was then in Paris; everybody had come up to see about equipment and clothes for attendance on the King, who was to escort the Queen of Spain. Monsieur de Nemours went to see him, therefore, and confessed frankly all he had hidden from him until then — except the state of Madame de Clèves' feelings, which he did not wish to appear to know.

The Vidame was very glad to hear all he had to say, and assured him that, without knowing his feelings, he had often thought, since Madame de Clèves had become a widow, that she was the only person worthy of him. Monsieur de Nemours begged him to say by what means he could talk to her and find out her intentions.

The Vidame proposed to take him to call on her, but Monsieur de Nemours thought that would displease her, because she had not yet received visitors. They were of the opinion that the Vidame must ask her to come to his apartment, on some pretext, and that Monsieur de Nemours should come there by a secret staircase, so as not to be seen by anyone. This plan was carried out. Madame de Clèves came, the Vidame went to meet her, and escorted her to a large room at the end of his apartment; some time after, Monsieur de Nemours came in, as if by chance. Madame de Clèves was extremely surprised to see him: she blushed and tried to hide her blushes. At first the Vidame talked of unimportant matters, and then left the room, pretending he had some orders to give. He begged Madame de Clèves to do the honours of his home, and said that he would be back in a moment.

No one could express what Monsieur de Nemours and Madame de Clèves felt upon finding themselves alone and for the first time free to speak. They remained for some time without saying a word; then, at last, Monsieur de Nemours broke the silence. "Will you forgive Monsieur de Chartres, Madame," he asked, "for having given me the opportunity of seeing you and talking to you which you have always so cruelly denied me?"

"I ought not to pardon him," she replied, "for having forgotten my condition and to what he exposes my reputation."

As she spoke, she moved towards the door, but Monsieur de Nemours detained her, saying: "Fear nothing, Madame; no one knows I am here, and no interruption is to be feared. Listen to me, Madame, listen to me, if not from kindness, at least for your own sake, and to avoid the extremes to which I shall inevitably be driven by a love which I can no longer control."

Madame de Clèves gave way for the first time to the feelings she had for Monsieur de Nemours, and, looking at him with eyes full of tenderness and charm, she said: "But what do you expect from the favour you ask of me? You will perhaps regret having obtained it, and I shall certainly regret granting it. You deserve a happier lot than you have had so far, and than you will have in future unless you seek it elsewhere."

"I, Madame," he exclaimed, "seek happiness elsewhere? And is there any other than to be loved by you? Although I have never declared it, I cannot believe, Madame, that you are unaware of my love, and that you do not know it to be the truest and most ardent that will ever be. How it has been tried by things unknown to you, and how you have tried it by your severity!"

"Since you wish me to talk to you, and I consent," replied Madame de Clèves, taking a seat, "I shall do so with a frankness you will not easily find in persons of my sex. I shall not tell you that I have not perceived your love for me — perhaps you would not believe me if I did. I admit, then, not only that I have seen it, but that I saw it as you would have wished it to appear to me."

"And, if you perceived it, Madame," he interrupted, "can it be that you were not affected by it, and dare I ask you whether it made no impression on your heart?"

"You must have judged this by my conduct," she replied; "but I should like to know what you thought."

"I should have to be in a more privileged condition to dare tell you," he replied, "and my lot has too little relation to what I should say. All I can tell you, Madame, is that I have ardently wished you had not told Monsieur de Clèves what you were hiding from me, and that you had hidden from him what you let me see."

"How were you able to find out," she asked, blushing, "that I confessed something to Monsieur de Clèves?"

"I learned it from you, Madame," he replied; "but, to absolve me for my boldness in listening to you, recall whether I took advantage of what I heard, whether my hopes were raised thereby, and whether I showed more boldness in trying to speak to you."

He began to tell her how he had heard her conversation with Monsieur de Clèves, but she interrupted him before he had finished, saying: "Do not tell me any more. I see now why you were so well informed; you seemed to me already too much so at the Dauphiness', who had heard about the incident from those to whom you had told it."

Monsieur de Nemours then told her how this came about.

"Do not excuse yourself," she said. "I forgave you long ago without having heard the reason from you; but, since you learned from me what I intended to keep from you all my life, I admit that you awakened feelings in me that were unknown to me before I met you, and of which I knew so little that they caused in me at first a surprise that only accentuated the agitation they always produce. I admit this to you with less shame because my admission comes at a time when it is not a sin, and because you have seen that my conduct has not been dictated by my feelings."

"What you have said, Madame," exclaimed Monsieur de Nemours, kneeling at her feet, "overwhelms me with joy and rapture."

"I have told you nothing," she replied with a smile, "that you did not already know only too well."

"Ah, Madame," said he, "what a difference between finding it out by chance and hearing it from you when I see that you are willing for me to know it!"

"It is true," she said, "that I am willing you should know it, and that I find pleasure in telling you. I am not sure whether I am not telling you more from love of myself than from love of you; for, after all, this avowal will have no consequences, and I shall observe the strict rules my duty imposes."

"You do not intend to do that, Madame," replied Monsieur de Nemours. "Duty no longer binds you; you are free; and, if I dared, I would even say that it is for you so to act that your duty will some day require you to cherish the feelings you have for me."

"My duty," she replied, "requires me never to think of anyone, and of you less than anyone in the world, for reasons unknown to you."

"Perhaps they are not, Madame," he replied, "but they are not real reasons. I have cause to believe that Monsieur de Clèves thought me more fortunate than I was, and that he imagined you had approved the foolish action love made me perform without your consent."

"Let us not speak of that affair," she said; "I cannot bear the thought — I am ashamed of it, and the subject is also very painful to me because of its consequences. It is only too true that you caused Monsieur de Clèves' death; the suspicions your inconsiderate conduct aroused cost him his life, as if you had taken it with your own hand. See what my duty would be if you had both gone to such extremes and the same calamity had happened. I know it is not the same thing in the eyes of the world, but in mine there is no difference, since I know that he came to his death by you and because of me."

"Oh, Madame," said Monsieur de Nemours, "what phantom of duty do you oppose to my happiness! What, Madame! Shall a vain and baseless belief prevent you from making happy a man whom you do not regard with indifference! What! I entertain the hope of passing my life with you: my destiny leads me to love the most estimable woman in the world; I find in her all that goes to make an adorable Mistress; she does not regard me with indifference; and I find in her conduct everything that can be wished for in a wife — for, after all, Madame, you are perhaps the only person in whom these two things were ever found to the same degree as they are in you: all who marry Mistresses who love them tremble when they marry them, and have fears with regard to other men when they remember their wives' conduct with themselves; but in you, Madame, nothing is to be feared, and all in you is admirable. Have I looked forward to such great happiness, I say, only to see you put obstacles in the way? Oh, Madame, you forget that you have distinguished me from all other men; you were mistaken, and I only flattered myself."

"You did not flatter yourself," she replied. "The reasons for my decision would perhaps not seem so strong to me were it not for the distinction you suspect, and that is just what makes me foresee unhappiness if I bind myself to you."

"I have no answer," he replied, "when you indicate that you fear unhappiness; but I confess that after all you have been good enough to say to me, I did not expect to find such a cruel reason."

"It is so far from being uncomplimentary to you," replied Madame de Clèves, "that I have even great difficulty in telling it to you."

"Alas! Madame," he replied, "how can you fear to flatter me too much after what you have recently said?"

"I mean to speak further with the same frankness as I have just shown," said she, "and I am going to ignore all the reserve and all the subtleties that I ought to practise during a first interview, but I beg you to listen without interrupting.

"I believe I owe to your faithfulness the slight reward of not hiding from you any feelings of mine, but of letting you see them just as they are. This will be probably the only time in my life that I shall allow myself to show them to you; nevertheless, I cannot admit to you without shame that the certainty of being no longer loved by you, as I now am, appears to me such a terrible misfortune that, were there not already insurmountable claims of duty, I doubt whether I could decide to expose myself to such a misfortune. I know you are free; that I am free; and that things are such that the public would perhaps have no cause to censure you, or me, if we united ourselves forever. But do men remain in love during these eternal unions? Ought I to expect a miracle in my favour, and can I put myself in a position to see the inevitable death of the love that would be my sole happiness? Monsieur de Clèves was perhaps the only man in the world capable of retaining love after marriage. My fate was opposed to my enjoying this happiness; perhaps, also, his love survived only because he found none in me. But I could not keep yours in that way; I even imagine that the obstacles account for your constancy. You found enough of them to incite you to win, and my involuntary actions, or things you learned by chance, gave you hope enough for you not to be discouraged."

"Ah, Madame," cried Monsieur de Nemours, "I cannot maintain the silence you imposed on me. You do me too great an injustice, and you show me too plainly how far you are from being prejudiced in my favour."

"I admit," she replied, "that love may lead me, but it cannot blind me; nothing can prevent my knowing that you were born with a disposition for gallantry and all the qualities likely to bring success therein. You have already had several love-affairs; you would have others; I should no longer make you happy; I should see you become to another woman what you have been to me; I should be mortally hurt; and I should not even be sure of not suffering from jealousy. I have told you too much to hide from you that I have already felt it on your account, and that I suffered so cruelly the evening the Queen gave me Madame de Thémines' letter, supposed to have been addressed to you, that an impression remains leading me to believe that jealousy is the greatest of all sufferings.

"Vanity or liking makes all women want to enthral you; there are few you do not attract; my experience leads me to believe that there are none you could not attract. I should always be thinking you were in love and loved, and I should not often be wrong. Yet, in this state of affairs, I should have no choice but to suffer — I do not know whether I should even dare to complain. One reproaches a lover, but can one reproach a husband, when his only fault is that he no longer loves? Even if I could get used to this kind of suffering, could I get used to thinking I saw Monsieur de Clèves ever accusing you of his death, reproaching me for having loved you, for marrying you, and making me feel the difference between his love and yours? It is impossible to ignore reasons so strong; I must stay as I am, and keep my resolution never to change my state."

"Oh, do you think you can, Madame?" cried Monsieur de Nemours. "Do you believe your resolution can hold out against a man who adores you and who is fortunate enough to be loved in return? It is harder than you think, Madame, to resist him who is loved and who loves you. You have done so by an austere virtue that is almost without parallel, but this virtue is no longer opposed to your feelings, and I hope you will be guided by them in spite of yourself."

"I well know that there is nothing more difficult than what I am undertaking," replied Madame de Clèves. "I mistrust my strength in the midst of my reasoning; what I think I owe to the memory of Monsieur de Clèves would be weak were it not upheld by the claims of my own peace; and the claims of my peace need the support of my duty, but, although I mistrust myself, I believe I shall never conquer my scruples, nor do I hope to overcome the affection I have for you. It will make me unhappy, and I shall avoid seeing you, however painful this may be. I entreat you, by all the influence I have over you, not to seek any opportunity of seeing me. I am in a state that makes sinful all that would be permitted at any other time, and propriety alone absolutely forbids our meeting."

Monsieur de Nemours threw himself at her feet, and gave way to all the feelings that agitated him. He showed her by his words and by his tears the tenderest passion with which a heart has ever been touched; Madame de Clèves was not insensible; and, looking at the Duke with eyes somewhat swollen with tears, she cried:

"Why is it that I must accuse you of the death of Monsieur de Clèves? Why did I not meet you for the first time after I was free, or why did I not know you before I was married? Why does fate separate us with such an insurmountable obstacle?"

"There is no obstacle, Madame," replied Monsieur de Nemours; "you alone oppose my happiness, and you alone impose on yourself a law that virtue and reason could not impose on you."

"It is true," she said, "that I am sacrificing much to a duty that exists only in my imagination. Wait and see what time can do. Monsieur de Clèves has only just died, and this terrible event is too near to allow me to see clearly and distinctly. Enjoy the pleasure of winning the love of a woman who never would have loved had she not met you; rest assured that the feelings I have for you will be eternal, and that they will remain unchanged whatever I do. Good-bye — this conversation shames me — repeat it to the Vidame; I consent to this, and beg you to do it."

With these words, she left the room, without Monsieur de Nemours' being able to retain her.

(Madame de La Fayette: *La Princesse de Clèves*, 1678)

7

Reason and Religion

In an age of reason and science, religion posed a number of serious problems. To be sure, St. Thomas Aquinas had demonstrated that the existence of God could be proved by the proper exercise of reason; but what of revelation, faith, and miracles? By what means (rational, scientific, or experiential) was it possible to explain and accept the Immaculate Conception, the reincarnation, the crossing of the Red Sea? How could these be "clear and distinct" to the mind?

Generally speaking, the seventeenth-century philosophers adopt a Janus-faced attitude toward these questions. Even if they may be in disagreement, matters of faith and of science are both true; faith, being of a superior truth, is not subject to scientific investigations. But it is this stand which leads Descartes to divorce religion and philosophy, since revelation cannot be

*attained by the application of reason. This divorce, however, is
not complete, for three religious beliefs, it is felt by most, can
be proved by reason: the existence of God, the immortality of
the soul, and the gift of human free will; on the last of these,
however, opinions are far from unanimous.*

*Another aspect of religion was bound to disturb writers who
thought in universal terms: the diversity of religions. If all men
are endowed with reason and God is supreme reason, why did
he not reveal himself in the same manner to all men? Lord
Herbert of Cherbury was among the first to propose a rational
religion drawn from the universal consent of religious beliefs
throughout the ages, i.e. the common notions that remain once
ceremonies and individual claims to revelation have been removed from the various religions of mankind. This is already
an outline of deism, although the full-scale attack against revelation will not occur until much later.*

A.   FAITH AND REASON

Sacred theology must be drawn from the word and oracles of God, not
from the light of nature, or the dictates of reason.

[With respect to theology] we must quit the small vessel of human reason,
and put ourselves on board the ship of the Church, which alone possesses
the divine needle for justly shaping the course.

We are obliged to believe the word of God, though our reason be
shocked at it. For if we should believe only such things as are agreeable to
our reason, we assent to the matter, and not to the author.

And therefore, the more absurd and incredible any divine mystery is, the
greater honor we do to God in believing it; and so much the more noble
the victory of faith.

Undoubtedly a superficial tincture of philosophy may incline the mind
to atheism, yet a farther knowledge brings it back to religion; for on the
threshold of philosophy, where second causes appear to absorb the attention, some oblivion of the highest cause may ensue; but when the mind
goes deeper, and sees the dependence of causes and the works of Providence, it will easily perceive, according to the mythology of the poets, that
the upper link of Nature's chain is fastened to Jupiter's throne.

(Francis Bacon: *De Augmentis*, 1605)

B. RELIGIOUS BELIEFS PROVED BY REASON

1. THE EXISTENCE OF GOD

Descartes uses a proof very similar to the one that had already been proposed, in the twelfth century, by St. Anselm.

After that I reflected upon the fact that I doubted, and that, in consequence, my spirit was not wholly perfect, for I saw clearly that it was a greater perfection to know than to doubt. I decided to ascertain from what source I had learned to think of something more perfect than myself, and it appeared evident that it must have been from some nature which was in fact more perfect. As for my ideas about many other things outside of me, as the sky, earth, light, heat, and thousands of other things, I was not so much troubled to discover where they came from, because I found nothing in them superior to my own nature. If they really existed, I could believe that whatever perfection they possessed might be derived from my own nature; if they did not exist, I could believe that they were derived from nothingness, that is, that they were derived from my own defects. But this could not be the explanation of my idea of a being more perfect than my own. To derive it from nothingness was manifestly impossible, and it is no less repugnant to good sense to assume what is more perfect comes from and depends on the less perfect than it is to assume that something comes from nothing, so that I could not assume that it came from myself. Thus the only hypothesis left was that this idea was put in my mind by a nature that was really more perfect than I was, which had all the perfections that I could imagine, and which was, in a word, God. To this I added that since I knew some perfections which I did not possess, I was not the only being in existence (I will here use freely, if you will pardon me, the terms of the schools), and that it followed of necessity that there was someone else more perfect upon whom I depended and from whom I had acquired all that I possessed. For if I had been alone and independent of anything else, so that I had bestowed upon myself all that limited quantity of value which I shared with the perfect Being, I would have been able to get from myself, in the same way, all the surplus which I recognize as lacking in me, and so would have been myself infinite, eternal, immutable, omniscient, omnipotent, and, in sum, I would possess all the perfections that I could discover in God.

For, following the reasoning which I have just explained, to know the nature of God as far as I was capable of such knowledge, I had only to consider each quality of which I had an idea, and decide whether it was or was not a perfection to possess it. I would then be certain that none of those which had some imperfection was in him, but that all the others were. I saw that doubt, inconstancy, sorrow and similar things could not be part of God's nature, since I would be happy to be without them myself. In addition, I had ideas of many sensible and corporeal entities, for although I might suppose that I was dreaming and that all that I saw or imagined was false, I could not at any rate deny that the ideas were truly in my consciousness. Since I had already recognized very clearly that intelligent nature is distinct from corporeal nature, I considered that composition is an evidence of dependency and that dependency is manifestly a defect. From this I judged that it could not be a perfection in God to be composed of these two natures, and that consequently he was not so composed. But if there were in the world bodies, or even intelligences or other natures that were not wholly perfect, their being must depend on God's power in such a way that they could not subsist without him for a single moment.

At this point I wished to seek for other truths, and proposed for consideration the object of the geometricians. This I conceived as a continuous body, or a space infinitely extended in length, breadth, and height or depth; divisible into various parts which can have different shapes and sizes and can be moved or transposed in any way: all of which is presumed by geometricians to be true of their object. I went through some of their simplest demonstrations and noticed that the great certainty which everyone attributes to them is only based on the fact that they are evidently conceived, following the rule previously established. I noticed also that there was nothing at all in them to assure me of the existence of their object; it was clear, for example, that if we posit a triangle, its three angles must be equal to two right angles, but there was nothing in that to assure me that there was a single triangle in the world. When I turned back to my idea of a perfect Being, on the other hand, I discovered that existence was included in that idea in the same way that the idea of a triangle contains the equality of its angles to two right angles, or that the idea of a sphere includes the equidistance of all its parts from its center. Perhaps, in fact, the existence of the perfect Being is even more evident. Consequently, it is at least as certain that God, who is this perfect Being, exists, as any theorem of geometry could possibly be.

What makes many people feel that it is difficult to know of the existence of God, or even of the nature of their own souls, is that they never consider things higher than corporeal objects. They are so accustomed never to think of anything without picturing it — a method of thinking suitable only for material objects — that everything which is not picturable seems to them unintelligible. This is also manifest in the fact that even philosophers hold it as a maxim in the schools that there is nothing in the understanding which was not first in the senses, a location where it is clearly evident that the ideas of God and of the soul have never been. It seems to me that those who wish to use imagery to understand these matters are doing precisely the same thing that they would be doing if they tried to use their eyes to hear sounds or smell odors. There is even this difference: that the sense of sight gives us no less certainty of the truth of objects than do those of smell and hearing, while neither our imagery nor our senses could assure us of anything without the co-operation of our understanding.

Finally, if there are still some men who are not sufficiently persuaded of the existence of God and of their souls by the reasons which I have given, I want them to understand that all the other things of which they might think themselves more certain, such as their having a body, or the existence of stars and of an earth, and other such things, are less certain. For even though we have a moral assurance of these things, such that it seems we cannot doubt them without extravagance, yet without being unreasonable we cannot deny that, as far as metaphysical certainty goes, there is sufficient room for doubt. For we can imagine, when asleep, that we have another body and see other stars and another earth without there being any such. How could one know that the thoughts which come to us in dreams are false rather than the others, since they are often no less vivid and detailed? Let the best minds study this question as long as they wish, I do not believe they can find any reason good enough to remove this doubt unless they presuppose the existence of God. The very principle which I took as a rule to start with, namely, that all those things which we conceived very clearly and very distinctly are true, is known to be true only because God exists, and because he is a perfect Being, and because everything in us comes from him. From this it follows that our ideas or notions, being real things which come from God insofar as they are clear and distinct, cannot to that extent fail to be true. Consequently, though we often have ideas which contain falsity, they can only be those ideas which contain some confusion and obscurity, in which respect they participate in nothingness. That is to say, they are confused in us only because we are not wholly perfect. It is evident that it is no less repugnant to good sense to assume that falsity or imperfection as such is derived from God, as that truth or perfection is derived from nothingness. But if we did not know that all reality and truth within us came from a perfect and infinite Being,

however clear and distinct our ideas might be, we would have no reason
to be certain that they were endowed with the perfection of being true.

(René Descartes: *Discourse on Method,* Part IV; 1637)

2. *THE IMMORTALITY OF THE SOUL*

I then described the rational soul, and showed that it could not possibly
be derived from the powers of matter, like the other things I have spoken
about, but must have been specially created. I showed also that it would
not suffice to place it in the human body, as a pilot in a ship, unless
perhaps to move its parts, but that it must be more intimately joined and
united with the body in order to have feelings and appetites like ours,
and so constitute a real man. For the rest, I elaborated a little on the topic
of the soul on account of its great importance; because, next to the error
of those who deny God, which I think I have sufficiently refuted, there is
none which is so apt to make weak characters stray from the path of virtue
as the idea that the souls of animals are of the same nature as our own,
and that in consequence we have no more to fear or to hope for after this
life than have the flies and ants. Actually, when we know how different
they are, we understand more fully the reasons which prove that our soul
is by nature entirely independent of the body, and consequently does not
have to die with it. Therefore, as long as we see no other causes which
might destroy it, we are naturally led to conclude that it is immortal.

(René Descartes: *Discourse on Method,* Part V; 1637)

PROP. XXIII. The human mind cannot be absolutely destroyed with the
human body, but something of it remains, which is eternal.

Proof. — There is necessarily in God the conception or idea which
expresses the essence of the human body, which therefore is something
necessarily which appertains to the essence of the human mind. But we
attribute to the human mind no duration which can be defined by time,
save in so far as it expresses the actual essence of the human body, which
is explained by means of duration and is defined by time, that is, we do
not attribute duration save as long as the body lasts. But as there is nevertheless something else which is conceived under a certain eternal necessity
through the essence of God, this something, which pertains to the essence
of the mind, will necessarily be eternal.

Note. — This idea, as we have said, which expresses under a certain
species of eternity the essence of the body, is a certain mode of thought
which appertains to the essence of the mind, and which is necessarily
eternal. It cannot happen, however, that we can remember that we existed

before our bodies, since there are no traces of it in the body, neither can eternity be defined by time nor have any relation to time. But nevertheless we feel and know that we are eternal. For the mind no less feels those things which it conceives in understanding than those which it has in memory. For the eyes of the mind by which it sees things and observes them are proofs. So although we do not remember that we existed before the body, we feel nevertheless that our mind in so far as it involves the essence of the body under the species of eternity is eternal, and its existence cannot be defined by time or explained by duration. Our mind therefore, can only be said to last, and its existence can be defined by a certain time only in so far as it involves the actual existence of the body, and thus far only it has the power of determining the existence of things by time and of conceiving them under the attribute of duration.

(Baruch Spinoza: *Ethics,* Part V; 1677)

3. FREEDOM OF THE WILL

Descartes, as we have seen on several occasions, considered the will completely free; this view is explained in rational theological terms by Milton. Both Hobbes and Spinoza, however (for different reasons), were determinists who held that every human choice is the necessary effect of causes in the infinite chain of causes.

The Case For

Milton was enough of a rationalist to be disturbed by the inexplicable aspects of the Fall of Man. He resolved this enigma by having God relate why he gave man free will.

> Thus to his only Son, foreseeing spake:
> "Only-begotten Son, seest thou what rage
> Transports our Adversary? whom no bounds
> Prescribed, no bars of Hell, nor all the chains
> Heaped on him there, nor yet the main Abyss
> Wide interrupt, can hold; so bent he seems
> On desperate revenge, that shall redound
> Upon his own rebellious head. And now,
> Through all restraint broke loose, he wings his way
> Not far off Heaven, in the presence of light,
> Directly towards the new-created World,

And Man there placed, with purpose to assay
If him by force he can destroy, or, worse,
By some false guile pervert: and shall pervert;
For Man will hearken to his glozing lies;
And easily transgress the sole command,
Sole pledge of his obedience; so will fall
He and his faithless progeny. Whose fault?
Whose but his own? Ingrate, he had of me
All he could have; I made him just and right,
Sufficient to have stood, though free to fall.   .
Such I created all the ethereal powers
And Spirits, both them who stood and them who failed:
Freely they stood who stood, and fell who fell.
Not free, what proof could they have given sincere
Of true allegiance, constant faith, or love,
Where only what they needs must do appeared,
Not what they would? what praise could they receive,
What pleasure I, from such obedience paid,
When will and reason — reason also is choice —
Useless and vain, of freedom both despoiled,
Made passive both, had served necessity,
Not me? They therefore, as to right belonged,
So were created, nor can justly accuse
Their Maker, or their making, or their fate,
As if predestination overruled
Their will, disposed by absolute decree
Of high foreknowledge. They themselves decreed
Their own revolt, not I: if I foreknew,
Foreknowledge had no influence on their fault,
Which had no less proved certain unforeknown.
So without least impulse, or shadow of fate,
Or aught by me immutably foreseen,
They trespass, authors to themselves in all,
Both what they judge and what they choose; for so
I formed them free, and free they must remain
Till they enthrall themselves: I else must change
Their nature, and revoke the high decree
Unchangeable, eternal, which ordained
Their freedom; they themselves ordained their fall."

(John Milton: *Paradise Lost*, III, 79–128; 1667)

The Case Against

PROP. XLVIII. There is in no mind absolute or free will, but the mind is determined for willing this or that by a cause which is determined in its turn by another cause, and this one again by another, and so on to infinity.

Proof. — The mind is a fixed and determined mode of thinking, and therefore cannot be the free cause of its actions, or it cannot have the absolute faculty of willing and unwilling: but for willing this or that it must be determined by a cause which is determined by another, and this again by another, etc.

.   .   .

Thus an infant thinks that it freely desires milk, an angry child thinks that it freely desires vengeance, or a timid child thinks it freely chooses flight. Again, a drunken man thinks that he speaks from the free will of the mind those things which, were he sober, he would keep to himself. Thus a madman, a talkative woman, a child, and people of such kind, think they speak by the free decision of the mind, when, in truth, they cannot put a stop to the desire to talk, just as experience teaches as clearly as reason that men think themselves free on account of this alone, that they are conscious of their actions and ignorant of the causes of them; and moreover that the decisions of the mind are nothing save their desires, which are various according to various dispositions of the body. For each one moderates all his actions according to his emotion, and thus those who are assailed by conflicting emotions know not what they want: those who are assailed by none are easily driven to one or the other. Now all these things clearly show that the decision of the mind and the desire and determination of the body are simultaneous in nature, or rather one and the same thing, which when considered under the attribute of thought and explained through the same we call decision, and when considered under the attribute of extension and deduced from the laws of motion and rest we call determination. . . . For there is another point which I wish to be noted specially here, namely, that we can do nothing by a decision of the mind unless we recollect having done so before, *e.g.*, we cannot speak a word unless we recollect having done so. Again, it is not within the free power of the mind to remember or forget anything. Wherefore it must only be thought within the free power of the mind in so far as we can keep to ourselves or speak according to the decision of the mind the thing we recollect. But when we dream that we speak, we think that we speak from the free decision of the mind, yet we do not speak, or if we do, it is due to a spontaneous motion of the body. We dream again that we conceal something from men, and think that we do so by the same decision of the mind as that by which, when we are awake, we are silent concerning what we know. In the third place, we dream that we do certain things by a decision of the mind which were we awake we would dare not: and therefore I should like to know whether there are in the mind two sorts of decisions, fantastic and free? But if our folly is not so great as that, we must necessarily admit that this decision of the mind, which is thought to be free, cannot be distinguished from imagination or memory, nor is it anything else than the affirmation which an idea, in so far as it is an idea, necessarily involves. And therefore these decrees of the mind arise in the mind from the same necessity as the ideas of things actually existing. Those therefore, who believe that they speak, are silent, or do anything from the free decision of the mind, dream with their eyes open.

(Baruch Spinoza: *Ethics,* Parts II, III; 1677)

C. TOWARD DEISM

Lord Herbert of Cherbury (1583–1648) has been called the father of deism. His five principles, which he considers innate ideas, will be attacked by Locke, who denies innate ideas, but they serve as the basis of future deistic attitudes.

. . . Profiting from these dissensions, a new sect unknown heretofore has formed that has attempted to establish its doctrines, contrary to the precepts of Reason, based on a certain implicit Faith which is close to the opinion of those who hold that we can know nothing.

But this procedure is iniquitous and offends our faculties; for by preferring Faith to Reason, they judge before knowing the true state of affairs. Is there anything, no matter how extravagant, that cannot be maintained by this attitude? And could not everybody use the same procedure in order to impose his dreamings as real? We must therefore explain what is meant by Truth attributed to common opinion, namely that there are things which surpass Reason and which have to be believed on faith, that we must receive and accept common notions, and to consider them as demonstrations, even without any prior consent of our faculties.

We shall thus accept as truthful everything consented to by all, for what is done everywhere cannot happen without the universal providence of God.

Now we derive this universal consent not only from laws, religions, philosophies and the writings bequeathed to us by all sorts of authors, but we claim furthermore that there are certain faculties innate in us by means of which these truths are vouched for. . . .

Before speaking of revelation, it must be noted that a few matters take precedence over it; for not every Religion that boasts of having revelations is good, not every doctrine that uses it is always necessary or useful. The doctrine of Common Notions is so useful for this purpose that it is impossible to recognize and discern revelation, even Religion, without their help. . . . For example, when it is said that human reason is blind and should yield to Faith, . . . that we should not trust the strength of our intelligence so much as to examine the power and the authority of Prelates and of those who convey the word of God, that there are good reasons for everything that is being preached (although it is beyond the reach of the human mind), that are so true that we should adore rather than examine them, that God can do all these things and more. For all these and similar arguments . . . can be used as easily to establish a false Religion as the true one, since any impostor could utilize such language to persuade people of the truth of his dreamings and imagined laws. . . .

Suffice it to know that nothing can be established in the true Religion without these Common Notions which I esteem so greatly that I believe the book, the Religion, and the Prophet that observe them most closely are also the best. At any rate, it suffices to note without additional explanation that these Notions have been accepted throughout the ages by all sorts of persons of good judgment.

I say therefore that these Common Notions are the universal or Catholic doctrine of the Church of God which does not nor will fail us, and in which alone the divine universal Providence triumphs, and which recognize and confess

That there is a Supreme Power.

People do not agree on the names of Gods, as they do on God, but there is no Religion that does not admit, has not admitted or will admit in the future that there is a Supreme one amongst all those one can imagine. . . . Whatever the case may be, all agree that there is a universal Providence.

That this Supreme Power must be worshipped.

Although there is no agreement about the worship of the Gods, of saints and angels, still the Common Notion, or universal consent, teaches that the Supreme Power must be worshipped. Whence the divine Religion has been established everywhere, not only because of the benefactions received

from the common providence of all things in the universe, but also because of the favors of particular providence.

*That the good ordering or disposition of human faculties constitutes the
principal or best part of divine worship, and that this has always been
believed.*

People are not in agreement on ceremonies and written traditions the
way they are, in all religions, concerning the good and complete ordering
of our faculties.

I come now to *conscience,* which does not rest or stay content, unless
all the faculties are well ordered; now, all our inner senses are subject to
the faculty of conscience, which sets up and composes the entire army of
affections, so that it is the common sense of the inner senses. Its objective
is thus the ordering of all the other faculties. Consequently, the legitimate
use of the faculties depends on *conscience,* whether it concerns the
analogies between things and God, the mutual analogy between men and
things or that of things among themselves.

That all vices and crimes should be expiated and effaced by repentance.

Not all agree that sins are effaced by different lustrations, purgatory,
purifications, sacrifices, and other ceremonies invented for this purpose,
but the general view of the Religions, the quality of divine goodness and
particularly conscience teach that they are removed by the grace of God
after true penitence which can help us to become reconciled with God,
for our inner feelings show that conscience, which prohibits and condemns
crimes, can efface and abolish them in this manner.

That there are rewards and punishments in the life hereafter.

All Religions, all sorts of laws and philosophies, and, what is more,
conscience teach overtly or implicitly that we shall be punished or re-
warded in the life hereafter.

People everywhere agree that there are rewards and punishments in the
life hereafter, although they argue about the following questions: in what
they consist, what they are like, and what is their extent.

(Lord Edward Herbert of Cherbury: *Of Truth,* 1625.
Translated from the French version, third edition, 1639)

NOTES

1. Thomas Corneille, *Le feint astrologue,* 1651.
2. An anonymous adaptation, 1668.
3. The nobility and the clergy.
4. In the sixth verse of the Eighty-second Psalm.
5. Jeremiah 29.
6. Jeremiah 13.

PART

V

The Countercurrents

No age is completely dominated by one attitude. The rational and the irrational, the factual and the mystical, the dryly scientific and the wildly imaginative exist side by side. It is primarily a matter of emphasis that imprints a particular aspect upon a given period. Besides, as rationalism had been, in part, a reaction against chaotic religious wars, disorderly political situations, and stifling philosophical authority, so, in turn, it created reactions once it had attained a position of dominance.

The reaction, as might be expected, was most strongly expressed in matters of religion. The philosophers, although apparently respectful of religion, had emphasized its rational aspects to the point of paying mere lip service to faith and revelation. To fervent believers this presented a serious impoverishment of religion against which they reacted by showing the limits of reason by pointing to miracles or by various kinds of mysticism. Some, like Glanvill, who had acclaimed rationalism at first, soon had second thoughts about the matter and attempted to prove the existence of witches and spirits. Finally, in regard to government and history, efforts were made to reestablish the unquestioned authority of God.

Two other fields seriously affected by rationalism were poetry and passionate emotions. Where clarity and definitions are demanded there is little room indeed for poetic expression, for it takes more than meter and rhyme to make poetry. And yet there were good, even great poets in the seventeenth century. Love too could not indefinitely be kept within the bounds of reason. In Mme de La Fayette's La Princesse de Clèves passion had already threatened to create chaos; in Racine's Andromache it will turn into madness.

The rationalist philosophers had been concerned with questions of truth and reality. But suppose all of life is a dream? No one has expressed this doubt more brilliantly than Calderón.

Finally, there were those who simply did not like the new science and the new universe; and according to whether they found these innovations alarming or pretentious, they expressed their disapproval in complaints or in satire.

1

Religion Beyond Reason

A. PASCAL: THE LIMITS OF REASON

None was better qualified to make a critique of rationalism than Blaise Pascal (1623–1662), for he was not only a philosopher but an eminent scientist and a deeply religious man. Among his achievements were the invention of a calculating machine, a treatise on vacuum, and a study on the equilibrium of fluids. His family was closely attached to Port-Royal, the headquarters of Jansenism, a Catholic group which, in opposition to the powerful Jesuits, insisted on the necessity of God's grace for salvation. In 1656, Pascal published his Provincial Letters, *which satirically exposed the casuistic Jesuit practice of granting absolution.*

Pascal died before he was able to complete his Thoughts, *leaving only. unarranged notes and fragments. It is generally agreed, however, that the author addressed himself to mundane people in order to show them how, after surveying the condition of man and the inability of philosophies and other religions to answer their questions, they would necessarily have to wager on the existence of God and accept the Christian religion.*

1. On Reason and Philosophers

The heart has its reasons, of which Reason knows nothing; we feel it in a thousand ways. It is the heart which feels God, and not reason. This indeed is perfect faith, God sensible to the heart.

The highest attainment of reason is to know that there are an infinite number of things beyond its reach. And it must be extremely feeble, if it does not go so far. A man ought to know, when to doubt, when to be

41. *Death Mask of Blaise Pascal.*

42. Mathieu Le Nain,
The Tric-Trac Players.
Photo: Giraudon.

certain, and when to submit. He who cannot do this does not understand the real strength of reason. Men violate these three principles either by being certain of every thing as demonstrative, for want of being acquainted with the nature of demonstration, or by doubting of every thing for want of knowing when to submit; or by submitting for want of knowing when they ought to judge.

If we submit every thing to reason, our religion will have nothing mysterious or supernatural. If we violate the principles of reason, our religion will be absurd and ridiculous.

On the philosophy of Des Cartes. —
We may say, in general, this is produced by figure and motion — for that is true; but to say, what figure and motion, and to compose a machine, is ridiculous, for it is useless, uncertain, and troublesome. And if it were true, we should not reckon all the philosophy in the world worth an hour's anxiety.

2. Attitudes Concerning the Life Hereafter

There are three sorts of persons: Those who have found God and serve him — those who are busy seeking him, but have not found him — and those, who not having found him, live without seeking him. The first are rational and happy; the last are foolish and unhappy; the other class are unhappy but rational.

.   .   .

A man in prison, who knows not whether the warrant be signed for his execution, and has only an hour for informing himself, but that hour probably sufficient to procure a pardon, would act most unnaturally if he employed this short period, not in taking measures to escape his doom, but in jollity and mirth. The persons I have been describing are in a similar situation, with this difference, that the evils which menace them are far other and weightier than the mere loss of life, or a punishment that will soon be over. Yet, having hood-winked themselves to hide the precipice from their view, they madly run towards it, and laugh at those who warn them of their danger.

3. The Difficulty of Proving the Existence of God.

Most persons who attempt to prove to unbelievers the existence of the Deity, begin with an appeal to the works of Nature, and they rarely succeed. Far be it from me to question the soundness of proofs which are consecrated by the inspired writings. They are conformable to the reason of man, I allow; but they are not sufficiently conformable to the dispositions of those whom they are employed to convince. . . .

It is not in this manner that the inspired writers, who understood the things of God better than we do, have treated the subject. The Scriptures declare, in general terms, that God is a God concealed from men — "Verily thou art a God that hideth thyself"; and that, since the fall, man have been left in a state of blindness, from which they are rescued only by Jesus Christ, separate from whom all communication between God and ourselves is cut off. This language cannot be used respecting an object that is perfectly luminous and exposed to view. We cannot be said to search for what manifests itself at once to us.

The metaphysical proofs of a Deity are so intricate, and so far removed from the usual track of men's thoughts, that they strike the mind with little force, and the persons most capable of entering into them feel the impression only while the demonstration is before their eyes; an hour after, they cannot trust their own conclusions.

4. The Human Condition.

What is the rank man occupies in Nature? A nonentity, as contrasted with infinity; a universe, contrasted with nonentity; a middle something between every thing and nothing. He is infinitely remote from these two extremes: his existence is not less distant from the nonentity out of which he is ingulfed. His intellect holds the same rank, in the order of intelligences, as his body in the material universe, and all it can attain is, to catch some glimpses of objects that occupy the middle, in eternal despair of knowing either extreme. — All things have sprung from nothing and are borne forward to infinity. Who can follow out such an astonishing career? The Author of these wonders, and he alone, can comprehend them.

Such is our real state; our acquirements are confined within limits which we cannot pass, alike incapable of attaining universal knowledge or of remaining in total ignorance. We are in the middle of a vast expanse, always unfixed, fluctuating between ignorance and knowledge; if we think of advancing further, our object shifts its position and eludes our grasp; it steals away and takes an eternal flight that nothing can arrest. This is our natural condition, altogether contrary, however, to our inclinations. We are inflamed with a desire of exploring every thing, and of building a tower that shall rise into infinity, but our edifice is shattered to pieces, and the ground beneath it discloses a profound abyss.

Man is the feeblest reed in existence, but he is a thinking reed. There is no need that the universe be armed for his destruction; a noxious vapour, a drop of water is enough to cause his death. But though the universe were to destroy him, man would be more noble than his destroyer, for he would know that he was dying, while the universe would know nothing of its own achievement. Thus all our dignity consists in the thinking principle. This and not space and duration, is what elevates us. — Let us labour then to think aright; here is the foundation of morals.

5. *The Wager*

A Dialogue Between a Sceptic and a Believer.

B. I would argue on principles admitted by yourself; and shall undertake to show you, by the mode of your reasoning every day on things of far inferior moment, in what manner you ought to reason on this infinitely important question, and which side you ought to take in deciding on the truth or falsehood of the existence of the Deity. You assert, then, that we are incapable of knowing that God exists. Now, it is certain that either there is a God, or there is not; there is no other alternative. But which side shall we take? Reason, again you assert, can do nothing towards deciding the point. A chaos of infinity separates man from God. At this infinite distance the game is played, whether it will turn up *cross* or *pile;* which do you wager? By reason, you cannot be certain of either; by reason, you cannot deny either. Do not blame those who have made a choice, for that they have acted unwisely, and made a bad choice, is more than you can tell.

S. I blame them not for choosing either one side or the other, but for making any choice whatever: he who takes *cross,* and he who takes *pile,* are both wrong: not to wager at all would be most proper.

B. Yes, but you must wager: it is not left to your option to be neutral: not to wager that there is a God, is to wager that there is no God. Which then do you choose? Consider which will be most for your own interest: there are two things you may fail to gain, truth and the supreme good; you have two things to pledge, your reason and your will, your knowledge and your happiness: and your nature has two things to avoid, error and misery. Do not hesitate then, to decide in the affirmative. Your reason will not be shocked by choosing one in preference to the other, since a choice must be made: that is a settled point. But your happiness: are you alarmed for that? Weigh the gain and the loss: by taking the affirmative, if you gain, you gain all; if you do not gain, you lose nothing. Oh! then, believe, if you can, that there is a God.

S. This is very forcible: I must believe; and yet I hesitate; shall I not hazard too much?

B. Consider; if there were two lives to be gained for one, on an equal chance of gain or loss, you would certainly not hesitate to wager. And if ten lives might be gained, would you not be foolish not to hazard your single life to gain ten, supposing the chances were equal? But here there are an infinity (so to speak) of infinitely happy lives to be gained, with an equal chance, as you allow, of gaining and losing: the stake, too, is an inconsiderable thing, which cannot be long at your disposal: to be chary therefore about parting with it now would be absurd. Nor is it any real objection to say, that the gain is uncertain, but the hazard certain; and that the infinite distance which exists between the certainty of what is hazarded, and the uncertainty of what may be gained, equalizes the finite good of which the risk is certain, and the infinite good of which the winning is uncertain. This is not a fair statement of the case: every gamester risks a certainty to gain an uncertainty, and yet he risks a finite good, to gain another finite good, without acting irrationally. It is not true that there is an infinite distance between the certainty of what he risks, and the uncertainty of what he hopes to gain. There is, indeed, an infinite distance between the certainty of winning, and the certainty of losing. But the uncertainty of gaining, is in proportion to the certainty of what is risked, according to the proportion of the chances of gain and loss: and hence, if the chances on both sides are equal, the risks are equal; the certainty of what we risk, in such a case, is equal to the uncertainty of the prize, instead of being infinitely distant from it. And our assertion acquires infinite force, when as in the present case, what is only finite, is hazarded on even chances of gain and loss, for what is infinite. This is demonstration: and if men's minds can admit any truth on rational grounds, they must admit this.

(Blaise Pascal: *Thoughts on Religion and Philosophy;*
written 1656–1658; published 1670)

B.   MIRACLES

The Jansenists in France were subject to attacks from the

*Jesuits and to persecution from the government which eventu-
ally disbanded them by scattering the nuns in different con-
vents and destroying their schools at Port-Royal. Faced with
this menace, the miracle of the Holy Thorn, on March 24,
1656, represented a ray of hope for this severe sect, for it seemed
to be a sign of divine approval and it happened to the niece of
Pascal. In what was perhaps his last literary effort, Racine, who
had been educated at Port-Royal and who, upon retiring from
the theater, had reconciled himself with his former teachers,
recounts this important event.*

The Miracle of the Holy Thorn

There was at Port-Royal a young boarder aged ten or eleven years by the
name of Mlle Perrier, a niece of M. Pascal. For three or four years she had
been afflicted with lachrymal fistula in the corner of her left eye, which
was very large on the outside and caused much harm inside. It had completely infected the nasal bone and pierced the palate; so that the puss
was affecting her cheeks, nostrils, and even her throat. Her eye had shrunk
considerably and all the surrounding parts were so much affected by the
inflammation that one could not touch that side of her head without
causing her much pain. One could not look at her without feeling a sort
of horror; and the puss coming out of the infection smelled so badly that,
on orders of the doctor, she had been separated from the other boarders
and placed in a room with an older woman, who was charitable enough to
keep her company. She had been sent to all sorts of occulists, surgeons,
and other specialists. But since the remedies only increased her illness and
since it was feared that the infection might extend over the entire face,
three of the most skillful surgeons in Paris, Cressé, Guillard, and Delancé,
proposed burning the infection. Informed of this proposal, M. Perrier had
set out at once to be present at the operation and was expected to arrive
any day.

At the same time, there was in Paris a churchman, both noble and
pious, by the name of M. de la Potterie who, among various holy relics he
had acquired, claimed to have one of the thorns from the crown of Our
Lord. . . . The nuns at Port-Royal had asked to see it and it was brought
to them on March 24, 1656. . . .

It was placed in the choir on a sort of altar and the Community was
informed that, after vespers, a procession in its honor would take place.
When vespers was finished, they sang the appropriate hymns and prayers
for the Holy Crown of thorns and the painful mystery of the Passion.

43. Magdeleine de Boulongne, *Port-Royal Nuns in Church.* Photo: Giraudon.

After which they filed by, according to rank, to kiss the relic: first the nuns, then the novices, and finally the boarders. When it was the turn of the little Perrier, the Supervisor of the Boarders, seeing her so disfigured, felt a mixture of a shudder and compassion and said to her: "Recommend yourself to God, my daughter, and touch the Holy Thorn with your sick eye." The little girl did as she was told and she stated later that she had no doubt that the Holy Thorn would cure her.

After this ceremony all the boarders retired to their rooms. As soon as she was in hers, she said to her roommate: "My sister, I feel no more pain. The Holy Thorn has cured me." And indeed, her roommate, after examining her attentively, found her left eye as healthy as the other, without any tumor, puss, or even a scar. . . .

The next morning, one of the nuns in charge of the boarders came to comb the hair of the little girl; and as she feared hurting her, she avoided as usual to brush hard on the left side of her head. But the girl said: "My sister, the Holy Thorn has cured me." "How is that, my sister, you are cured?" "Look for yourself," she replied. And the nun looked and saw that she was completely cured. She went to inform the Mother Superior who came to see her and thanked God for this miraculous effect of his power. But she deemed it advisable not to let the news get out, for she felt that, in view of the unfriendly attitude that prevailed against their convent, it was best to avoid drawing any attention to it. In fact, so great was the silence that reigned in this convent that six days after this miracle there were still some sisters who had not heard of it.

But God, who did not want it to remain secret, caused it that after three or four days Delancé, one of the three surgeons mentioned before, came to the convent for another patient. Before leaving, he asked to see the little girl with the fistula. She was brought in, but not recognizing her, he repeated that he wanted to see the little girl with the fistula. He was told simply that she was right in front of him. Delancé, surprised, looked at the nun who was speaking to him and concluded that they must have sent for some quack doctor who by means of some drug had momentarily stopped the ailment. So he examined his patient with special attention, pressed on her eye several times to make the puss come out, looked in her nose and at her palate and finally, beside himself, asked what was the meaning of all this. He was candidly told what had happened, and he hurried at once to see his colleagues, Guillard and Cressé. When the three arrived at the convent, they were all equally amazed and, after declaring that only God could have worked such a complete healing, they went to spread the news all over Paris.

The rumor of this miracle finally reached the Court, then at Compiègne, where the Queen Mother was greatly embarrassed. She found it difficult to believe that God would particularly favor a convent that had been depicted to her for a long time as infected with heresy; and that this miracle had been performed on one of the boarders of this convent, as if in this way God had wanted to show his approval of the education young people were receiving there. Trusting neither the letters she had received from several pious persons nor even the attestations of the Paris surgeons, she sent M. Félix, the First Surgeon of the King, a man esteemed for his skill and honesty, to give her an account of what he could find out about this miracle. M. Félix acquitted himself of his task with the greatest care. He questioned the nuns and the surgeons, inquired about the beginning, progress and end of the illness, examined the girl and declared finally that neither nature nor remedies had played any part in the healing and that it could only have been the working of God alone.

(Jean Racine: *An Abridged History of Port-Royal;*
published 1742 and 1767)

C. MYSTICISM

Religion was by no means entirely rational during the seven-
teenth century. In France, there appeared the quietism of Mme
Guyon, supported by Fénelon but condemned by Bossuet. In
Germany, pietism was preached by Philipp Jacob Spener. But
the most significant mystic of the century was probably Jakob
Boehme (1575–1624), a man of humble origin who had to suffer
a great deal for his writings.

Since thou desirest me to tell thee how to forsake thy own perverse
creaturely will, that the creatures might die, and that yet thou mightest
live with them in the world, I must assure thee that there is but one way
to do it, which is narrow and straight, and will be very hard and irksome
to thee at the beginning, but afterwards thou wilt walk in it cheerfully.

Thou must seriously consider, that in the course of this worldly life
thou walkest in the anger of God and in the foundation of hell; and that
this is not thy true native country; but that a Christian should, and must
live in Christ, and in his walking truely follow him; and that he cannot
be a Christian, unless the spirit and power of Christ so live in him, that
he becometh wholly subject to it. Now seeing the kingdom of Christ is not
of this world, but in heaven, therefore thou must always be in a continual
ascension towards heaven, if thou wilt follow Christ; though thy body
must dwell among the creatures and use them.

The narrow way to which perpetual ascension into heaven and imitation of Christ is this: Thou must despair of all thy own power and
strength, for in and by thy own power thou canst not reach the gates of
God; and firmly purpose and resolve wholly to give thyself up to the mercy
of God, and to sink down with thy whole mind and reason into the passion
and death of our Lord Jesus Christ, always desiring to persevere in the
same, and to die from all thy creatures therein. Also thou must resolve to
watch and guard thy mind, thoughts, and inclinations that they admit no
evil into them, neither must thou suffer thyself to be held fast by temporal
honour or profit. Thou must resolve likewise to put away from thee all
unrighteousness, and whatsoever else may hinder the freedom of thy motion and progress. Thy will must be wholly pure, and fixed in a firm
resolution never to return to its old idols any more, but that thou wilt that
very instant leave them, and separate thy mind from them, and enter into
the sincere way of truth and righteousness, according to the plain and full

44. Peter Paul Rubens, *Saint Louis de Gonzague.* Photo: Giraudon.

doctrine of Christ. And as thou dost thus purpose to forsake the enemies of thine own inward nature, so thou must also forgive all thine outward enemies, and resolve to meet them with thy love; that there may be left no creature, person, or thing at all able to take hold of thy will and captivate it; but that it may be sincere, and purged from all creatures. Nay further; if it should be required, thou must be willing and ready to forsake all thy temporal honour and profit for Christ's sake, and regard nothing that is earthly so as to set thy heart and affections upon it; but esteem thyself in whatsoever state, degree, and condition thou art, as to worldly rank and riches, to be but a servant of God and of thy fellow-Christians; or as a stewart in the office wherein thy Lord hath placed thee. All arrogance and self-exaltation must be humbled, brought low, and so annihilated that nothing of thine own or of any other creature may stay in thy will to bring thy thoughts or imagination to be set upon it.

Thou must also firmly impress it on thy mind, that thou shalt certainly partake of the promised grace in the merit of Jesus Christ, viz. of his out-flowing love, which indeed is already in thee, and which will deliver thee from thy creatures, and enlighten thy will, and kindle it with the flame of love, whereby thou shalt have victory of the devil. Not as if thou couldst will or do anything in thine own strength, but only enter into the suffer-

45. Giovanni Lorenzo Bernini, *Santa Teresa in Ecstasy*, detail. Photo: Giraudon.

ing and resurrection of Jesus Christ, and take them to thyself, and with them assault and break in pieces the kingdom of the devil in thee, and mortify thy creatures. Thou must resolve to enter into this way this very hour, and never to depart from it, but willingly to submit thyself to God in all thy endeavours and doings, that he may do with thee what he pleaseth.

When thy will is thus prepared and resolved, it hath then broken through its own creatures, and is sincere in the presence of God, and clothed with the merits of Jesus Christ. It may then freely go to the Father with the Prodigal Son, and fall down in his presence and pour forth its prayers; and putting forth all its strength in this divine work, confess its sins and disobedience; and how far it hath departed from God. This must be done not with bare words, but with all its strength, which indeed amounteth only to a strong purpose and resolution; for the soul of itself hath no strength or power to effect any good work.

Now when thou art thus ready, and that thy Heavenly Father shall see thy coming and returning to him in such repentance and humility, he will inwardly speak to thee, and say in thee, "Behold, this is my son which I had lost, he was dead and is alive again." And he will come to meet thee in thy mind with the grace and love of Jesus Christ, and embrace thee with the beams of his love, and kiss thee with his Spirit and strength; and then thou shalt receive grace to pour out thy confession before him and to pray powerfully. This indeed is the right place where thou must wrestle in the light of his countenance. And if thou standest resolutely here, and shrinkest not back, thou shalt see or feel great wonders. For thou shalt find Christ in thee assaulting hell, and crushing thy beasts in pieces, and that a great tumult and misery will arise in thee; also thy secret undiscovered sins will then first awake, and labour to separate thee from God, and to keep thee back. Thus shalt thou truely find and feel how death and life fight one against the other, and shalt understand by what passeth within thyself, what heaven and hell are. At all which be not moved, but stand firm and shrink not; for at length all thy creatures will grow faint, weak, and ready to die; and then thy will shall wax stronger, and be able to subdue and keep down the evil inclinations. So shall thy will and mind ascend into heaven every day, and thy creatures gradually die away. Thou wilt get a mind wholly new, and begin to be a new creature, and getting rid of the bestial deformity, recover the divine image. Thus shalt thou be delivered from thy present anguish, and return to thy original rest.

(Jakob Boehme: *A Discourse Between a Soul Hungry and Thirsty After the Fountain of Life and a Soul Enlightened,* 1624)

Richard Crashaw (1613–1649), educated at Cambridge and or-dained in 1639, exiled himself from England in 1644, living in Holland, Paris (where he was converted to Roman Catholi-cism), and Rome. His poem "The Flaming Heart" can perhaps be better understood by reference to a passage from the English translation of Saint Teresa's autobiography, attributed to Sir Toby Matthew: The Flaming Hart or the Life of the Glorious S. Teresa, *Antwerp, 1642:*

"It pleased our Blessed Lord, that I should haue sometimes, this following Vision. I saw an Angell very neer me, towards my left side, and he appeared to me, in a Corporeall forme; though yet I am not wont to see anie thing of that kind, but very rarely. For, though Angells be represented often to me, it is yet, without my seeing them, but only according to that other kind of Vision, whereof I spake before. But, in this Vision, our Lord was pleased, that I should see this Angell, after this other manner. He was not great; but rather little; yet withall, he was of very much beautie. His face was so inflamed, that he appeared to be of those most Superiour Angells, who seem to be, all in a fire; and he well might be of them, whome we call *Seraphins;* but as for me, they neuer tell me their names, or rankes; yet howsoeuer, I see thereby, that there is so great a difference in Heauen, between one Angell, and another, as I am no way able to expresse. I saw, that had a long Dart of gold in his hand; and at the end of the iron below, me thought, there was a little fire; and I conceaued, that he thrust it, some seuerall times, through my verie Hart, after such a manner, as that it passed the verie inwards, of my Bowells; and when he drew it back, me thought, it carried away, as much, as it had touched within me; and left all that, which remained, wholy inflamed with a great loue of Almightie God. The paine of it, was so excessiue, that it forced me to vtter those groanes; and the suauitie, which that extremitie of paine gaue, was also so very excessiue, that there was no desiring at all, to be ridd of it; nor can the Soule then, receaue anie contentment at all, in lesse, then God Almightie himself."

The Flaming Heart.

Upon the booke and picture of *Teresa.*
As she is usually expressed with a *Seraphim* beside her.

Well meaning Readers! you that come as Friends,
And catch the pretious name this piece pretends,
Make not so much hast to admire
That faire cheek't fallacie of fire.
That is a *Seraphim* they say,
And this the great *Teresia.*
Readers, be rul'd by me, and make,
Here a well plac't, and wise mistake.

You must transpose the picture quite,
And spell it wrong to reade it right;
Read *Him* for *Her,* and *Her* for *Him,*
And call the *Saint,* the *Seraphim.*
Painter, what did'st thou understand
To put her dart into his *Hand?*
See, even the yeares, and size of Him,
Shew this the Mother *Seraphim.*
This is the Mistrisse *Flame;* and duteous *hee*
Her happier *fire-works,* here, comes down to see.
O most poore spirited of men!
Had thy cold Pencill kist her Pen
Thou could'st not so unkindly err
To shew us this faint shade for Her.
Why man, this speakes pure mortall frame,
And mocks with Femall Frost Love's manly flame.
One would suspect thou mean'st to paint,
Some weake, inferior, *Woman Saint.*
But had thy pale-fac't purple tooke
Fire from the burning Cheekes of that *bright booke,*
Thou would'st on her have heap't up all
That could be form'd *Seraphicall.*
What e're this youth of fire wore faire,
Rosie Fingers, Radiant Haire,
Glowing cheekes, and glistring wings,
All those, faire and flagrant things,
But before All, that fierie Dart,
Had fill'd the *Hand* of this great *Heart.*
Do then as equall Right requires,
Since *his* the blushes be, and *hers* the fires,
Resume and rectifie thy rude designe,
Undresse thy *Seraphim* into *mine.*
Redeeme this injury of thy art,
Give *him* the *veyle,* give *her* the *Dart.*
Give *him* the *veyle,* that he may cover,
The red cheekes of a rivall'd Lover;
Asham'd that our world now can show
Nests of new *Seraphims* here below.
Give *her* the *dart,* for it is *she*
(Faire youth) shoot's both thy shafts and *thee.*

Say, all ye wise and well pierc't Hearts
That live, and dye amid'st Her darts,
What is't your tast-full spirits doe prove
In that rare Life of *her,* and Love?
Say and beare witnesse. Sends she not,
A *Seraphim* at every shot?
What *Magazins* of immortall armes there shine!
Heav'ns great *Artillery* in each *Love-spun-line.*
Give then the *Dart* to *Her,* who gives the *Flame;*
Give *Him* the *veyle,* who kindly takes the shame.

.   .   .

O thou undaunted daughter of desires!
By all thy dowr of *Lights* & *Fires;*
By all the eagle in thee, all the dove;
By all thy lives & deaths of love;
By thy large draughts of intellectuall day,
And by thy thrists of love more large then they;
By all thy brim-fill'd Bowles of feirce desire
By thy last Morning's draught of liquid fire;
By the full kingdome of that finall kisse
That seiz'd thy parting Soul, & seal'd thee his;
By all the heav'ns thou hast in him
(Fair sister of the *Seraphim!*)
By all of *Him* we have in *Thee;*
Leave nothing of my *Self* in me.
Let me so read thy life, that I
Unto all life of mine may dy.

(Richard Crashaw: *The Flaming Heart,* 1648)

D. SPIRITS AND WITCHES

*As rationalism began to gather strength, those who did not
want to abandon supernatural religion became increasingly
concerned, for Satan, spirits, and witches could not be proved
as rationally as the existence of God. In turn, Sir Thomas
Browne, Henry More, and Joseph Glanvill rallied to defend
the reality of witchcraft while accusing those who denied this
of being close to atheism.*

If any thing were to be much admired in an *Age* of Wonders, it would be to me Matter of *Astonishment,* that Men, otherwise witty and ingenious, are fallen into the Conceit, that there is no such Thing as a *Witch,* or *Apparition;* but that these are the creatures of *Melancholy* and *Superstition,* foster'd by Ignorance and Design; which, comparing the confidence of their disbelief with the evidence of the things denied, and the weakness of their grounds, would almost suggest that themselves are argument of what they deny; and that so confident an opinion could not be held, upon such inducements, but by some kind of witchcraft and fascination in the fancy. . . .

And in order to the proof that there have been, and are unlawful confederacies with evil Spirits, by virtue of which the hellish Accomplices perform things above their natural powers, I must premise that this, being Matter of Fact, is only capable of the evidence of authority and sense; and by both these, the being of Witches and diabolical contracts is most abundantly confirm'd. All histories are full of the exploits of those instruments of darkness, and the testimony of all Ages, not only of the rude and barbarous, but of the most civilized and polished world, brings tiding of their strange performances. We have the attestation of thousands of Eye and Ear-witnesses, and those not of these easily deceived vulgar only, but of wise and grave discerners; and that, when no interest could oblige them to agree together in a common lie.

Objections

The Notion of a Spirit is impossible and contradictious, and consequently, so is that of Witches; the Belief of which is founded on that doctrine.

To which I answer, First, that if the *Notion* of a *Spirit* be absurd, as is pretended, that of God and a Soul distinct from Matter, and immortal, are likewise absurdities; and that our Souls are only parts of Matter that came together, we know not whence, nor how; that all our Conceptions are but the thrusting of one part of Matter against another; and the *Ideas* of our Minds mere blind and casual motion. . . .

And yet secondly, tho' it should be granted them, that a Substance immaterial is as much a contradiction as they can fancy; yet why should they not believe that the Air, and all the Regions above us, may have their invisible intellectual Agents of Nature, like unto our Souls, be that what it will, and some of them, at least, as much degenerate as the vilest and most mischievous among Men. . . . The certainty of which I believe microscopical observations will discover. . . .

I come to another *Prejudice* against the *Being* of *Witches;* which is, that 'tis very improbable that the Devil, who is a wise and mighty Spirit, should be at the beck of a poor Hag, and have so little to do, as to attend the Errands and impotent Lusts of a silly old Woman.

To which I might answer, (1.) that 'tis much more *improbable* that all the World should be *deceiv'd* in Matters of Fact, and circumstances of the clearest evidence and conviction, than that the *Devil,* who is *wicked,* should be also *unwise;* and that he, that persuades all his Subjects and Accomplices out of their Wits, should himself act like his own Temptations and Persuasions. In Belief, there is nothing more strange in this Objection, than that *Wickedness* is *Baseness* and *Senility;* and that the *Devil* is at leisure to serve those he is at leisure to *tempt,* and industrious to *ruin.* And again, (2.) I see no *Necessity* to believe that the Devil is always the *Witch's Confederate;* but perhaps it may be fitly consider'd, whether the *Familiar* be not some *departed human Spirit,* forsaken of God and Goodness and swallowed up by the unsatiable desire of Mischief and Revenge; which, possibly, by the *Laws* and *Capacity* of its *State,* it cannot execute *immediately.* . . .

That Cartesius is the Prince of the *Nullibists,* and wherein chiefly consists the Force of their Opinion.

We will now propose and confute the Reasons, first of the *Nullibists,* of whom the Chief Author and Leader seems to have been that pleasant Wit, *Renatus des Cartes;* who, by his jocular *metaphysical Meditations,* has so luxated and distorted the rational Faculties of some otherwise sober and quick-witted Persons; but in this Point, by Reason of their over-great Admiration of *Des Cartes,* not sufficiently cautious, that deceived partly by his counterfeit and prestigious Subtlety, and partly by his Authority, have persuaded themselves that such Things were most *true* and *clear* to them; which, had they not been blinded with these Prejudices, they could never have thought to have been so much as possible. . . .

The Question is, whether there are *Witches* or not. Mr. *Webster* accuseth the Writers on the Subject of Defect, in not laying down a perfect Description of a *Witch* or *Witchcraft,* or explaining what they mean. . . . The Conception which I, and I think most Men have is, that *a Witch is one, who can do, or seems to do strange Things, beyond the known Power of Art and ordinary Nature, by virtue of a Confederacy with evil Spirits.* . . . The *strange Things* are *really* performed, and are not at all *Impostures* and *Delusions.* The Witch *occasions* but is not the principal Efficient; she seems to do it, but the *Spirit* performs the Wonder; sometimes immediately, as in *Transportations* and *Possessions;* sometimes by applying other natural causes, as in raising *Storms,* and inflicting *Diseases;* sometimes using the *Witch* as an *Instrument,* and either by the Eyes, or Touch, conveying malign Influences. And these Things are done by Virtue of a *Covenant,* or *Compact* betwixt the *Witch* and an *evil Spirit.*

(Joseph Glanvill: *Sadducismus Triumphatus;* first published 1666)

E. RELIGION IN GOVERNMENT AND HISTORY

Galileo's discovery of the law of inertia had left God in the role of the benevolent prime mover who merely had had to set the universe into motion and could watch it thereafter without any additional effort. But there were those who insisted that God was actively directing all events and who advocated a theocracy, a government directly governed by God or his ministers. Such men were Richard Baxter (1615–1691), an English Puritan theologian, and Bishop Jacques Bénigne Bossuet (1627–1704), famous for his sermons and the most influential man in religious matters in France during the century.

Thes. 69. That is the best form of Government to this or that People, that all things considered, doth most powerfully tend to their spiritual and everlasting welfare, and their Holiness, Obedience, and pleasing of God.

Thes. 74. Of all the three ordinary sorts of Government, Democracy is to most people, and usually the worst.

Thes. 81. That Democracy or Popular Government is ordinarily the worst, is provided by all these Arguments: 1. Because it comes nearest to the utter confounding of the Governors and Governed: the Ranks that God hath separated by his Institutions.

Thes. 82. 2. Nothing is more incident to corrupted nature than for self-love to blind men, and every man to be partial in his own cause. Now it is the people that are to be Governed, judged, punished, etc. and therefore how likely are they by partiality to themselves to make the Government next to none.

Thes. 88. 8. Democracy is furthest from Unity, and therefore furthest from perfection; and therefore the most imperfect sort of Government.

Thes. 90. 10. It is ordinarily the most imperfect form of Government which is furthest from the Angelical order. But such is popular Government.

Thes. 93. 13. The Government that recedeth furthest from that which

Christ hath settled in the Church is the most imperfect and the worst. But such is popular Government.

Thes. 96. 16. A safe and good Government must be able speedily to determine and execute in cases of great weight, that require haste: But the Popular Government is dilatory, and will the Common-wealth be lost, while they are debating.

Thes. 191. That Common-wealth is likely to be most Happy, which in the Constitution and Administration is fullyest suited to this Heavenly End; and therefore that is the best form of Government.

Thes. 192. The more Theocratical, or truly Divine any Government is, the better it is.

Thes. 194. In a Divine Common-wealth, God the Universal King is the Soveraign; and none that Rule pretend to a Power that is not from him, nor do any else claim the honour of being the Original of Power.

Thes. 205. By this it appeareth that in a true Theocracy, or Divine Common-wealth, the Matter of the Church and Common-wealth should be altogether or almost the same, though the form of them and administration are different.

(Richard Baxter: *A Holy Common-wealth,* 1659)

From on high God holds the reins of all kingdoms; every heart is in his grasp; sometimes he restrains the passions, at other times he unbridles them and thereby unsettles all of mankind. Suppose he wants to create conquerors — he has terror march ahead of them and he inspires in them and in their soldiers invincible boldness. Suppose he wants to create legislators — he sends them his spirit of wisdom and foresight; he makes them anticipate the dangers that threaten the State and has them create the basis of public tranquility. He knows that human wisdom is always deficient in some respects; he enlightens it, extends its limits, and then abandons it to its ignorance; he blinds it, plunges it into darkness, and he confounds it through itself; it gets entangled and stumbles over its own subtleties, and its precautions turn into traps.

By these means God carries out his fear-inspiring judgments according to the rules of his justice, which is always infallible. He is the one who prepares effects by the most remote causes and who strikes those terrible blows whose repercussions extend so widely. When he wants to overthrow empires, their councils become weak and unsteady. Egypt, formerly so wise, acts as if drunk, heedless and staggering, because the Lord has spread the spirit of intoxication into its councils; she no longer knows what she is doing, she is lost. But let men not be misled: God sets straight the erring sense when it pleases him; and the one who mocked the blindness of others falls himself into deepest darkness, often without any other cause being required to upset his mind than his long years of prosperity.

Thus God reigns over all peoples. Let us speak no more of chance or luck, or else let us use these words only to cover our ignorance. What appears as chance to our uncertain interpretations is a deliberate design in a council above, that is to say, in the eternal council that contains all causes and all effects in one scheme. Thus everything contributes to the same end; and it is for want of understanding the whole that we find chance or disorder in particular series of events.

All those who govern feel themselves subject to a superior power: they do more or less than they think they are doing, and their decisions never fail to have unforeseen effects. They are neither masters of the state of affairs with which past centuries have provided them nor can they foresee what the future holds. Only he holds everything in his power who knows the name of what is and what is not yet, who rules over all ages, and who presides over all councils.

(Jacques Bénigne Bossuet: *Discourse on Universal History,* 1681)

2
The Rights of Passion

Jean Racine (1639–1699) was, along with his older contemporary Pierre Corneille, the greatest French writer of tragedy in the seventeenth century. While Corneille's heroes demonstrate that reason and will can win out over passions, Racine's principal characters usually are left only with two choices: complete possession of the person desired or vengeance through death. Such is the situation in Andromache, *where four characters are chained together by love: Andromache, Hector's widow, is loved by her captor Pyrrhus, the son of Achilles; he, in turn, is loved by Hermione to whom he is betrothed; she finally is loved by Orestes who has come to Epirus as envoy of the Greeks in order to demand that Pyrrhus surrender Andromache's baby son. Faced with this threat, Andromache, who is faithful to and*

loves only the memory of Hector, has agreed to marry Pyrrhus.
This news causes Hermione to send for Orestes.

ORESTES: Can it really be that for once you want to see Orestes as much as he wants to see you? Or am I flattering myself? Do your eyes look at me with pleasure at last? Now what is it you want?

HERMIONE: Sir, I want to know if you love me.

ORESTES: I think you are perfectly well informed of that. My oaths, my perjuries, my flight from you and return to you, my pleas, my wounds, and finally my despair are surely witnesses to my sincerity.

HERMIONE: If you avenge me, I shall believe you.

ORESTES: Madam, I shall. Let there be a new war like the war against Troy. You shall be Helen, I, Agamemnon. We shall bring on this land all the horrors of Troy.

HERMIONE: Not so fast, my lord. I don't want to avenge an insult to that point. My aim is not to exalt the insolence of an enemy. I would rather be less extreme, more prudent, and get the kind of revenge I want. Why risk everything in a battle which I am not certain to win? But if you are going to avenge me, you must do so within the hour and in your own person. If you delay I shall think that you are refusing my request. You must hurry to the temple, you must kill him. . . .

ORESTES: I must kill whom?

HERMIONE: Pyrrhus.

ORESTES: Pyrrhus!

HERMIONE: Can it be that you hesitate? Aren't you afraid that I'll tell you not to kill him? And do not tell me that he has rights of any kind. Whatever they are, I want to forget about them.

ORESTES: Never fear that, madam. Your appeal to me makes him a criminal. We shall be avenged, I agree. But not as you suggest. Let us be his enemies, not his murderers. Let's bring about his ruin honestly. Do you want me to bring the Greeks his head instead of his answer to them? I am the envoy of Greece. Do you want me to behave like an assassin? Let Greece decide his fate. Let him die publicly, hated by all. Remember, though, here he reigns, here he is master.

HERMIONE: Isn't it enough for you that I have sentenced him? Isn't it enough for you that I, offended, ask you that a victim be sacrificed to me? Is Hermione not worth the corpse of a tyrant? And isn't it enough

for you, sir, that I hate this man, and that I once loved him? I will be
frank. This traitor knew how to please me. Whether because of my
feelings or because of my father matters not at all now. I want you to
know this: Despite my pledges which he shamefully spurned, despite
the horror of his treachery to me, as long as he lives you must fear that
I may forgive him. As long as he lives you cannot be sure that I will
continue to hate him. I am capable of loving him tomorrow, Orestes.
I am asking you to kill him — today.

ORESTES: You want me to kill him? Otherwise you'll forgive him? So be it.
If I must, I can. But it will take some planning. I must find a way to
him. Remember I have only just come to Epirus. You expect me with
one blow to overthrow an empire; and you give me a day, an hour, a
single moment in which to achieve all that? I am to kill Pyrrhus in
front of all his subjects? Very well, but I must consider how. Tonight.
Yes. . . . Tonight I'll avenge you.

HERMIONE: Tonight? But by then he'll have married Andromache! The
wedding takes place today. The temple is now being prepared, my
shame is about to be made public, and his crime against me consummated. Nor is there reason for you to delay. Pyrrhus goes to the ceremony unguarded; he has ordered his men to watch over Hector's son.
Pyrrhus is at your mercy, Orestes. He is careless of his life. Are you
going to be more careful than he is? Arm my followers and your men.
Pyrrhus has betrayed me, deceived you, and scorned us all. I am not
now the only one who hates him. . . . Well, speak up. He can't escape
you. Lead your men to the temple. The thing done by your men or by
you — it does not matter. Return to me with his blood upon you and
then tell me you love me.

ORESTES: But, wait, madam, think. . . .

HERMIONE: I have thought, sir. I choose not to argue. I wanted to give you
a chance to please me, but I see that you, as always, prefer losing to
doing. Leave me. Boast of your constancy to others, and let me prepare my vengeance. I have offered my heart twice today; it has been
refused twice. I shall go myself to the temple where you are afraid to
go to win my favor. I'll be able to come close to my enemy and pierce
that heart I could not move. Then, I'll pierce my own heart, and
despite him, unite us in death. He deceived me, betrayed me. . . . All
the same, Orestes, I think I would rather die with him than live to
love you.

ORESTES: He shall die by my hand. You shall owe his death to me.

HERMIONE: And I will be your reward. But go at once. See that our ships are ready to sail.

(*Exit* ORESTES.)

.   .   ..

(*Enter* PYRRHUS *and* PHOENIX.)

PYRRHUS: I know you were not expecting me, but I had to see you, and I assure you my aim is not to justify what I am doing with false arguments. I don't argue well for what I don't believe, and I know my guilt toward you. Yes, I am about to marry Hector's widow, and I plan for her what I promised you. Do you know what I would say to you if I were not the kind of man I am? I would tell you that your father and mine on the battlefield of Troy promised each other that you and I would marry without asking you or me what we ourselves wished. But I won't insist on this point; I did agree to the marriage when it was proposed. My ambassadors came to your court and promised my heart to you; in so doing they spoke for me, or at least not against my wishes. You came to Epirus, but when I saw you at last it was with the eyes of a man who had already seen another beauty he could not resist. I tried to free myself from the spell cast on me by Andromache; I really wanted to be constant and keep the vows I had made you. I received you as if you were already my bride and believed until today that my word had more power over me than the violence in my heart. How wrong I was! Andromache has taken from me this heart she herself hates. She will break her sacred vows to Hector; I, my vows to you. So, madam, vent your rage against me. I have betrayed you, I have sacrificed you, not for happiness, no — only for sorrow, and yet I could not do otherwise. I think the rage you feel against me is just; express it and you will help me, too. Heap insults on me; madam, whatever you omit to say against me my own heart will supply.

HERMIONE: Perhaps you mean what you say, my lord, but for my part, I think you do not rate yourself highly enough; cannot you commit crimes without thinking yourself culpable? After all, is it right that a conqueror should be obliged to keep his promise to a woman? Inconstancy has its delights. Should you be denied them? I think you come here with no other aim than to show me the pleasure you feel in breaking your vows to me. Why should your pledged word or any duty tie you to me? Woo a princess of Greece, fall in love with a Trojan woman, break off with me, beg me for my hand again, and then turn once more from the daughter of Helen toward Hector's widow. Why not? Crown in turn the princess and the slave; sacrifice Troy to the Greeks and after that all Greece to Hector's son! Will not these actions show the world that you are master of your destiny, a hero not enslaved by his own words? Let people call you perjurer or traitor, why should that matter to you? In any case you will have pleased your wife. I think you came to inspect my pallor so as to be able to describe it to her when you hold her in your arms. I am sure you would like to see me following her chariot in tears, but, my lord, I think you have enjoyed yourself enough today. Why look for more conquests, you who already have so many hollow victories to your credit? Didn't you beat down Hector's old father and, watching him die in front of his grandchildren, stab him yet again with your sword to draw out every last drop of his old man's blood? Didn't you butcher all the Trojans? Didn't you kill Polyxena with your own hands in front of all the Greeks who begged you to spare her life? Why shouldn't I expose my breast to those blows which only you know how to give?

PYRRHUS: Madam, I well remember and regret what I did in avenging your mother. I could charge her with the blood I've spilled, but I've decided to forget what's past, and I thank heaven that you have no admiration for me; now I can be innocent and hope for happiness. My heart is too prone to blame itself; it should have known you better. I see that my guilt toward you was really insulting. I condemned myself for being inconstant, assuming that I was loved. You don't want me, I know that. Our hearts were never involved. You were going to yield to duty in marrying me, and I the same. Nothing forced you to love me.

HERMIONE: You think I never loved you. You can say that to me when for your sake I scorned all the princes of Greece! I came seeking you here in your land and I am still here despite your infidelity. I have told my Grecian warriors to keep your cruelty to me secret, and I waited for your heart to show itself again faithful to me. I believed that sooner or later you would yield me what you promised and what you owed. You were faithless, still I loved you. Think what I would have felt for you if you had been constant. At this very moment when your cruel lips calmly tell me my fate, I am forced to wonder, traitor, if I am not still in love with you. But, my lord, if the happiness of pleasing you has been granted her by heaven, then marry her. I consent, but do not force me to witness the ceremony. Perhaps these are the last words I shall ever say to you. Postpone the marriage for just one day. Tomorrow you can do what you will. But you do not answer me. I know what is in your mind. You are counting the minutes spent with me as minutes lost to you. You want to be with Andromache and can barely even speak to me. You are talking to her right now in your heart. Your eyes are looking for her. I shall not detain you. Go. Swear to her the vows you made me. Go, and profane the gods who have not forgotten the oaths that bound you to me. Take your heart which has forgotten me to the holy altar. Go, and go quickly; Hermione may be there before you.

.　　.　　.

ACT V

HERMIONE: Lost! What have I done? What should I do now? I don't know whether what I feel is pleasure or pain. Aimless in this palace, I cannot now tell love from hate. . . . That cruel traitor! How coldly he dismissed me, not even feigning the slightest pity. Did he show any sign of grief or regret, for even one moment? Was I able to extract from him a single sigh? Deaf to my sighs, calm when I showed fear, did he even notice that I was on the point of weeping? And still I pity him. My weak heart pleads for him! The thought of the blow now threatening him makes me tremble. Ready to avenge myself, I am also ready to forgive! But no, I must be angry! Let the blow fall. Let Pyrrhus fall! I lose him; he, life. At this very moment my rage causes him to smile, and he calculates that the storm within me will end when I cry. He thinks me weak; he thinks, too, that with one hand I'll thrust aside the dagger my other hand holds. He thinks of me as I was; I was loving. He counts on that. Right now at the temple he thinks he will get what he desires. He has not tried to find out whether I desire his life or his death. And I have to decide which I prefer and without any help from him. Kill him, Orestes! Strike him again! I shall let Orestes act. Pyrrhus must die if for no other reason than that he could not foresee his death. . . . And because he forced me to want his death. Is it that I want? Did I really order it? Is the death of the man I love to be my act of love? My heart was so delighted in the past to talk about this prince's deeds, this prince to whom I was destined, before he planned the marriage which today he will not live to enjoy. . . . But did I come from so far, cross so many seas, only to bring about his ruin, only to assassinate him? May he, before he dies . . . (*Enter* CLEONE.) What have I done, Cleone? What have you come to tell me? . . . Tell me of Pyrrhus.

CLEONE: He is the proudest and most loving of men, at the height of his desires. I saw him go toward the temple, triumphantly leading his new conquest, his eyes lit with joy and hope, drunk with the pleasure of seeing Andromache, who, for her part, did not seem to hear the joyous shouts of the crowd, but always remembering Troy, incapable of either loving or hating, seemed to obey the wishes of Pyrrhus without pleasure but without protest.

HERMIONE: But what of Pyrrhus? Has he consummated his crime? And, Cleone, did you see his face? Did you observe his expression? Did he seem to you calm in his great joy? Did he once look toward the palace? Tell me, did he notice you were there? And did he blush at seeing you? Did he admit his guilt, showing uneasiness, or was he proud to the end?

CLEONE: Madam, he sees no one, nothing. His fame and safety seem not to be in his mind any more than you are. He does not seem to know who is following him, so intent is he on his new adventure. He has placed his picked men around Hector's son, apparently thinking the boy the only one in danger. Phoenix himself is in charge of the boy and has taken him to a refuge far from the temple and the palace. The boy's safety seems to be the only thing that worries Pyrrhus.

HERMIONE: He must die. What did you learn from Orestes?

CLEONE: Orestes entered the temple with his Greek followers.

HERMIONE: So be it. Is he prepared to avenge me?

CLEONE: I cannot tell you that.

HERMIONE: You don't know? Why don't you know? Am I betrayed by Orestes, too?

CLEONE: Orestes worships you, but I think his mind, attacked by many scruples, counsels him to love, but also to think of honor. He respects Pyrrhus for his crown, because he is the son of Achilles, and I think he respects Pyrrhus for what he is. Orestes fears the Greeks; he fears the anger of the world. He would like to bring you the head of his rival, after having beaten him in battle, but he does not want to be called an assassin. . . . He entered the temple still undecided whether he had come there to be a spectator or a murderer.

HERMIONE: No, he'll do nothing, he'll watch the spectacle and not inter-
fere with it. I know his lack of courage. He is afraid of death. Yes,
death is what he fears. My mother armed all of Greece to fight for her.
For ten long years she watched twenty kings die whom she had never
before seen. All I am asking for is the death of a traitor, and I have
entrusted a lover to avenge me. . . . He can do it without risk. Am I
to be guilty and not avenged? Come, I must myself act in my own
cause. May cries of grief fill the temple, preventing the consummation
of the ceremony. Perhaps the couple has already been joined; they
shall not be united long! In the confusion I shall not pick or choose a
victim. Everyone there, even Orestes, will seem to me like Pyrrhus.
I will die but, at least, in dying, I will be avenged. And I shall not
die alone.

(*Enter* ORESTES.)

ORESTES: Madame, the deed is done. You have been obeyed. Pyrrhus is
dying now at the altar where he was to be married.

HERMIONE: He is dead!

ORESTES: He is dying, and my Greek followers have washed away the stain
to your honor with his blood. I promised you the deed, and against
my inclination, raced to the temple where my Greek followers were
placed in the crowd around the altar. Pyrrhus recognized me at once,
but never lost heart. His audacity seemed to be excited by my presence. Perhaps he thought that all of Greece, defied in her ambassador,
would add a new luster to his marriage. Joyfully placing his crown on
the brow of Andromache, he said: "I give you my crown and my vows
of faith. I promise your son a father's friendship; I call the Gods to
witness: this is my oath to the boy's mother. All his enemies are mine;
I recognize him as the king of Troy." These words, applauded by the
people of Epirus, caused our Greeks to answer with cries of rage. The
faithless king was hemmed in on all sides. I could not get close enough
to strike him. Everyone fought for the glory of being his killer. I saw
him struggle for a while, all bloody, trying to escape their blows: finally, he fell by the altar. I pushed my way through the terrified crowd
to reach you, my princess, and bring you to the port where soon we
shall meet our friends smoking with the blood of him you wanted
dead.

HERMIONE: What have they done?

ORESTES: You must forgive their impatience. I know you think they betrayed your vengeance. I know you wanted my own hand to strike the

first blows, so that Pyrrhus, in dying, would know you ordered his death. But it was my fever which inspired them to act; I was the one who brought them to the temple, and you can take credit for the death their arms simply executed. You really were the one who struck Pyrrhus.

HERMIONE: Traitor, your crime belongs to you, only to you. Go, get your Greeks to admire your fury. Go! I disavow your deed. You fill me with horror. Savage, what have you done! You have cut off a glorious life. How could you, cruel Orestes, strike him today? And tell me this. Who made you the arbiter of his fate? Why did you assassinate him? What had he done? By what right did you act? Who told you to do this?

ORESTES: Didn't you yourself, madam, order his death?

HERMIONE: Did you have to believe the words of a woman mad with love? Couldn't you read my real thoughts behind my words? Didn't you notice that in my rage my heart always gave the lie to what I said? When I wished his death, did you have to agree? Shouldn't you have asked me to repeat my words at least a hundred times in order to be sure of their real meaning? Shouldn't you have come to consult me before the deed, come back to consult me again, or perhaps even have avoided me entirely? Why not leave my revenge to me? What brought you to this place, which I came to in order not to see you? Here is the result of your detested love: you brought me the unhappiness which pursues you. Your mission here made Pyrrhus incline to my rival, to his misfortune. At least I could have gone to him when he was in trouble. Perhaps he would have loved me. At least he pretended to love me once. Good-by. You can go. I shall stay in Epirus. I renounce Greece, Sparta, my whole family. I think of Greece now as the land which produced the monster you are.

(*Exit* HERMIONE.)

ORESTES: Is this Hermione I heard? For whom, then, did I make myself guilty of murder? She has called me a traitor and an assassin. Is it Pyrrhus who is dying? Am I still Orestes? Gods! I stifled my own reason. I murdered a king I honored. In one day I violated the rights of a sovereign, the duty of an envoy, and my duty to men. I also violated the sanctity of an altar. I have become a traitor and an assassin. And for whom did I make myself sin? For a thankless woman, who even if Pyrrhus had not died would have refused to see me again, a woman to whose hatred I am wedded! And when I did what she bid, she asked me to give her back his blood and his life. She loves him! And I am the monster! She will not let me see her again. And in fleeing me she leaves in payment all the ill I did to please her.

(*Enter* PYLADES.)

PYLADES: We must go quickly, my lord. Either we leave this palace now or we may never leave it. For the moment our Greek soldiers are holding the gateway, but they are being attacked on all sides by the people of Epirus, who support Andromache, treating her as their queen and us as their enemies. Andromache herself, who was so unyielding to Pyrrhus, now shows him all the devotion of a faithful widow, orders that he be avenged, and perhaps sees a chance now to get revenge for Troy and for Hector. Let us go before we are entirely surrounded. Our friends will join us; and while Hermione occupies the populace, we can slip out and save our skins.

ORESTES: Hermione? I'll go with her. I do not want to survive her sentence of me. Go! I committed the crime; I am ready to expiate it.

PYLADES: Hermione, my lord? I think you should forget her. You were always the instrument and the object of her anger. Are you going to attempt some new outrage in the land of the dead? Because she is dying, must you perish, too?

ORESTES: Did I hear that Hermione is dying?

PYLADES: You didn't know? Returning here, we met her racing madly toward the temple. She found Pyrrhus borne by his soldiers, anxious to avenge him. Doubtless she was overwhelmed by the sight of the dead hero. . . . From the gateway we saw her lean over the body of Pyrrhus, dagger in hand, raise her eyes to heaven, stab herself, and fall.

ORESTES: Praised be the Gods! My bad luck is even worse than I could have hoped for! Yes, I praise you, heavens above, for your preserverance, devoted without respite to my punishment. You have led me to the very height of sorrow. Your hatred is pleased by my grief. After all, what was I born for, except to be an instance of your anger, the paradigm of all those who are unhappy? Well, I can die content that my fate is perfect. Where are the two lovers? To consummate my joy, I must drown myself in their blood and in mine; I would like to see the two of them even as I die; let the three hearts which could not beat to the same rhythm be reunited. The thickness of night surrounds me suddenly. From whence did all this blackness come? Why do I shudder? What horror seizes me? May heaven be praised. I see around me such pools of blood. . . .

PYLADES: My lord!

ORESTES: Pyrrhus, must I meet you again? Must I find, no matter where, a rival whom I hate? Pierced by so many dagger blows, how can you still be alive? Wait, wait! Here is the blow I kept for you. But what do I see now? Hermione embraces him. She arrives just in time to ward off the blow that would really kill him. What hatred for me there is in her glance! What are those demons and serpents that follow in her train? Daughters of Hell, are your hands ready to seize me? Is it because of me that those serpents in your hair hiss with hate? Have you come to take me off to eternal night? Come then, Orestes yields to you, Furies. Only one thing I ask: do not substitute yourselves for Hermione. She knows how to torture me better than you can. I bring her my heart. Let her devour it!

PYLADES: He has lost his senses. Time presses. Let us use to best advantage this moment of his transport. Now that his rage, like his reason, is subdued, let us try to save him.

(Jean Racine: Andromache, Acts IV and V; 1667)

3
The Poetic Witness

That seventeenth-century philosophy was not particularly favorable to poetry need hardly surprise us, for if there is a type of writing which tends not to be "clear and distinct," it is poetry. John Locke, in An Essay Concerning Human Understanding, *Book II, Chap. 11, Sect. 2, sums up this general attitude in his distinction between wit and judgment:*

Wit [lies] most in the assemblage of *ideas,* and putting those together with quickness and variety, wherein can be found any resemblance or congruity, thereby to make up pleasant pictures and agreeable visions in the fancy; *judgment,* on the contrary, lies quite on the other side, in separating carefully, one from another, *ideas* wherein can be found the least difference, thereby to avoid being misled by similitude, and by affinity to take one thing for another. This is a way of proceeding quite contrary to metaphor and allusion, wherein for the most part lies that entertainment and pleasantry of wit, which strikes so lively on the fancy, and therefore is so acceptable to all people: because its beauty appears at first sight, and there is required no labour of thought to examine what truth or reason there is in it. The mind, without looking any further, rests satisfied with the agreeableness of the picture and the gaiety of the fancy; and it is a kind of affront to go about to examine it by the severe rules of truth and good reason; whereby it appears that it consists in something that is not perfectly conformable to them.

Of the styles of poetry employed during the century, the most celebrated is that of "metaphysical poetry," whose best-known
• *representative is John Donne. This style is characterized by conceits that differ from those we have already encountered in John Lyly and poets of Mannerism by blending passion and thought, feeling and ratiocination in direct, unconventional, at times colloquial speech. When dealing with universal problems of mankind, "metaphysical poetry" maintains an antithetical tension between passion and paradox, flesh and spirit, a characteristic that can also be found in other baroque arts.*

While no attempt can be made here to present a survey of seventeenth-century poetry, a few recurring themes will be exposed. The poems chosen are preferably those dealing with a subject that was also treated in other art forms.

A.   RELIGIOUS POETRY

Batter my heart, three person'd God; for, you
As yet but knocke, breathe, shine, and seeke to mend;
That I may rise, and stand, o'erthrow mee,'and bend
Your force, to breake, blowe, burn and make me new.
I, like an usurpt towne, to'another due,
Labour to'admit you, but Oh, to no end,
Reason your viceroy in mee, mee should defend,
But is captiv'd, and proves weake or untrue.
Yet dearely'I love you,'and would be loved faine,
But am betroth'd unto your enemie:
Divorce mee,'untie, or breake that knot againe,
Take mee to you, imprison mee, for I
Except you'enthrall mee, never shall be free,
Nor ever chast, except you ravish mee.

(John Donne, 1572–1631: *Holy Sonnets*, 14)

46. Vignola and Giacomo della Porta, *Facade of the Gesù Church,* Rome. Photo: Anderson-Giraudon.

47. Balthazar Longhena, *Salute Church,* Venice. Photo: Anderson-Giraudon.

48. Georges de La Tour, *The Adoration of the Shepherds.* Photo: Giraudon.

49. Alonzo Cano, *Ecce Homo.* Photo: Giraudon.

50. Diego Rodriguez de Silva
y Velásquez, *Dead Friar*.
Photo: Alinari-Giraudon.

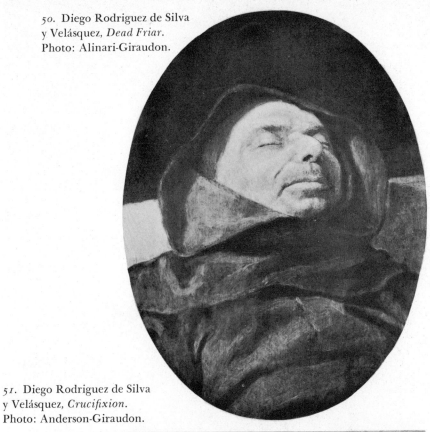

51. Diego Rodriguez de Silva
y Velásquez, *Crucifixion*.
Photo: Anderson-Giraudon.

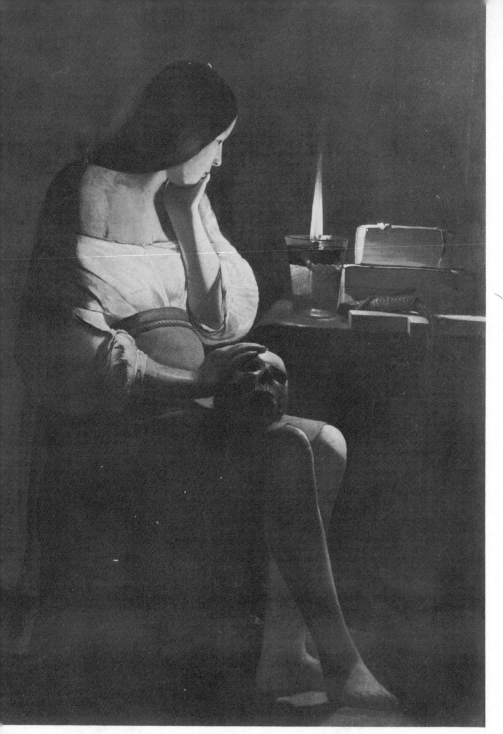

52. Georges de La Tour, *The Wake of Maria Magdalena*. Photo: Giraudon.

To the Suffering Countenance of Jesus Christ

Oh head of blood and gashes,
Of pain and mocked with scorn!
Oh head, in spite of lashes,
Bound with a crown of thorn!
Oh head else well adorned
With greatest glory and care,
But now unfairly scorned!
I honor your despair.

What you, my Lord, have suffered,
Is now my burden too;
My guilt to you is offered
For what you took 'pon you.
See, here I stand, poor sinner,
Deserving scorn in place;
Turn to me, with a glimmer,
Your countenance of grace.

Right by you I'll abide,
Refuse me not my wake;
I shall not leave your side
The day your heart will break;
When your heart is to gasp
In death's last agony,
It's then you I shall grasp
And place you 'pon my knee.

The day I must depart,
Do not depart from me;
When death will seize my heart,
You by my side shall be.
When I am struck by fear
And my heart stops to beat,
Then let me feel you're near
To overcome defeat.

Appear and be my shield,
And comfort me in death;

53. Anonymous, Italian, *Judith and Holophernes*. Photo: Giraudon.

Your image to me yield
When you gave up your breath.
To you I'll raise my eyes
And clasp you to my breast.
Blessed one who thus dies,
That death of all is best.

(Paul Gerhardt, 1607–1676)

Marie Magdalene

When blessed Marie wip'd her Saviours feet,
(Whose precepts she had trampled on before)
And wore them for a jewell on her head,
    Shewing his steps should be the street,
    Wherein she thenceforth evermore
With pensive humblenesse would live and tread:

She being stain'd her self, why did she strive
To make him clean, who could not be defil'd?
Why kept she not her tears for her own faults,

And not his feet? Though we could dive
In tears like seas, our sinnes are pil'd
Deeper then they, in words, and works, and thoughts.

Deare soul, she knew who did vouchsafe and deigne
To bear her filth; and that her sinnes did dash
Ev'n God himself: wherefore she was not loth,
    As she had brought wherewith to stain,
    So to bring in wherewith to wash:
And yet in washing one, she washed both.

                  (George Herbert, 1593–1633)

On the Triumph of Judith

Blood from the shoulder drips from couch to floor,
Blood from the savage tyrant who in vain
Besieged Bethulia's wall, and caused a rain
Of bolts from Heaven to strike him down in war.

The left hand's anguished rigor, like a claw,
Grips back the scarlet curtain, and again
Horror reveals itself: the attitude of pain,
The hideous torso, one blind mass of gore.

Wine's spilt; the heavy mail has disarrayed
The ornaments; the table's overturned;
The guards asleep forget their vicious lord;

And on the rampart the chaste Hebrew maid,
To Israel's people splendidly returned,
Holds up the armored head as a reward.

                  (Lope de Vega, 1562–1635)

B. LOVE

The Extasie

Where, like a pillow on a bed,
    A Pregnant banke swel'd up, to rest
The violets reclining head,
    Sat we two, one anothers best.

Our hands were firmely cimented
  With a fast balme, which thence did spring,
Our eye-beames twisted, and did thred
  Our eyes, upon one double string;
So to'entergraft our hands, as yet
  Was all the meanes to make us one,
And pictures in our eyes to get
  Was all our propagation.
As 'twixt two equal Armies, Fate
  Suspends uncertaine victorie,
Our soules, (which to advance their state,
  Were gone out,) hung 'twixt her, and mee.
And whil'st our soules negotiate there,
  Wee like sepulchrall statues lay;
All day, the same our postures were,
  And wee said nothing, all the day.
If any, so by love refin'd,
  That he soules language understood,
And by good love were growen all minde,
  Within convenient distance stood,
He (though he knew not which soule spake,
  Because both meant, both spake the same)
Might thence a new concoction take,
  And part farre purer then he came.
This Extasie doth unperplex
  (We said) and tell us what we love,
Wee see by this, it was not sexe,
  Wee see, we saw not what did move:
But as all severall soules containe
  Mixture of things, they know not what,
Love, these mixt soules doth mixe againe,
  And makes both one, each this and that.
A single violet transplant,
  The strength, the colour, and the size,
(All which before was poore, and scant,)
  Redoubles still, and multiplies.
When love, with one another so
  Interinanimates two soules,
That abler soule, which thence doth flow,
  Defects of lonelinesse controules.

Wee then, who are this new soule, know,
    Of what we are compos'd, and made,
For, th'Atomies of which we grow,
    Are soules, whom no change can invade.
But O alas, so long, so farre
    Our bodies why doe wee forbeare?
They'are ours, though they'are not wee, Wee are
    The intelligences, they the spheare.
We owe them thankes, because they thus,
    Did us, to us, at first convay,
Yeelded their forces, sense, to us,
    Nor are drosse to us, but allay.
On man heavens influence workes not so,
    But that it first imprints the ayre,
Soe soule into the soule may flow,
    Though it to body first repaire.
As our blood labours to beget
    Spirits, as like soules as it can,
Because such fingers need to knit
    That subtile knot, which makes us man:
So must pure lovers soules descend
    T'affections, and to faculties,
Which sense may reach and apprehend,
    Else a great Prince in prison lies.
To'our bodies turne wee then, that so
    Weake men on love reveal'd may looke;
Loves mysteries in soules doe grow,
    But yet the body is his booke.
And if some lover, such as wee,
    Have heard this dialogue of one,
Let him still marke us, he shall see
    Small change, when we'are to bodies gone.

(John Donne, 1572–1631)

54. Peter Paul Rubens (attributed to), *Coronation of a Woman.* Photo: Giraudon.

55. Jacob van Ruysdael, *River Landscape.* Photo: Giraudon.

56. François Girardon, *Nymphs Bathing*, detail. Photo: Giraudon.

57. Jacob van Ruysdael, *Landscape with Waterfall*. Photo: Giraudon.

58. Claude Gelée, called Le Lorrain, *The Enchanted Castle*. Photo: Giraudon.

59. Jacob van Ruysdael, *A Tempest in Holland*. Photo: Alinari-Giraudon.

60. Anonymous, Southern Italy, *Gamblers Surprised by Death*.

C. NATURE AND DEATH

The Mariners

The daintiest Loves to our oars do cling,
Tritons by tens caress our cheeks,
Calm winds, calm waves gently sing
Where'er our boat a passage seeks.

To our fate the stars are close,
The tempest does not make us pale,
To sea Alcyone his nestlings daren't expose
Without first glancing at our sail.

In happy climes, far from the thunder's cries,
We spend in leisure days on end;
And there with some disdain we scan the skies,
Nor do our eyes strain to discover land.

Delightful beauties, for whom our sweet sighs aim,
Come join us in our gay abode;
And ne'er a ship, we shall proclaim,
Contained as cargo such a precious load.

Epigram

This woman acted as once Troy:
Nice men besieged her with their plight
Ten years and more, but she was coy —
A horse succeeded in one night.

(Théophile de Viau, 1590–1626)

Solitude

Oh, how I love solitude!
How these sacred spots at night
Calm my mind, my plight,
Away from noise and multitude! . . .

How sweet I find the sound
Of those roving torrents there up high,
Which, rushing on and with gigantic sigh,
Into the valley down below bound!
Then, gliding under bushes green,
Like slippery snakes crawl on the herb,
They change into a pleasant stream,
Where some lovely nymphs superb,
From their beds in posture prone,
Reign from above a crystal throne! . . .

How I love to see the decadence
Of those old, ruined castles nether,
'Gainst which both time and weather
Have used up all their insolence!
The sorcerers there their sabbath hold;
Mad demons there make their abode,
And, malicious, fierce, and bold,
Deceive our senses they corrode.
Lo and behold! there snakes are found,
And owls peep out with eyes all round.

(Antoine Girard de Saint-Amant, 1594–1661)

They Are All Gone

They are all gone into the world of light!
    And I alone sit lingring here;
Their very memory is fair and bright,
    And my sad thoughts doth clear.

It glows and glitters in my cloudy brest
    Like stars upon some gloomy grove,
Or those faint beams in which this hill is drest,
    After the Sun's remove.

I see them walking in an Air of glory,
    Whose light doth trample on my days:
My days, which are at best but dull and hoary,
    Meer glimering and decays.

O holy hope! and high humility,
    High as the Heavens above!
These are your walks, and you have shew'd them me
    To kindle my cold love,

Dear, beauteous death! the Jewel of the Just,
    Shining no where, but in the dark;
What mysteries do lie beyond thy dust;
    Could man outlook that mark!

He that hath found some fledg'd birds nest, may know
    At first sight, if the bird be flown;
But what fair Well, or Grove he sings in now,
    That is to him unknown.

And yet, as Angels in some brighter dreams
    Call to the soul, when man doth sleep:
So some strange thoughts transcend our wonted theams,
    And into glory peep.

If a star were confin'd into a Tomb
    Her captive flames must needs burn there;
But when the hand that lockt her up, gives room,
    She'l shine through all the sphære.

O Father of eternal life, and all
    Created glories under thee!

> Resume thy spirit from this world of thrall
> Into true liberty.
>
> Either disperse these mists, which blot and fill
> My perspective (still) as they pass,
> Or else remove me hence until that hill,
> Where I shall need no glass.

(Henry Vaughan, 1622–1695)

4

The Unreality of Life

Opposed to the philosophical and scientific search for truth, necessarily based on reality, another view that maintains that life is a dream recurs throughout the century. This doubt, it will be remembered, had haunted Descartes to a great extent. In thinkers such as Pascal, La Bruyère, and especially Calderón, the tension between reality and dream continues to be present.

If we should dream every night the same thing, it would, perhaps, affect us as much as the objects we see every day: and if a mechanic were invariably to dream for twelve hours, every night, that he was a king, I believe he would be almost as happy as a king who should dream twelve hours, every night, that he was a mechanic. Were we to dream every night that we were pursued by enemies, or haunted by frightful spectres; or that we passed all our time in various occupations — in travelling for instance; we should dread going to sleep as much as we should dread to awake, if we apprehended meeting with such misfortunes in actual life. In fact, such dreams would produce almost the same evils as reality. But because our dreams are all different, and varied, what we see in them affects us much less than what we see when awake, owing to the continuity of the latter, though that is not so constant and equable as never to change: but it does so less abruptly, except in some remarkable cases, as when travelling, and then we say, "Methinks I am dreaming"; for life is a dream, a little more regular than other dreams.

(Blaise Pascal: *Thoughts on Religion and Philosophy*,
published 1670)

Life is a kind of sleep; old men have slept longer than others, and only begin to wake again when they are to die. If, then, they take a retrospect of the whole course of their lives, they frequently discover neither virtues nor commendable actions to distinguish one year from another; they confound one time of their life with another time, and see nothing of sufficient note by which to measure how long they have lived. They have dreamt in a confused, indistinct, and incoherent way; but, nevertheless, they are aware, as all people who wake up, that they have slept for a long while.

(Jean de La Bruyère: "Of Mankind," § 48;
The Characters, 1669)

Pedro Calderón de la Barca (1600–1681) was the last in the brilliant series of dramatists of the Spanish Golden Age. Of his immense production, some 120 dramas and numerous religious plays are extant. Life Is a Dream *is his most famous play. Its hero, Segismund, has been imprisoned by his father, the King of Poland, because the stars had forecast that the child would kill his father. Overcome by scruples, the King releases Segismund, who suddenly finds himself installed as ruler. But he acts so violently that his father has him reimprisoned. Segismund's reflections expose the theme of the play.*

CLOTALDO. What? Do you have to spend all day asleep?
    Since I was following the eagle's flight
    With tardy discourse, have you still lain here
    Without awaking?

SEGISMUND.   No. Nor even now
    Am I awake. It seems I've always slept,
    Since, if I've dreamed what I've just seen and heard
    Palpably and for certain, then I am dreaming
    What I see now — nor is it strange I'm tired,
    Since what I, sleeping, see, tells me that I
    Was dreaming when I thought I was awake.

CLOTALDO. Tell me your dream.

SEGISMUND.   That's if it *was* a dream!
    No, I'll not tell you what I dreamed; but what
    I lived and saw, Clotaldo, I *will* tell you.
    I woke up in a bed that might have been
    The cradle of the flowers, woven by Spring.

A thousand nobles, bowing, called me Prince,
Attiring me in jewels, pomp, and splendour.
My equanimity you turned to rapture
Telling me that I was the Prince of Poland.

CLOTALDO. I must have got a fine reward!

SEGISMUND.   Not so:
For as a traitor, twice, with rage and fury,
I tried to kill you.

CLOTALDO.   Such cruelty to me?

SEGISMUND. I was the lord of all, on all I took revenge,
Except I loved one woman . . . I believe
That *that* was true, though all the rest has faded.

.   .   .

CLOTALDO. Talking of eagles made you dream of empires,
But even in your dreams it's good to honour
Those who have cared for you and brought you up.
For Segismund, even in dreams, I warn you
Nothing is lost by trying to do good.

SEGISMUND. That's true, and therefore let us subjugate
The bestial side, this fury and ambition,
Against the time when we may dream once more,
As certainly we shall, for this strange world
Is such that but to live here is to dream.
And now experience shows me that each man
Dreams what he is until he is awakened.
The king dreams he's a king and in this fiction
Lives, rules, administers with royal pomp.
Yet all the borrowed praises that he earns
Are written in the wind, and he is changed
(How sad a fate!) by death to dust and ashes.
What man is there alive who'd seek to reign
Since he must wake into the dream that's death.
The rich man dreams his wealth which is his care
And woe. The poor man dreams his sufferings.
He dreams who thrives and prospers in this life.
He dreams who toils and strives. He dreams who injures,
Offends, and insults. So that in this world

Everyone dreams the thing he is, though no one
Can understand it. I dream I am here,
Chained in these fetters. Yet I dreamed just now
I was in a more flattering, lofty station.
What is this life? A frenzy, an illusion,
A shadow, a delirium, a fiction.
The greatest good's but little, and this life
Is but a dream, and dreams are only dreams.

.   .   .

ACT III
The Tower

.   .   .

Shouts within.
Long life to Segismund!

SEGISMUND. Once more, you heavens will that I should dream
Of grandeur, once again, 'twixt doubts and shades,
Behold the majesty of pomp and power
Vanish into the wind, once more you wish
That I should taste the disillusion and
The risk by which all human power is humbled,
Of which all human power should live aware.
It must not be. I'll not be once again
Put through my paces by my fortune's stars.
And since I know this life is all a dream,
Depart, vain shades, who feign, to my dead senses,
That you have voice and body, having neither!
I want no more feigned majesty, fantastic
Display, nor void illusions, that one gust
Can scatter like the almond tree in flower,
Whose rosy buds, without advice or warning,
Dawn in the air too soon and then, as one,
Are all extinguished, fade, and fall, and wither
In the first gust of wind that comes along!
I know you well. I know you well by now.
I know that all that happens in yourselves
Happens as in a sleeping man. For me

There are no more delusions and deceptions
Since I well know this life is all a dream.

SECOND SOLDIER. If you think we are cheating, just sweep
Your gaze along these towering peaks, and see
The hosts that wait to welcome and obey you.

SEGISMUND. Already once before I've seen such crowds
Distinctly, quite as vividly as these:
And yet it was a dream.

SECOND SOLDIER. No great event
Can come without forerunners to announce it
And this is the real meaning of your dream.

SEGISMUND. Yes, you say well. It was the fore-announcement
And just in case it was correct, my soul,
(Since life's so short) let's dream the dream anew!
But it must be attentively, aware
That we'll awake from pleasure in the end.
Forewarned of that, the shock's not so abrupt,
The disillusion's less. Evils anticipated
Lose half their sting. And armed with this precaution —
That power, even when we're sure of it, is borrowed
And must be given back to its true owner —
We can risk anything and dare the worst.

.   .   .

SEGISMUND. Heavens! If it is true I'm dreaming,
Suspend my memory, for in a dream
So many things could not occur. Great heavens!
If I could only come free of them all!
Or never think of any! Who ever felt
Such grievous doubts? If I but dreamed that triumph
In which I found myself, how can this woman
Refer me to such sure and certain facts?
Then all of it was true and not a dream.
But if it be the truth, why does my past life
Call it a dream? This breeds the same confusion.
Are dreams and glories so alike, that fictions
Are held for truths, realities for lies?
Is there so little difference in them both

That one should question whether what one sees
And tastes is true or false? What? Is the copy
So near to the original that doubt
Exists between them? Then if that is so,
And grandeur, power, majesty, and pomp,
Must all evaporate like shades at morning,
Let's profit by it, this time, to enjoy
That which we only can enjoy in dreams.
But with my own opinions, I begin
Once again to convince myself. Let's think.
If it is but vainglory and a dream,
Who for mere human vainglory would lose
True glory? What past blessing is not merely
A dream? Who has known heroic glories,
That deep within himself, as he recalls them,
Has never doubted that they might be dreams?
But if this all should end in disenchantment,
Seeing that pleasure is a lovely flame
That's soon converted into dust and ashes
By any wind that blows, then let us seek
That which endures in thrifty, lasting fame
In which no pleasures sleep, nor grandeurs dream.

(Pedro Calderón de la Barca: *Life Is a Dream*, 1635)

5

Barriers Against the Tide of Science

Innovations and scientific progress are not always universally hailed. There are always those who (not without justification) fear the havoc caused when mechanics run ahead of mind; others find it difficult to adjust to the changes they have to face; still others greet the latest discoveries with scorn and mockery.

Samuel Butler (1612–1680) is best known for his satire Hudibras. *Rankled by what he felt to be the pretentiousness*

61. Franz Hals, *The Administrators of the Elisabeth Hospital.* Photo: Hanf-staengl-Giraudon.

of the members of the Royal Society, he took up his pen in order to cover them with ridicule. The result was The Elephant in the Moon, *the second version of which, in long verse, is presented below.*

> A virtuous, learn'd Society, of late
> The pride and glory of a foreign state,
> Made an agreement, on a summer's night,
> To search the Moon at full by her own light;
> To take a perfect inventory of all
> Her real fortunes, or her personal,
> And make a geometrical survey
> Of all her lands, and how her country lay. . . .
> This was the only purpose of their meeting,
> For which they chose a time and place most fitting,
> When, at the full, her equal shares of light
> And influence were at their greatest height.
> And now the lofty telescope, the scale,
> By which they venture heav'n itself t'assail,
> Was rais'd, and planted full against the Moon,
> And all the rest stood ready to fall on,
> Impatient who should bear away the honour
> To plant an ensign, first of all, upon her.
> When one, who for his solid deep belief

Was chosen virtuoso then in chief,
Had been approv'd the most profound and wise
At solving all impossibilities,
With gravity advancing, to apply
To th'optic glass his penetrating eye,
Cry'd out, O strange! then reinforc'd his sight
Against the Moon with all his art and might,
And bent the muscles of his pensive brow,
As if he meant to stare and gaze her through. . . .

*He recounts seeing a fierce battle between the old inhabit-
ants of the moon, who dwell in cellars, and the mountaineers,
named Privolvans.*

  At this a famous great philosopher
Admir'd, and celebrated, far and near
As one of wondrous, singular invention,
And equal universal comprehension;
"By which he had compos'd a pedler's jargon,
For all the world to learn, and use in bargain,
An universal canting idiom,
To understand the swinging pendulum,
And to communicate, in all designs,
With th'Eastern virtuosi Mandarines;"
Apply'd an optic nerve, and half a nose,
To th'end and centre of the engine close:
For he had very lately undertook
To vindicate, and publish in a book
That men, whose native eyes are blind, or out,
May by more admirable art be brought
To see with empty holes, as well and plain
As if their eyes had been put in again. . . .

*This scientist gives further account of the progress of the battle
he is observing.*

  While thus the virtuoso entertains
The whole assembly with the Privolvans,
"Another sophist, but of less renown,
Though longer observation of the Moon,"
Who, after poring tedious and hard
In th'optic engine, gave a start, and star'd,

And thus began — A stranger sight appears
Than ever yet was seen in all the spheres!
A greater wonder, more unparallel'd
Than ever mortal tube or eye beheld;
A mighty Elephant from one of those
Two fighting armies is at length broke loose,
And, with the desp'rate horror of the fight
Appears amaz'd, and in a dreadful fright! . . .
It is a large one, and appears more great
Than ever was produc'd in Afric yet;
From which we confidently may infer,
The Moon appears to be the fruitfuller. . . .
That Elephants are really in the Moon,
Although our fortune had discover'd none,
Is easily made plain and manifest,
Since from the greatest orbs, down to the least,
All other globes of stars and constellations
Have cattle in'em of all sorts and nations. . . .
And if the Moon can but produce by Nature
A people of so large and vast a stature,
'Tis more than probable she should bring forth
A greater breed of beasts, too, than the earth;
As by the best recounts we have, appears
Of all our crediblest discoveries,
And that those vast and monstrous creatures there
Are not such far-fet rarities as here. . . .
          This said, the whole assembly gave consent
To drawing up th'authentic Instrument,
And, for the nation's gen'ral satisfaction,
To print and own it in their next Transaction:
But while their ablest men were drawing up
The wonderful memoir o'th'telescope,
A member peeping in the tube by chance,
Beheld the Elephant begin t'advance,
That from the west-by-north side of the Moon
To th'east-by-south was in a moment gone.
This being related, gave a sudden stop
To all their grandees had been drawing up,
And every person was amaz'd anew,
How such a strange surprisal should be true,

Or any beast perform so great a race,
So swift and rapid, in so short a space,
Resolv'd, as suddenly, to make it good,
Or render all as fairly as they cou'd,
And rather chose their own eyes to condemn,
Than question what they had beheld with them.
  While every one was thus resolv'd, a man
Of great esteem and credit thus began — . . .
That Elephant may chance to differ so
From those with us upon the earth below,
Both in his bulk, as well as force and speed,
As being of a different kind and breed,
That though, 'tis true, our own are but slow-pac'd,
Theirs there, perhaps, may fly, or run as fast,
And yet be very Elephants, no less,
Than those deriv'd from Indian families.
  This said, another member of great worth,
Fam'd for the learned works he had put forth, . . .
Look'd wise a while, then said — All this is true,
And very learnedly observed by you;
But there's another nobler reason for't,
That, rightly observ'd, will fall but little short
Of solid mathematic demonstration
Upon a full and perfect calculation;
And that is only this — As th'earth and moon
Do constantly move contrary upon
Their several axes, the rapidity
Of both their motions cannot fail to be
So violent, and naturally fast,
That larger distances may well be past
In less time than the Elephant has gone,
Although he had no motion of his own,
Which we on earth can take no measure of,
As you have made it evident by proof.
This granted, we may confidently hence
Claim title to another inference,
And make this wonderful phenomenon
(Were there no other) serve our turn alone
To vindicate the grand hypothesis,
And prove the motion of the earth from this. . . .

But while their grandees were diverted all
With nicely wording the Memorial,
The foot-boys, for their own diversion, too, . . .
Began to stare and gaze upon the Moon,
As those they waited on before had done:
When one, whose turn it was by chance to peep,
Saw something in the lofty engine creep,
And, viewing carefully, discover'd more
Than all their masters hit upon before.
Quoth he, O strange!.a little thing is slunk
On th'inside of the long star-gazing trunk,
And now is gotten down so low and nigh,
I have him here directly 'gainst mine eye.
   This chancing to be overheard by one
Who was not, yet, so largely overgrown
In any philosophic observation,
As to conclude with mere imagination,
And yet he made immediately a guess
At fully solving all appearances
A plainer way, and more significant
Than all their hints had prov'd o' th'Elephant,
And quickly found, upon a second view,
His own conjecture, probably, most true;
For he no sooner had apply'd his eye
To th'optic engine, but immediately
He found a small field-mouse was gotten in
The hollow telescope, and shut between
The two glass windows, closely in restraint,
Was magnify'd into an Elephant,
And prov'd the happy virtuous occasion
Of all this deep and learned dissertation.
And as a mighty mountain, heretofore,
Is said t' have begot with child, and bore
A silly mouse, this captive mouse, as strange,
Produc'd another mountain in exchange.

There is general consternation, but a specialist "in frogs and toads, as well as rats and mice" admonishes his colleagues:

It is no wonder that we are cry'd down,
And made the table-talk of all the town, . . .

If every one have liberty to doubt,
When some great secret's more than half made-out,
Because, perhaps, it will not hold out true,
And put a stop to all w'attempt to do.
As no great action ever has been done,
Nor ever's like to be, by Truth alone,
If nothing else but only truth w'allow,
'Tis no great matter what w'intend to do;
"For Truth is always too reserv'd and chaste,
T'endure to be by all the Town embraced;" . . .
For truth is never without danger in't,
As here it has depriv'd us of a hint
The whole assembly had agreed upon
And utterly defeated all we'ad done,
"By giving foot-boys leave to interpose,
And disappoint whatever we propose;" . . .
How much, then, ought we have a special care
That none presume to know above his share. . . .
    This said, the whole Society allow'd
The doctrine to be orthodox and good,
And from th'apparent truth of what they'ad heard,
Resolv'd, henceforth, to give Truth no regard,
But what was for their interests to vouch,
And either find it out, or make it such:
That 'twas more admirable to create
Inventions, like truth, out of strong conceit,
Than with vexations study, pains, and doubt
To find, or but suppose t'have found, it out.
    This being resolv'd, th'assembly, one by one,
Review'd the tube, the Elephant, and Moon;
But still the more and curiouser they pry'd,
They but became the more unsatisfy'd;
In no one thing they gaz'd upon agreeing,
As if they'ad different principles of seeing.
Some boldly swore, upon a second view,
That all they had beheld before was true,
And damn'd themselves they never would recant
One syllable they'ad seen of th'Elephant,
Avow'd his shape and snout could be no Mouse's,
But a true nat'ral Elephant's proboscis.

*Some propose to put the matter to a vote, but it is finally
agreed to take the telescope apart. As the optic tube is let down,
they discover they had mistaken flies and gnats for warring
armies.*

But when, at last, they had unscrewd'd the glass
To find out where the sly imposter was,
And saw 'twas but a Mouse, that by mishap
Had catch'd himself, and them, in th'optic trap,
Amaz'd, with shame confounded, and afflicted
To find themselves so openly convicted,
Immediately made haste to get them gone,
With none but this discovery alone:
That learned men, who greedily pursue
Things that are rather wonderful than true,
And, in their nicest speculations, choose
To make their own discoveries strange news,
And nat'ral hist'ry rather a Gazette
Of rarities stupendous and far-fet;
Believe no truths are worthy to be known,
That are not strongly vast and overgrown,
And strive to explicate appearances,
Not as they're probable, but as they please,
In vain endeavour Nature to suborn,
And, for their pains, are justly paid with scorn.

(Samuel Butler: *The Elephant in the Moon,* published 1759)

The Triumph of
Reason and Science

The application of the rational method to all fields of endeavor had led to revolutionary developments. Yet, as we have seen, the seventeenth-century rationalists were not truly revolutionaries. In religion, they wanted to do away with superstition, but at the same time they insisted that certain ideas were innate; in philosophy and science, they rebelled against the authority of the ancients, but they continued to take pride in imitating ancient literary authors; still more paradoxically, they failed to extend their rational inquiry to social and political conditions, or, if they did, they arrived at results that justified authoritarian regimes.

It was not until late in the century that these conclusions, implicit in the rational method, were being suggested. Descartes had accepted knowledge through innate ideas, as had Lord Herbert of Cherbury, but Locke rejects them, thus giving rise to a more empirical and relativistic approach to problems. Similarly, in the Quarrel of the Ancients and the Moderns, the latter widen the attack on ancient authority to include literary authors.

As religious authority grows more intolerant, reaction quickens. Earlier in the century, blind faith and belief in miracles had already been attacked by Hobbes and Spinoza. But the revocation of the Edict of Nantes by Louis XIV in 1685, putting an end to religious tolerance in France, brings strong protests from the Huguenots. One of these, Pierre Bayle, devises the method the eighteenth-century encyclopedists will use in his examination of Biblical texts. Finally, Locke's Letter Concerning Toleration will contribute to the passage of the Act of Toleration by the English Parliament in 1689.

At last the social and political fields are being invaded by the new ideas. As the aging Louis XIV grows more tyrannical and intolerant, voices are heard that complain of unjust social inequalities and that even dare question the entire political rule of the Sun King himself.

These are as yet only murmurs, but the two-pronged attack against royal and religious authority forecasts some of the major concerns of the next century. For these murmurs will grow until all established authority will be engulfed by the giant waves of the French and American revolutions.

1
The Rejection of Innate Ideas

John Locke (1632–1704) was educated at Christ Church, Oxford, where he later became a lecturer in Greek and rhetoric. From 1667 to 1681 he was physician and secretary to Anthony Ashley Cooper, who later became the Earl of Shaftesbury. Elected to the Royal Society in 1668, Locke held various government offices, but in 1684, when he was deprived of his appointment to Christ Church, he went into voluntary exile in Holland until 1689. After his return to England, he was named Commissioner to the Board of Trade, a post he held until 1700.

Locke's thorough examination of human knowledge goes beyond the concepts of earlier seventeenth-century philosophers, who had included innate ideas among the knowledge we possess. Locke denies this type of knowledge; and the eighteenth-century thinkers, while using Descartes' method, will prefer Locke's estimate of knowledge to that of Descartes, not only because it seems more plausible to them but also because the denial of innate ideas will permit them to attack established authority more effectively.

A short passage from Descartes' Meditations will illustrate how his views on innate ideas differed from those of Locke.

But before examining whether any such objects as I conceive exist outside of me, I must consider the ideas of them in so far as they are in my thought, and see which of them are distinct and which confused.

In the first place, I am able distinctly to imagine that quality which philosophers commonly call continuous, or the extension in length, breadth, or depth, that is in this quality, or rather in the object to which it is attributed. Further, I can number in it many different parts, and attribute to each of its parts many sorts of size, figure, situation and local movement, and, finally, I can assign to each of these movements all degrees of duration.

And not only do I know these things with distinctness when I consider them in general, but, likewise [however little I apply my attention to the matter], I discover an infinitude of particulars respecting numbers, figures, movements, and other such things, whose truth is so manifest, and so well accords with my nature, that when I begin to discover them, it seems to me that I learn nothing new, or recollect what I formerly knew — that is to say, that I for the first time perceive things which were already present to my mind, although I had not as yet applied my mind to them.

And what I find here to be the most important is that I discover in myself an infinitude of ideas of certain things which cannot be esteemed as pure negations, although they may possibly have no existence outside of my thought, and which are not framed by me, although it is within my power either to think or not to think them, but which possess natures which are true and immutable. For example, when I imagine a triangle, although there may nowhere in the world be such a figure outside my thought, or ever have been, there is nevertheless in this figure a certain determinate nature, form, or essence, which is immutable and eternal, which I have not invented, and which in no wise depends on my mind, as appears from the fact that diverse properties of that triangle can be demonstrated, viz. that its three angles are equal to two right angles, that the greatest side is subtended by the greatest angle, and the like, which now, whether I wish it or do not wish it, I recognise very clearly as pertaining to it, although I never thought of the matter at all when I imagined a triangle for the first time, and which therefore cannot be said to have been invented by me.

Nor does the objection hold good that possibly this idea of a triangle has reached my mind through the medium of my senses, since I have sometimes seen bodies triangular in shape; because I can form in my mind an infinitude of other figures regarding which we cannot have the least conception of their ever having been objects of sense, and I can nevertheless demonstrate various properties pertaining to their nature as well as to that of the triangle, and these must certainly all be true since I conceive them clearly. Hence they are something and not pure negation; for it is perfectly clear that all that is true is something, and I have already fully demonstrated that all that I know is clearly true. And even although I had not demonstrated this, the nature of my mind is such that I could not prevent myself from holding them to be true so long as I conceive them clearly; and I recollect that even when I was still strongly attached to the objects of sense, I counted as the most certain those truths which I conceived clearly as regards figures, numbers, and the other matters which pertain to arithmetic and geometry, and, in general, to pure and abstract mathematics.

(René Descartes: *Meditations on First Philosophy,*
Meditation V; published 1641)

Since it is the *understanding* that sets man above the rest of sensible beings, and gives him all the advantage and dominion which he has over them, it is certainly a subject, even for its nobleness, worth our labour to inquire into. The understanding, like the eye, whilst it makes us see and perceive all other things, takes no notice of itself; and it requires art and pains to set it at a distance and make it its own object.

. . .

If by this inquiry into the nature of the understanding, I can discover the powers thereof: *how far* they reach; to what things they are in any degree proportionate; and where they fail us, I suppose it may be of use to prevail with the busy mind of man to be more cautious in meddling with things exceeding its comprehension; to stop when it is at the utmost extent of its tether; and to sit down in a quiet ignorance of those things which upon examination are found to be beyond the reach of our capacities. We should not then perhaps be so forward, out of an affectation of an universal knowledge, to raise questions and perplex ourselves and others with disputes about things to which our understandings are not suited, and of which we cannot frame in our minds any clear or distinct perceptions, or whereof (as it has perhaps too often happened) we have not any notions at all. If we can find out how far the understanding can extend its view, how far it has faculties to attain certainty, and in what cases it can only judge and guess, we may learn to content ourselves with what is attainable by us in this state.

. . .

When we know our own *strength,* we shall the better know what to undertake with hopes of success; and when we have well surveyed the *powers* of our own minds, and made some estimate what we may expect from them, we shall not be inclined either to sit still and not set our thoughts on work at all, in despair of knowing anything, nor, on the other side, question everything and disclaim all knowledge, because some things are not to be understood. It is of great use to the sailor to know the length of his line, though he cannot with it fathom all the depths of the ocean. It is well he knows that it is long enough to reach the bottom, at such places as are necessary to direct his voyage, and caution him against running upon shoals that may ruin him. Our business here is not to know all things, but those which concern our conduct. If we can find out those measures whereby a rational creature, put in that state in which man is in this world, may and ought to govern his opinions and actions depending thereon, we need not be troubled that some other things escape our knowledge.

No Innate Principles in the Mind

It is an established opinion amongst some men that there are in the *understanding* certain *innate principles,* some primary notions, κοιναὶ ἔννοιαι, characters, as it were, stamped upon the mind of man, which the soul receives in its very first being and brings into the world with it. It would be sufficient to convince unprejudiced readers of the falseness of this supposition, if I should only show (as I hope I shall in the following parts of this discourse) how men, barely by the use of their natural faculties, may attain to all the knowledge they have, without the help of any innate impressions, and may arrive at certainty without any such original notions or principles. For I imagine anyone will easily grant that it would be impertinent to suppose the *ideas* of colours innate in a creature to whom God has given sight, and a power to receive them by the eyes, from external objects; and no less unreasonable would it be to attribute several truths to the impressions of nature and innate characters, when we may observe in ourselves faculties, fit to attain as easy and certain knowledge of them, as if they were originally imprinted on the mind.

But because a man is not permitted without censure to follow his own thoughts in the search of truth, when they lead him ever so little out of the common road, I shall set down the reasons that made me doubt of the truth of that opinion, as an excuse for my mistake, if I be in one; which I leave to be considered by those who, with me, dispose themselves to embrace truth, wherever they find it.

.   .   .

For if they are not notions naturally imprinted, how can they be innate? And if they are notions imprinted, how can they be unknown? To say a notion is imprinted on the mind, and yet at the same time to say that the mind is ignorant of it, and never yet took notice of it, is to make this impression nothing. No proposition can be said to be in the mind, which it never yet knew, which it was never yet conscious of. For if any one may, then by the same reason all propositions that are true and the mind is capable ever of assenting to, may be said to be in the mind and to be imprinted: since, if any one can be said to be in the mind which it never yet knew, it must be only because it is capable of knowing it; and so the mind is of all truths it ever shall know. Nay, thus truths may be imprinted on the mind which it never did nor ever shall know; for a man may live long, and die at last in ignorance of many truths which his mind was capable of knowing, and that with certainty. So that if the capacity of knowing be the natural impression contended for, all the truths a man ever comes to know will, by this account, be every one of them innate; and this great point will amount to no more, but only to a very improper way of speaking; which, whilst it pretends to assert the contrary, says nothing different from those who deny innate principles. For nobody, I think, ever denied that the mind was capable of knowing several truths. The capacity they say is innate, the knowledge acquired. But then to what end such contest for certain innate maxims? If truths can be imprinted on the understanding without being perceived, I can see no difference there can be between any truths the mind is capable of knowing, in respect of their original: they must all be innate, or all adventitious. In vain shall a man go about to distinguish them. He therefore that talks of innate notions in the understanding, cannot (if he intend thereby any distinct sort of truths) mean such truths to be in the understanding as it never perceived, and is yet wholly ignorant of. For if these words (*to be in the understanding*) have any propriety, they signify to be understood. So that to be in the understanding and not to be understood, to be in the mind and never to be perceived, is all one as to say: anything is and is not in the mind or understanding. If therefore these two propositions, *Whatsoever is, is* and *It is impossible for the same thing to be and not to be,* are by nature imprinted, children cannot be ignorant of them; infants, and all that have souls, must necessarily have them in their understandings, know the truth of them, and assent to it.

To avoid this, it is usually answered that all men know and *assent* to them, *when they come to the use of reason;* and this is enough to prove them innate. I answer:

Doubtful expressions, that have scarce any signification, go for clear reasons to those who, being prepossessed, take not the pains to examine even what they themselves say. For, to apply this answer with any tolerable sense to our present purpose, it must signify one of these two things: either, that as soon as men come to the use of reason these supposed native inscriptions come to be known and observed by them; or else, that the use and exercise of men's reason assists them in the discovery of these principles, and certainly makes them known to them.

If they mean that by the *use of reason* men may discover these principles, and that this is sufficient to prove them innate, their way of arguing will stand thus: viz. that whatever truths reason can certainly discover to us and make us firmly assent to, those are all naturally imprinted on the mind, since that universal assent, which is made the mark of them, amounts to no more but this: that by the use of reason we are capable to come to a certain knowledge of and assent to them; and, by this means, there will be no difference between the maxims of the mathematicians and theorems they deduce from them: all must be equally allowed innate, they being all discoveries made by the use of reason, and truths that a rational creature may certainly come to know, if he apply his thoughts rightly that way.

But how can these men think the *use of reason* necessary to discover principles that are supposed innate, when reason (if we may believe them) is nothing else but the faculty of deducing unknown truths from principles or propositions that are already known? That certainly can never be thought innate which we have need of reason to discover, unless, as I have said, we will have all the certain truths that reason ever teaches us to be innate. We may as well think the use of reason necessary to make our eyes discover visible objects, as that there should be need of reason, or the exercise thereof, to make the understanding see what is originally engraven in it, and cannot be in the understanding before it be perceived by it. So that to make reason discover those truths thus imprinted is to say that the use of reason discovers to a man what he knew before; and if men have those innate, impressed truths originally, and before the use of reason, and yet are always ignorant of them till they come to the use of reason, it is in effect to say that men know and know them not at the same time.

·   ·   ·

Indoctrination Does Not Constitute Innate Ideas

I easily grant that there are great numbers of *opinions* which, by men of different countries, educations, and tempers are received and *embraced as first and unquestionable principles; many whereof,* both for their absurdity as well as oppositions one to another, *it is impossible should be true*. But yet all those propositions, how remote soever from reason, are so sacred somewhere or other, that men even of good understanding in other matters will sooner part with their lives, and whatever is dearest to them, than suffer themselves to doubt, or others to question, the truth of them.

This, however strange it may seem, is that which every day's experience confirms; and will not, perhaps, appear so wonderful, if we consider the *ways* and *steps by which* it is brought about, and how really it may come to pass that *doctrines* that have been derived from no better original than the superstition of a nurse or the authority of an old woman, may, by length of time and consent of neighbours, *grow up to the dignity of principles* in religion or morality. For such who are careful (as they call it) to principle children well (and few there be who have not a set of those principles for them which they believe in) instil into the unwary and, as yet, unprejudiced understanding (for white paper receives any characters) those doctrines they would have them retain and profess. These, being taught them as soon as they have any apprehension and still as they grow up confirmed to them, either by the open profession or tacit consent of all they have to do with, or at least by those of whose wisdom, knowledge, and piety they have an opinion, who never suffer those propositions to be otherwise mentioned but as the basis and foundation on which they build their religion or manners, come by these means to have the reputation of unquestionable, self-evident, and innate truths.

.   .   .

Idea of God Not Innate

If any *idea* can be imagined *innate*, the *idea of God* may, of all others, for many reasons be thought so, since it is hard to conceive how there should be innate moral principles without an innate *idea* of a *deity*. . . .

But had all mankind everywhere a *notion of a God* (whereof yet history tells us the contrary) it would *not* from thence follow that the *idea* of him was *innate*. For, though no nation were to be found without a name and some few dark notions of him, yet that would not prove them to be natural impressions on the mind, no more than the names of fire or the sun, heat, or number do prove the *ideas* they stand for to be innate; because the names of those things and the *ideas* of them, are so universally received and known amongst mankind. Nor on the contrary is the want of such a name, or the absence of such a notion out of men's minds, any argument against the being of a god; any more than it would be a proof that there was no load-stone in the world, because a great part of mankind had neither a notion of any such thing nor a name for it. . . .

.   .   .

I grant that *if* there were *any ideas* to be found *imprinted* on the minds of men, we have reason to expect *it should be the notion of his maker,* as a mark GOD set on his own workmanship, to mind man of his dependence and duty; and that herein should appear the first instances of human knowledge. But how late is it before any such notion is discoverable in children? And when we find it there, how much more does it resemble the opinion and notion of the teacher than represent the true God? He that shall observe in children the progress, whereby their minds attain the knowledge they have, will think that the objects they do first and most familiarly converse with are those that make the first impressions on their understandings; nor will he find the least footsteps of any other. It is easy to take notice how their thoughts enlarge themselves, only as they come to be acquainted with a greater variety of sensible objects, to retain the *ideas* of them in their memories, and to get the skill to compound and enlarge them, and several ways put them together. How by these means they come to frame in their minds an *idea* men have of a deity, I shall hereafter show.

.   .   .

If it be said that *wise men* of all nations came to *have true conceptions* of the unity and infinity *of the Deity,* I grant it. But then this,

First, excludes universality of consent in anything but the name, for those wise men being very few, perhaps one of a thousand, this universality is very narrow.

Secondly, it seems to me plainly to prove that the truest and best notions men had of God were not imprinted but acquired by thought and meditation and a right use of their faculties: since the wise and considerate men of the world, by a right and careful employment of their thoughts and reason, attained true notions in this as well as other things; whilst the lazy and inconsiderate part of men, making the far greater number, took up their notions by chance from common tradition and vulgar conceptions, without much beating their heads about them. And if it be a reason to think *the notion of God innate,* because all wise men had it, virtue too must be thought innate, for that also wise men have always had.

.   .   .

If the Idea of God Is Not Innate,
No Other Can Be Supposed Innate

.   .   .

Since then, though the knowledge of a GOD be the most natural discovery of human reason, yet *the idea of him* is *not innate,* as I think is
evident from what has been said; I imagine there will be scarce any other
idea found that can pretend to it; since, if God had set any impression,
any character on the understanding of men, it is most reasonable to expect
it should have been some clear and uniform *idea* of himself, as far as our
weak capacities were capable to receive so incomprehensible and infinite
an object. But our minds being at first void of that *idea* which we are
most concerned to have, it *is a strong presumption against all other innate
characters.* I must own, as far as I can observe, I can find none and would
be glad to be informed by any other.

.   .   .

To which let me add: if there be any innate *ideas,* any *ideas* in the mind
which the mind does not actually think on, they must be lodged in the
memory and from thence must be brought into view by remembrance, i.e.
must be known when they are remembered to have been perceptions in
the mind before, unless remembrance can be without remembrance. For
to remember is to perceive anything with memory, or with a consciousness, that it was known or perceived before; without this, whatever *idea*
comes into the mind is new and not remembered: this consciousness of its
having been in the mind before being that which distinguishes remembering from all other ways of thinking. Whatever *idea* was never perceived by
the mind was never in the mind. Whatever *idea* is in the mind is either an
actual perception or else, having been an actual perception, is so in the
mind that by the memory it can be made an actual perception again.
Whenever there is the actual perception of an *idea* without memory, the
idea appears perfectly new and unknown before to the understanding.
Whenever the memory brings any *idea* into actual view, it is with a consciousness that it had been there before and was not wholly a stranger to
the mind. Whether this be not so, I appeal to everyone's observation. And
then I desire an instance of an *idea* pretended to be innate which (before
any impression of it by ways hereafter to be mentioned) anyone could
revive and remember as an *idea* he had formerly known: without which
consciousness of a former perception there is no remembrance; and whatever *idea* comes into the mind without that consciousness is not remem-

bered, or comes not out of the memory, nor can be said to be in the mind before that appearance. For what is not either actually in view, or in the memory, is in the mind no way at all, and is all one as if it never had been there. Suppose a child had the use of his eyes till he knows and distinguishes colours; but then cataracts shut the windows and he is forty or fifty years perfectly in the dark; and in that time perfectly loses all memory of the *ideas* of colours he once had. This was the case of a blind man I once talked with, who lost his sight by the smallpox when he was a child and had no more notion of colours than one born blind. I ask whether anyone can say this man had then any *ideas* of colours in his mind, any more than one born blind? And I think nobody will say that either of them had in his mind any *idea* of colours at all. His cataracts are couched and then he has the *ideas* (which he remembers not) of colours, *de novo*, by his restored sight conveyed to his mind, and that without any consciousness of a former acquaintance. And these now he can revive and call to mind in the dark. In this case all these *ideas* of colours, which when out of view can be revived with a consciousness of a former acquaintance, being thus in the memory, are said to be in the mind. The use I make of this is that whatever *idea*, being not actually in view, is in the mind is there only by being in the memory; and if it be not in the memory, it is not in the mind; and if it be in the memory, it cannot by the memory be brought into actual view without a perception that it comes out of the memory: which is this, that it had been known before and is now remembered. If therefore there be any innate *ideas*, they must be in the memory or else nowhere in the mind; and if they be in the memory, they can be revived without any impression from without; and whenever they are brought into the mind, they are remembered, i.e. they bring with them a perception of their not being wholly new to it. This being a constant and distinguishing difference between what is and what is not in the memory, or in the mind: that what is not in the memory, whenever it appears there, appears perfectly new and unknown before; and what is in the memory or in the mind, whenever it is suggested by the memory, appears not to be new, but the mind finds it in itself and knows it was there before. By this it may be tried whether there be any innate *ideas* in the mind before impression from *sensation* or *reflection*. I would fain meet with the man who, when he came to the use of reason or at any other time, remembered any of them, and to whom, after he was born, they were never new. If anyone will say there are *ideas* in the mind that are not in the memory, I desire him to explain himself and make what he says intelligible.

.   .   .

All Ideas Come from Sensation or Reflection

. . .

Let us then suppose the mind to be, as we say, white paper void of all characters, without any *ideas*. How comes it to be furnished? Whence comes it by that vast store which the busy and boundless fancy of man has painted on it with an almost endless variety? Whence has it all the materials of reason and knowledge? To this I answer, in one word, from *experience;* in that all our knowledge is founded, and from that it ultimately derives itself. Our observation, employed either about *external sensible objects, or about the internal operations of our minds perceived and reflected on by ourselves, is that which supplies our understandings with all the materials of thinking.* These two are the fountains of knowledge, from whence all the *ideas* we have, or can naturally have, do spring.

(John Locke: *An Essay Concerning Human Understanding,* 1690)

2

The Quarrel of the Ancients and the Moderns

It was inevitable that the attack against ancient philosophical authority would be extended to ancient literature. The resulting quarrel concerns an age-old question: How do the present times compare to a golden age in the past? The answer to this question tells us a great deal about what has been called the "height" of the times, i.e. whether people think they are living in a period of progress or decadence. The very fact that the dispute raged so furiously demonstrates the optimistic outlook which science and the rational method had created by the close of the century.

The question had already been debated in Italy in the sixteenth century and it was to find an echo in England late in the seventeenth, but the most heated arguments were exchanged in France between 1687 and 1700. It began in 1687, during a ses-

sion of the French Academy, with the reading of a poem by Charles Perrault supposedly celebrating Louis XIV but actually stating the superiority of the Moderns over the Ancients. Boileau walked out of the meeting, muttering to himself. But Perrault, best known for his fairy tales, gathered supporters, especially Fontenelle. Boileau, backed by La Fontaine and La Bruyère, fired back an angry reply in 1693, but finally wrote an apparently conciliatory letter to Perrault in 1700, which officially closed the quarrel. Meanwhile Swift had rallied to the defense of the Ancients with a biting satire; yet the net result represented a victory for the Moderns, whose thesis of progress in the arts was taken up again in the nineteenth century by ~omantic critics, such as Chateaubriand and Mme de Staël.

A. THE ARGUMENTS OF THE MODERNS

1. THE MODERNS ARE OLDER THAN THE ANCIENTS

As for antiquity, the opinion touching it which men entertain is quite a negligent one, and scarcely consonant with the world itself. For the old age of the world is to be accounted the true antiquity; and this is the attribute of our own times, not of that earlier age of the world in which the ancients lived; and which, though in respect of us it was the elder, yet in respect of the world it was the younger. And truly as we look for greater knowledge of human things and a riper judgment in the old man than in the young, because of his experience and of the number and variety of the things which he has seen and heard and thought of; so in like manner from our age, if it but knew its own strength and chose to essay and exert it, much more might fairly be expected than from the ancient times, inasmuch as it is a more advanced age of the world, and stored and stocked with infinite experiments and observations.

(Francis Bacon: *Novum Organum*, Aphorism LXXXIV; 1620)

2. NATURE IS THE SAME THROUGHOUT THE AGES

To form bodies, and to form minds
Nature at all times the same means finds;
Her being's unchanging and that strength
Of her creative drive is unweakened at length.

(Charles Perrault: *The Age of Louis the Great*, 1687)

The whole dispute for pre-eminence between the Ancients and Moderns being well understood, has this short issue, *viz.* to know whether the trees which formerly grew in our fields were larger than these of the present time. If they were, *Homer, Plato, Demosthenes* cannot possibly be equalled in these later ages: but if otherwise, they can.

Let us explain this paradox. If the Ancients had more wit or capacity than the Moderns, then brains must have been better formed, of stronger or more delicated fibres, and filled with more animal spirits. But what could be the cause of this? Their trees must have been larger and more beautiful: for if nature at that time was younger and more vigorous, plants, as well as human brains, must have shared of this youth and vigour.

Let the adorers of the Ancients take care what they say, when they tell us, *they* are the sources of good taste and reason, and the luminaries destined to give light to all mankind: that nobody has wit or judgment, but in proportion to his veneration for them; that nature has exhausted herself in producing those great originals: for, in truth, they make them of a species different from us, and philosophy does by no means agree with all those fine expressions. Nature has between her hands a kind of clay, which is always the same, which she forms and reforms into a thousand shapes, and of which she makes men, and beasts, and plants: And it is ridiculous to fancy that she composed *Plato, Demosthenes* or *Homer* of a finer mold, or better prepared than the philosophers, orators, and poets of the present time. For, though our minds are immaterial, I regard here only their union with the brain, which is material, and which, according to its various dispositions, produces all the difference between them. . . .

However it be, this seems to me to be the whole matter of the grand question concerning the Ancients and the Moderns. Ages make no natural difference between men: the climate of *Greece* or *Italy* and that of *France,* are too near to create any sensible difference between the *Greeks,* or *Latins,* and the *French;* or when they do create any, it would be easy to efface it: And, in short, this difference would be no more to their advantage than to ours. It follows then that we are all upon an equality, Ancients and Moderns, *Greeks, Latins,* and *French.*

(Bernard Le Bovier de Fontenelle: *A Discourse Concerning the Ancients and Moderns,* 1688)

3. GENIUS IS A PRODUCT OF POLITICAL
AND OTHER CONDITIONS

The centuries, 'tis true, are indeed quite diff'rent,
Some were enlightened and others ignorant;
But if the reign of a brilliant monarch
Always impressed on them his glory and his mark,
Which age, whether for kings or men 'twas praised,
Could to the great century of Louis be raised?

(Charles Perrault: *The Age of Louis the Great,* 1687)

Nature remembers, no doubt, how she formed the heads of *Cicero* and *Titus Livius.* She produces in all ages, some that are capable of being great men; but those ages do not always permit them to exert their talents. The inundation of barbarous nations; governments, either absolutely opposite, or little favourable to the arts and sciences; prejudices and fancies, which may take a thousand different forms, such as the superstition they have in *China* for dead bodies, which prevents their making any dissections; and universal wars, often established, and for a long time, ignorance and bad taste: Add to this, all the various dispositions of particular fortunes and conditions, and you will easily apprehend how nature sows in vain *Ciceros* and *Virgils* in the world, and how rarely it is that they come up to good.

(Fontenelle: *A Discourse Concerning the Ancients and Moderns,* 1688)

In cases where we merely wish to know what has been committed to writing, as in history, geography, the languages, or theology; in short, for whatever rests on simple facts, or institution, divine or human; we necessarily have recourse to books, since they contain all that can be known; to them, it is evident, we must be indebted for our information, without the possibility of adding to it. . . .

It is very different with respect to subjects that fall under the cognizance of the senses and the discursive faculty. Authority becomes useless; our only appeal is to reason. . . . Thus it is, that geometry, arithmetic, natural philosophy, medicine, and architecture, and all the sciences which can be submitted to the test of reasoning and experiment, must be cultivated, in order to arrive at perfection. The ancients worked upon the rude sketches of their predecessors; and we, again, shall leave them to our posterity in a more finished state than we received them. As their perfection is the result of time and labour, it is evident that, even should we have been less successful than former ages, yet our united exertions must produce greater results than those of either, separately taken. . . .

The secrets of nature are concealed; her agency is perpetual, but we do not always discover its effects; time reveals them from age to age, and although she is always the same in herself, she is not always equally well known. The experiments that make us acquainted with her, are constantly multiplying, and as these alone are the sources of natural science, our deductions multiply in the same proportion.

In this manner we can adopt, at the present day, different sentiments and new opinions, without despising the ancients or treating them with ingratitude, since the elementary knowledge they gave us served as steps for us. We are indebted to them for our superiority, and, standing on an elevation to which they have conducted us, the least effort raises us still higher; and with less toil, and less glory too, we find ourselves above them.

(Blaise Pascal: Fragment of a *Treatise on Vacuum;*
written in 1647, published in 1663)

4. THE MODERNS ARE NOT ONLY EQUAL TO THE ANCIENTS BUT SUPERIOR TO THEM

When we shall have found that the Ancients have arrived to the point of perfection in any thing, let us content ourselves to say, they cannot be excelled; but let us not say, they cannot be equalled, a manner so common among their admirers. Why should we not equal them? As we are men, we have always a right to pretend to it. . . .

And, in effect, it is certain that the principal part in philosophy, and the manner of reasoning . . . has been brought to a great perfection in this age. . . . Let the subject be what it will, the Ancients are too apt to be uncorrect in their reasoning. Slight agreements, little similitudes, trifling fancies, rambling and confused harangues pass with them for proofs; so that to prove costs them nothing. But what an Ancient would demonstrate in play, would be a task to make a poor Modern sweat; for how severe are we now upon reasonings? We require them to be intelligible, just, conclusive. We have the malice to unravel the least equivocation either of thought or expression, and the boldness to condemn the most ingenious turn in the world, if it does not reach the matter. Before *Descartes* appeared, people reasoned much more commodiously; and it was happy for preceding ages, that they had not this man to disturb them. . . .

Let us have patience, and by a long succession of ages, we shall become, as it were, contemporaries with the *Greeks* and *Latins.* And when we are thus all Ancients, it is easy to foresee that there will be no scruple in giving us, in many things, the preference. The best works of *Sophocles, Euripides, Aristophanes,* will scarcely stand before the *Cinna, Horace* [both by Pierre Corneille], *Ariadne* [by Thomas Corneille], the *Misanthrope* and many other tragedies and comedies written at a good time.

(Fontenelle: *A Discourse Concerning the Ancients and Moderns,* 1688)

B.   THE REPLY OF THE ANCIENTS

It must not be thought that, among the number of writers approved by all the ages, I mean to include those authors, Ancient indeed, but who have acquired but moderate esteem, such as . . . Nonnus, Silius, Italicus and several others, with whom one cannot only compare, but to whom, in my opinion, one can justly prefer many modern writers. I admit to this exalted rank only that small number of marvelous writers whose very name stands for praise, like Homer, Plato, Cicero, Virgil, etc.

Nor is the esteem in which I hold these determined by the time their works have been lasting, but rather by the time they have been admired. It is desirable to point this out to many people who might erroneously believe . . . that the Ancients are praised because they are ancient and the Moderns berated because they are modern; there is no truth to this, since there are many Ancients who are not at all admired and many Moderns who are praised by everybody. The Antiquity of a writer is not a sure indication of his merit; but the durable and constant admiration his works have always enjoyed is a certain and infallible proof that they should be admired.

Since only posterity can judge the true value of a work, we must not place a modern writer, however admirable he may seem to us, on the same level as those authors who have been admired for so many centuries, since it is not even certain that his works will pass on gloriously to the next century.

(Boileau: *Reflections about Longinus,* 7th Reflection; 1693)

Jonathan Swift (1667–1745), best known for Gulliver's Travels, *was secretary to Sir William Temple between 1692 and 1699, although from 1694 until 1696 he lived in Ireland, where he was ordained. In 1713 he became Dean of St. Patrick's in Dublin. The last years of his life his mind gave way and from 1742 on he remained in a state of apathy.*

*Swift's participation in the Quarrel was caused by an essay
Temple wrote in favor of the Ancients in 1692 to which William Wotton replied. Temple was supported by Charles Boyle,
while Richard Bentley took the opposite side. Swift, rallying
to the defense of his patron, pretends that the Quarrel has
spread to the books of St. James Library, of which Bentley was
curator.*

1. The Cause of the Quarrel

This quarrel first began, as I have heard it affirmed by an old dweller in
the neighbourhood, about a small spot of ground, lying and being upon
one of the two tops of the hill Parnassus; the highest and largest of which
had, it seems, been time out of mind in quiet possession of certain tenants,
called the Ancients; and the other was held by the Moderns. But these,
disliking their present station, sent certain ambassadors to the ancients,
complaining of a great nuisance; how the height of that part of Parnassus
quite spoiled the prospect of theirs, especially toward the *east;* [1] and therefore, to avoid a war, offered them the choice of this alternative, either that
the ancients would please to remove themselves and their effects down to
the lower summit, which the moderns would graciously surrender to them,
and advance into their place; or else the said ancients will give leave to
the moderns to come with shovels and mattocks, and level the said hill as
low as they shall think it convenient. To which the ancients made answer,
how little they expected such a message as this from a colony whom they
had admitted, out of their own free grace, to so near a neighbourhood.
That, as to their own seat, they were aborigines of it, and therefore to talk
with them of a removal or surrender was a language they did not understand. That if the height of the hill on their sides shortened the prospect
of the moderns, it was a disadvantage they could not help; but desired
them to consider whether that injury (if it be any) were not largely recom-
pensed by the shade and shelter it afforded them. That as to the levelling
or digging down, it was either folly or ignorance to propose it if they did
or did not know how that side of the hill was an entire rock, which would
break their tools and hearts, without any damage to itself. That they
would therefore advise the moderns rather to raise their own side of the
hill than dream of pulling down that of the ancients; to the former of
which they would not only give licence, but also largely contribute. All
this was rejected by the moderns with much indignation, who still insisted
upon one of the two expedients; and so this difference broke out into a
long and obstinate war, maintained on the one part by resolution, and by

the courage of certain leaders and allies; but, on the other, by the greatness of their number, upon all defeats affording continual recruits. In this quarrel whole rivulets of ink have been exhausted, and the virulence of both parties enormously augmented. Now, it must be here understood that ink is the great missive weapon in all battles of the learned, which, conveyed through a sort of engine called a quill, infinite numbers of these are darted at the enemy by the valiant on each side, with equal skill and violence, as if it were an engagement of *porcupines*. This malignant liquor was compounded, by the engineer who invented it, of two ingredients, which are, gall and copperas; by its bitterness and venom to suit, in some degree, as well as to foment, the genius of the combatants.

.   .   .

2. The Arguments of the Moderns
(On the library shelves, the ancient books
have been mixed in among the modern ones.)

While things were in this ferment, discord grew extremely high; hot words passed on both sides, and ill blood was plentifully bred. Here a solitary ancient, squeezed up among a whole shelf of moderns, offered fairly to dispute the case, and to prove by manifest reason that the priority was due to them from long possession, and in regard of their prudence, antiquity, and, above all, their great merits toward the moderns. But these denied the premises, and seemed very much to wonder how the ancients could pretend to insist upon their antiquity, when it was so plain (if they went to that) that the moderns were much the more ancient of the two. As for any obligations they owed to the ancients, they renounced them all. It is true, said they, we are informed some few of our party have been so mean to borrow their subsistence from you; but the rest, infinitely the greater number, (and especially we French and English,) were so far from stooping to so base an example, that there never passed, till this very hour, six words between us. For our horses were of our own breeding, our arms of our own forging, and our clothes of our own cutting out and sewing. Plato was by chance up on the next shelf, and observing those that spoke to be in the ragged plight mentioned a while ago; their jades lean and foundered, their weapons of rotten wood, their armour rusty, and nothing but rags underneath; he laughed aloud, and in his pleasant way swore, by ——, he believed them.

.   .   .

3. *The Spider and the Bee*
(The spider's dwelling is invaded by a bee,
and the following discussion ensues.)

. . . — Rogue, rogue, replied the spider, yet methinks you should have more respect to a person whom all the world allows to be so much your betters. — By my troth, said the bee, the comparison will amount to a very good jest; and you will do me a favour to let me know the reasons that all the world is pleased to use in so hopeful a dispute. At this the spider, having swelled himself into the size and posture of a disputant, began his argument in the true spirit of controversy, with resolution to be heartily scurrilous and angry to urge on his own reasons, without the least regard to the answers or objections of his opposite; and fully predetermined in his mind against all conviction.

Not to disparage myself, said he, by the comparison with such a rascal, what art thou but a vagabond without house or home, without stock or inheritance? born to no possession of your own, but a pair of wings and a drone-pipe. Your livelihood is a universal plunder upon nature; a freebooter over fields and gardens; and, for the sake of stealing, will rob a nettle as easily as a violet. Whereas I am a domestic animal, furnished with a native stock within myself. This large castle (to show my improvements in the mathematics [2]) is all built with my own hands, and the materials extracted altogether out of my own person.

I am glad, answered the bee, to hear you grant at least that I am come honestly by my wings and my voice; for then, it seems, I am obliged to Heaven alone for my flights and my music; and Providence would never have bestowed on me two such gifts, without designing them for the noblest ends. I visit indeed all the flowers and blossoms of the field and garden; but whatever I collect thence enriches myself, without the least injury to their beauty, their smell, or their taste. Now, for you and your skill in architecture and other mathematics, I have little to say: in that building of yours there might, for aught I know, have been labour and method enough; but, by woful experience for us both, it is too plain the materials are naught; and I hope you will henceforth take warning, and consider duration and matter, as well as method and art. You boast indeed of being obliged to no other creature, but of drawing and spinning out all from yourself; that is to say, if we may judge of the liquor in the vessel by what issues out, you possess a good plentiful store of dirt and poison in your breast; and, though I would by no means lessen or disparage your genuine stock of either, yet I doubt you are somewhat obliged, for an increase of both, to a little foreign assistance. Your inherent portion of dirt does not fail of acquisitions, by sweepings exhaled from below; and one insect furnishes you with a share of poison to destroy another. So that, in short, the question comes all to this; whether is the nobler being of the two, that which, by a lazy contemplation of four inches round, by an overweening pride, feeding and engendering on itself, turns all into excrement and venom, producing nothing at all but flybane and a cobweb; or that which, by a universal range, with long search, much study, true judgment, and distinction of things, brings home honey and wax.

.   .   .

4. *The Parable Explained by Aesop*

. . . The disputants, said he, have admirably managed the dispute between them, have taken in the full strength of all that is to be said on both sides, and exhausted the substance of every argument *pro* and *con*. It is but to adjust the reasonings of both to the present quarrel, then to compare and apply the labours and fruits of each, as the bee has learnedly deduced them, and we shall find the conclusion fall plain and close upon the moderns and us. For pray, gentlemen, was ever anything so modern as the spider in his air, his turns, and his paradoxes? he argues in the behalf of you his brethren and himself with many boastings of his native stock and great genius; that he spins and spits wholly from himself, and scorns to own any obligation or assistance from without. Then he displays to you his great skill in architecture and improvement in the mathematics. To all this the bee, as an advocate retained by us the ancients, thinks fit to answer, that, if one may judge of the great genius or inventions of the moderns by what they have produced, you will hardly have countenance to bear you out in boasting of either. Erect your schemes with as much method and skill as you please; yet, if the materials be nothing but dirt, spun out of your own entrails (the guts of modern brains), the edifice will conclude at last in a cobweb; the duration of which, like that of other spiders' webs, may be imputed to their being forgotten, or neglected, or hid in a corner. For anything else of genuine that the moderns may pretend to, I cannot recollect; unless it be a large vein of wrangling and satire, much of a nature and substance with the spider's poison; which, however they pretend to spit wholly out of themselves, is improved by the same arts, by feeding upon the insects and vermin of the age. As for us the ancients, we are content, with the bee, to pretend to nothing of our own beyond our wings and our voice: that is to say, our flights and our language. For the rest, whatever we have got has been by infinite labour and search, and ranging through every corner of nature; the difference is, that, instead of dirt and poison, we have rather chosen to fill our hives with honey and wax; thus furnishing mankind with the two noblest of things, which are sweetness and light.

(Jonathan Swift: *The Battle of the Books*, written 1697–1698, published 1704)

C. THE RECONCILIATION

What is the reason that made you shout so much against the Ancients? Are you afraid the Moderns would spoil their talents by imitating them? But can you deny that, on the contrary, our greatest poets owe their successes to that very imitation? Can you deny that it is from Titus Livy, from Plutarch, and from Seneca that M. de Corneille has taken his great ideas that have enabled him to invent a new type of tragedy unknown to Aristotle? Can you, finally, fail to agree that Sophocles and Euripides have formed M. Racine and that Molière has learned the greatest refinements of his art from Plautus and Terence?

Yet, our opinions are not so far apart as you may think. For, what are you attempting to prove? . . . It seems to me, your purpose is to show that, as far as the knowledge, especially of the fine arts, and the worth of letters are concerned, our age . . . is not only comparable but superior to all of the famous century of Antiquity, and even to the Augustan age. It will no doubt surprise you to learn that on that point I entirely agree with you and would even, if my health and time permitted me to, gladly offer to prove this proposition with my pen. It is true that I would draw on reasons different from yours, for everybody has his own way of reasoning; and I would take precautions you have failed to take.

I would not set up, as you, our nation and our century against all the other nations and all the other centuries taken together. This attempt, to my way of thinking, cannot succeed. I would examine each nation and each century in turn, and after carefully weighing wherein they are superior to us and wherein we rank above them, I would be very much mistaken if I could not prove that the advantage is on our side. Thus, when coming to the Augustan age, I would begin by admitting frankly that we have neither heroic poets nor orators comparable to Virgil and Cicero. I would admit that our most skilled historians are insignificant compared to Titus Livy and Sallust; I would avow defeat in satire and elegy, even though there are admirable satires by Régnier and highly pleasant elegies by Voiture. But at the same time I would point out that we are far superior to the Latins in theater, where they could oppose so many excellent tragic plays in our language only with pompous rather than reasonable declamations attributed to Seneca and with the little acclaim received, in their time, by the *Thyestes* of Varius and Ovid's *Medea*. I would point out, furthermore, that, far from having better comic poets than we, they did not have a single one whose name deserves to be remembered, since Plautus, Cecilius, and Terence had died in the previous century.

I would show that, while for odes we have no author so perfect as Horace, who is their only lyrical poet, we still have a rather great number who are not inferior to him in refinement of language and in propriety of expression, and that all their works together thrown into the balance would perhaps not give a less meritorious weight than the five books of odes bequeathed to us by that great poet. I would show that there are types of poetry in which the Latins not only fail to surpass us but that they did not even know; as, for example, those prose poems we call NOVELS, and of which we have models that cannot be too highly esteemed, except for their moral aspects which are very loose and which make them dangerous reading for young people. I would boldly maintain that, taking the Augustan age in its widest sense, that is to say from Cicero to Cornelius Tacitus, one could not find one single Latin philosopher comparable, in physics, to Descartes or even Gassendi. I would prove that, for knowledge and extent of competence, their Varron and Plinius, who are their most learned writers, would seem mediocre scientists next to our Bignon, Scaliger, Saumaize, our Fathers Sirmond and Pétare. I would take pride with you in their small knowledge of astronomy, geography, and navigation. I would defy them to cite, except for Vitravius (who is rather a professor of architecture than an excellent architect), one single good architect, one skillful Latin sculptor, one good painter, since those who received acclaim in Rome in all the arts were Greeks from Asia Minor who came to practice among the Latins arts the Latins did not know, so to speak; whereas the whole world is filled today by the reputation and the works of our Poussins, Lebruns, Girardons, and Mansards.

I could add many things to this list; but what I have said should suffice, I believe, to make you understand how I would handle the matter with respect to the Augustan age.

(Boileau: *Letter to Perrault*, 1700)

3

The Revolt Spreads

A. FAITH IS ATTACKED

Neverthelesse, we are not to renounce our Senses, and Experience; nor (that which is the undoubted Word of God) our naturall Reason. For they are the talents which he hath put into our hands to negotiate, till the coming again of our blessed Saviour; and therefore not to be folded up in the Napkin of an Implicite Faith, but employed in the purchase of Justice, Peace, and true Religion. For though there be many things in Gods Word above Reason; that is to say, which cannot by naturall reason be either demonstrated, or confuted; yet there is nothing contrary to it; but when it seemeth so, the fault is either in our unskilfull Interpretation, or erroneous Ratiocination.

Therefore, when any thing therein written is too hard for our examination, wee are bidden to captivate our understanding to the Words; and not to labour in sifting out a Philosophicall truth by Logick, of such mysteries as are not comprehensible, nor fall under any rule of naturall science. For it is with the mysteries of our Religion, as with wholsome pills for the sick, which swallowed whole, have the vertue to cure; but chewed, are for the most part cast up again without effect.

(Thomas Hobbes: *Leviathan,* Chap. 32; 1651)

B. BELIEF IN MIRACLES IS ATTACKED

Nothing, then, comes to pass in nature in contravention to her universal laws, nay, everything agrees with them and follows from them, for whatsoever comes to pass, comes to pass by the will and eternal decree of God; that is, as we have just pointed out, whatever comes to pass, comes to pass according to laws and rules which involve eternal necessity and truth; nature, therefore, always observes laws and rules which involve eternal necessity and truth, although they may not all be known to us, and there-

337

fore she keeps a fixed and immutable order. Nor is there any sound reason for limiting the power and efficacy of nature, and asserting that her laws are fit for certain purposes, but not for all; for as the efficacy and power of nature, are the very efficacy and power of God, and as the laws and rules of nature are the decrees of God, it is in every way to be believed that the power of nature is infinite, and that her laws are broad enough to embrace everything conceived by the Divine intellect; the only alternative is to assert that God has created nature so weak, and has ordained for her laws so barren, that He is repeatedly compelled to come afresh to her aid if He wishes that she should be preserved, and that things should happen as He desires: a conclusion, in my opinion, very far removed from reason. Further, as nothing happens in nature which does not follow from her laws, and as her laws embrace everything conceived by the Divine intellect, and lastly, as nature preserves a fixed and immutable order; it most clearly follows that miracles are only intelligible as in relation to human opinions, and merely mean events of which the natural cause cannot be explained by a reference to any ordinary occurrence, either by us, or at any rate, by the writer and narrator of the miracle. . . .

(Baruch Spinoza: *Ethics*, 1677)

C. A CRITICAL EXAMINATION OF THE BIBLE

Pierre Bayle (1647–1706), a French Protestant living in exile in Holland, supposedly wrote his General Dictionary, Historical and Critical *to correct errors in a previous one by Moreri; in reality, Bayle used his immense learning to criticize intolerance, and inconsistencies in the Scriptures. His method consists of a purposely confusing system of footnotes and cross references, some of them scholarly and others personal. By pointing out shortcomings in David, "a man after God's own heart," and errors in the sacred writings, Bayle sheds doubt on the basis that supports religious authority. In the article on David, below, only portions of Remarks A, D, G, and I have been selected to illustrate Bayle's method.*

DAVID, King of the Jews, was one of the greatest men in the World, though we should not consider him as a Royal Prophet, and a man after God's own heart. The first time the Scripture makes him appear on the stage

(a) I Samuel,
chap. xv,
ver. 13.

(a) is to acquaint us that Samuel appointed him King, and performed the ceremony of anointing him. David was then but a simple shepherd. He was the youngest of the eight sons of Jesse the Bethlemite. [A]

After this, the Scripture informs us that he was sent to Saul (b), to cure him of his fits of frenzy, by the sound of musical Instruments. A service of such importance made him so much beloved by Saul, that the Prince retained him in his family, and made him his Armour-bearer (c). The Scripture proceeds to tell us (d), that David from time to time returned home to his father's, to take care of the flocks, and that one day his father sent him to Saul's camp with some provisions, which he designed for three other of his sons who were in the army. David, in executing this order, heard the challenge which a Philistine named Goliath, proud of his strength and gigantic stature, came every day to offer the Israelites without any of them daring to accept it. He shewed a great desire to go and fight this giant; whereupon he was brought to the King, and assured him that he should triumph over the Philistine. Saul gave him his armour; but as David found it cumbersome, he put it off, and resolved to make use only

(b) Ibid. ver 20.

(c) Ibid. ver. 21.
(d) Ibid. chap.
xvii, ver. 15.

[A] *He was the youngest of the Sons of Jesse the Bethlemite.*]
Some modern Rabbins say, that when David was conceived, Jesse his father did not think he enjoyed his Wife, but his maid-servant; and hereby they explain the 7th Verse of the LIst Psalm, where David declares *that he was shapen in iniquity, and that his mother conceived him in sin.* This, they say, signifies that Jesse *his father committed Adultery when he begot him, because tho' he begot him on his wife, he thought he begot him on no other than the maidservant, whose chastity he had tried to corrupt* (1). This explication is not very conformable to the doctrine of original sin, for which reason Father Bartolocci (2), having reported this opinion of the modern Rabbins, has thought himself obliged occasionally to examine, whether the ancient Jews acknowledged the truth of this Doctrine. If the supposition of those Rabbins be true, they would be much in the right to say that Jesse committed adultery; but on the other hand, it must be owned that he would not have sinned, if he had gotten his maid with child, when he really believed he was enjoying his wife. . . . They who admit the impertinence of these Rabbins concerning the conception of David, might easily proceed to another impertinence and rank David among the illustrious bastards. The Physical reason which is given why bastards are so frequently born with such extraordinary natural talents, might be properly alledged here with regard to the father.

(1) See the
*Journal des
Savans* of the
14th of July
1692, pag. 465
of the Dutch
Edition.
(2) In *Biblio-
theca magna
Rabbinica,*
Part 2. pag. 4,
quoted in the
*Journal des
Savans,* ibid.

62. Rembrandt van Ryn, *David Playing the Harp for Saul*. Photo: Giraudon.

(e) Ibid.
ver. 49, 50.

of his sling; which he did with such success that he felled the boaster with a stone (e), and then killed him with his own sword, and cut off his head, which he presented to Saul. That Prince had asked his General, when he saw David march against Goliath, *Whose son is this youth* (f) [D]? The General answered that he did not know, and received orders from Saul to enquire whose son

(f) Ibid.
ver. 55.

[D] *Saul had asked his General . . . Whose son is this youth?*] It is a little strange that Saul did not know David that day, since the young man had several times played on instruments of music in his presence to calm the dismal vapours which disturbed him. If such a relation were found in Thucydides or Livy, all the Critics would unanimously conclude that the Transcribers had transposed the pages, forgotten something in one place, repeated something in another, or inserted additional passages in the Author's Work. But we must not entertain such suspicions with regard to the Bible. Notwithstanding some have been so bold as to pretend that all the Chapters, or all the Verses of the first Book of Samuel are not placed in their original order . . .

(g) Ibid.
ver. 58.

he was: but Saul himself learned it from the young man's mouth; for when he was brought to him after the Victory, he asked him, *Whose son art thou?* and David answered him he was the son of Jesse (g). . . . David's piety is so conspicuous in his Psalms, and in several of his actions, that it cannot be sufficiently admired. He is a Sun of holiness in the Church, through which by his writings he diffuses a light full of consolation and piety; but he had his spots. [G]. The Article of David, which I have lately read in the Dictionary of the Bible will furnish me with matter for a Remark [I].

(Pierre Bayle: *A General Dictionary, Historical and Critical,* 1697)

D.   INTOLERANCE IS ATTACKED

I esteem it above all things necessary to distinguish exactly the business of civil government from that of religion, and to settle the just bounds that lie between the one and the other. If this be not done, there can be no end put to the controversies that will be always arising between those that have, or at least pretend to have, on the one side, a concernment for the interest of mens souls, and on the other side, a care of the commonwealth.

The commonwealth seems to me to be a society of men constituted only

---

(17) 2 Sam. chap. xxiv.
(18) Ibid. chap. xi.

[G] *He had his spots.*] The numbring of the people was a thing which God looked on as a great sin (17). His amour with the wife of Uriah, and the orders he gave to destroy her husband (18), are the two most enormous crimes; but he was so grieved for them, and expiated them by so admirable a repentance, that this is not the passage of his life wherein he contributes the least to the instruction and edification of faithful souls. We therein learn the frailty of the Saints; and it is a precept of vigilance: we therein learn in what manner we ought to lament our sins; and it is an excellent model. . . .

(21) It is the *Dictionary of the Bible* composed by Mr. Simon, Priest, Doctor of Divinity, and printed at Lyons, 1693, in folio.
(22) There were 1090, according to Calvicius.

[I] *The Article of David . . . in the Dictionary of the Bible will furnish me with matter for a Remark.*] The Printers were got thus far when I was shewn a Dictionary (21), which I immediately consulted in the Article on the Prophet David. I have found some passages in it, which have given me occasion to make a few Observations. I. It is not true that David came into the world 110 years before the birth of Jesus Christ: there were above a thousand years (22) between the birth of the one and that of the other. . . .

for the procuring, the preserving, and the advancing their own civil interests.

Civil interests I call life, liberty, health, and indolency of body; and the possession of outward things, such as money, lands, houses, furniture, and the like.

It is the duty of the civil magistrate, by the impartial execution of equal laws, to secure unto all the people in general, and to every one of his subjects in particular, the just possession of these things belonging to this life. . . .

Now that the whole jurisdiction of the magistrate reaches only to these civil concernments; and that all civil power, right, and dominion, is bounded and confined to the only care of promoting these things, and that it neither can or ought in any manner to be extended to the salvation of souls; these following considerations seem unto me abundantly to demonstrate.

First, because the care of souls is not committed to the civil magistrate, any more than to other men. It is not committed unto him, I say, by God; because it appears not that God has ever given any such authority to one man over another, as to compel any one to his religion. Nor can any such power be vested in the magistrate by the consent of the people; because no man can so far abandon the care of his own salvation, as blindly to leave it to the choice of any other, whether prince or subject, to prescribe to him what faith or worship he shall embrace. For no man can, if he would, conform his faith to the dictates of another. All the life and power of true religion consists in the outward and full persuasion of the mind; and faith is not faith without believing. . . .

In the second place. The care of souls cannot belong to the civil magistrate, because his power consists only in outward force; but true and saving religion consists in the inward persuasion of the mind, without which nothing can be acceptable to God. And such is the nature of the understanding, that it cannot be compelled to the belief of any thing by outward force. Confiscation of estate, imprisonment, torments, nothing of that nature can have any such efficacy as to make men change the inward judgment that they have framed of things.

It may indeed be alleged, that the magistrate may make use of arguments, and thereby draw the heterodox into the way of truth, and procure their salvation. I grant it; but this is common to him with other men. In teaching, instructing, and redressing the erroneous by reason, he may certainly do what becomes any good man to do. Magistracy does not oblige him to put off either humanity or Christianity. But it is one thing to persuade, another to command; one thing to press with arguments, another with penalties. . . .

In the third place, the care of the salvation of mens souls cannot belong to the magistrate; because, though the rigour of laws and the force of penalties were capable to convince and change mens minds, yet would not that help at all to the salvation of their souls. For, there being but one truth, one way to heaven; what hope is there that more men would be led into it, if they had no other rule to follow but the religion of the court, and were put under a necessity to quit the light of their own reason, to oppose the dictates of their own consciences, and blindly to resign up themselves to the will of their governors, and to the religion, which either ignorance, ambition, or superstition had chanced to establish in the countries where they were born? . . .

Let us now consider what a church is. A church then I take to be a voluntary society of men, joining themselves together of their own accord, in order to the publick worshipping of God, in such a manner as they may judge acceptable to him, and effectual to the salvation of their souls.

I say, it is a free and voluntary society. Nobody is born a member of any church; otherwise the religion of parents would descend unto children, by the same right of inheritance as their temporal estates, and every one would hold his faith by the same tenure he does his lands; than which nothing can be imagined more absurd. Thus therefore that matter stands. No man by nature is bound unto any particular church or sect, but every one joins himself voluntarily to that society in which he believes he has found that profession and worship which is truly acceptable to God. . . .

[However] no opinions contrary to human society, or to those moral rules which are necessary to the preservation of civil society, are to be tolerated by the magistrate. . . .

Again: That church can have no right to be tolerated by the magistrate, which is constituted upon such a bottom, that all those who enter into it, do thereby *ipso facto,* deliver themselves up to the protection and service of another prince. For by this means the magistrate would give way to the settling of a foreign jurisdiction in his own country, and suffer his own people to be listed, as it were, for soldiers against his own government. . . .

Lastly, those are not at all to be tolerated who deny the being of God. Promises, covenants, and oaths, which are the bonds of human society, can have no hold upon an atheist. The taking away of God, though but even in thought, dissolves all. Besides also, those that by their atheism undermine and destroy all religion, can have no pretence of religion whereupon to challenge the privilege of a Toleration. As for other practical opinions, though not absolutely free from all error, yet if they do not tend to establish domination over others, or civil impunity to the church in which they are taught, there can be no reason why they should not be tolerated.

(John Locke: *A Letter concerning Toleration*, 1689)

E. SOCIAL AND POLITICAL PROTESTS

Certain wild animals, male and female, are scattered over the country, dark, livid, and quite tanned by the sun, who are chained, as it were, to the land they are always digging and turning up and down with an unwearied stubbornness; their voice is somewhat articulate, and when they stand erect they discover a human face, and, indeed, are men. At night they retire to their burrows, where they live on black bread, water, and roots; they spare other men the trouble of sowing, tilling the ground, and reaping for their sustenance, and, therefore, deserve not to be in want of that bread they sow themselves. ("Of Mankind," § 128)

If I compare the two most opposite conditions of men, I mean the great and the common people, the latter appear satisfied if they only have the necessities of life, and the former fretful and poor amidst superfluities. A man of the people can do no harm; a great man will do no good, and is capable of doing great mischief; the first only plans and practices useful things, the second adds to them what is hurtful. Here rusticity and frankness show themselves ingenuously; there a malignant and corrupt disposition lies hidden under a veneer of politeness. If the common people have scarcely any culture, the great have no soul; the first have a good foundation and no outward appearances; the latter are all outward appearances and but a mere superstratum. Were I to choose between the two, I should select, without hesitation, being a plebian. ("Of the Great," § 25)

There exist miseries in this world which wring the very heart; some people even want food; they dread the winter and are afraid to live; others eat hothouse fruits; the earth and the seasons are compelled to furnish forth delicacies; and mere citizens, simply because they have grown rich, dare to swallow in one morsel what would nourish a hundred families. Whatever may be brought forward against such extremes, let me be neither unhappy or happy if I can help it; I take refuge in mediocrity. ("Of the Gifts of Fortune," § 47)

Torture is an admirable invention, and infallibly destroys an innocent man who has a weak constitution, whilst it saves a guilty man who is hardy. . . .

The punishment of a villain is an example for his fellows; in the condemnation of an innocent man all honest men are concerned.

Speaking of myself, I would almost affirm never to become a thief or a murderer, but I would not be so bold as to infer that I might never be punished as such.

Deplorable is the condition of an innocent person whose trial has been hurried, and who is found guilty. Can even that of his judge be more lamentable? ("Of Certain Customs," § 51, 52)

(Jean de La Bruyère: *The Characters*, 1688)

François de Salignac de La Mothe-Fénelon (1651–1715), archbishop of Cambrai, published in 1699 Telemachus, *which contained veiled allusions to the government of Louis XIV. The authenticity of his Letter to Louis XIV was doubted until the manuscript was found in 1825. The letter was written after 1691. We do not know whether Louis XIV ever received it.*

Sire, the person who is taking the liberty of writing you this letter has no interest in this world. He has no axe to grind, nor any ambitions, nor any desire to become involved in affairs of state. He loves you without being known by you, and sees in you God's representative. Great as your power is, you cannot give him any good he desires and he is ready to suffer gladly any pain in order to reveal to you the truths you need to know for the sake of your salvation. Be not surprised at the fact that he speaks to you forcefully, for truth is free and strong.

You were born, Sire, with a just and fair heart; but those who taught you the art of governing instilled in you only mistrust, jealousy, a dislike of virtue, a preference for tractable and fawning men, haughtiness, and concern for your personal interest only.

For some thirty years now your important ministers have upset and uprooted the old rules of government in order to raise your authority to the skies. . . . Their concern was no longer with the state or rules, but the king and what was his pleasure. Your revenues and expenses exceeded all limits. You were raised up to heaven, because you had eclipsed, it was claimed, the grandeur of all your predecessors taken together, that is to say, that you had impoverished all of France so that you could display at your court a monstrous and incurable luxury. They tried to raise you up on the ruins of all the ranks of the state, as if you could be great while ruining all your subjects on whom your greatness is based.

Your Majesty was induced in 1672 to undertake the war against the Dutch for your glory and in order to punish the Dutch, who had made some slighting remarks because of their discontent with the interference with the rules of commerce established by Cardinal Richelieu. I particularly mention this war, because it was the source of all the others. As cause it had nothing but a motive of vengeance, which can never justify a war; hence all the territory annexed by that war has been unjustly acquired from the start. It is true, Sire, that the subsequent peace treaties seem to cover and to make up for this injustice, because they legitimized your conquests of these territories; but an unjust war remains no less unjust for being successful. The peace treaties signed by the losers were not signed freely. One signs because of the knife at one's throat; one signs in spite of oneself, to avoid still greater losses; one signs as one surrenders one's purse when the only alternative is death. We must therefore, Sire, go back to the origin of the Dutch War in order to examine, before God, all your conquests. It is of no use to claim that they were necessary for your State: the goods of others are never a necessity for us. What we really need is a scrupulous adherence to justice. . . .

You, Sire, who were capable of covering yourself with solid and peaceful glory by being the father of all your subjects and the arbiter of your neighbors, you have been led into becoming the common enemy of your neighbors and into being considered a hard master in your kingdom. . . .

The allied enemy nations prefer costly wars to concluding peace with you. . . . Thus the more victorious you are, the more they fear you and unite to avoid the enslavement which they believe threatens them. Unable to defeat you, they hope at least to wear you out at length. Briefly, their only hope for safety is to render you powerless to harm them. Put yourself for a moment in their place, Sire, and you will see what you have achieved by having preferred your advantage to justice and good faith.

Meanwhile your people, whom you ought to love like your children and who until now have been doting on you, are starving to death. The tilling of the soil has almost been abandoned; the towns and villages are being depopulated; all crafts are at a standstill and no longer feed the workmen; all commerce has been annihilated. Consequently, you have destroyed half of the real backbone inside your State in order to make and defend conquests abroad. Instead of taking money from these poor people, you should have been charitable and fed them. All of France is no longer but a huge, ravaged hospital deprived of the necessities of life. The magistrates are debased and worn out. The nobility, whose possessions are completely attached, lives only by governmental favors. You are molested by the crowd of people who petition and grumble. You, Sire, are the one who has brought all these embarrassments on yourself; for, since the kingdom is ruined, all is in your hands and nobody can live otherwise but by your gifts. That is the real state of this flourishing great kingdom under a king who every day is being depicted to us as the delight of the people and who would correspond to this description if he had not been poisoned by the flatteries of his councilors. . . .

Since you are the King, you should seek out the truth, urge people to tell it to you without sugar-coating it, and encourage those who are too timid to speak up. But, quite on the contrary, all you want is not to go to the bottom of things. But God will manage to lift the veil from your eyes and show you what you do not want to see. For a long time he has been holding his arm raised above your head; but he delays striking you, because he feels pity for a prince who all his life has been obsessed by flatterers, and because your enemies are also his. But he will soon separate his just cause from yours, which is unjust, and humiliate you in order to convert you; for you will become a Christian only through humiliation. You do not love God; it is hell you fear, not God. All you love is your glory and your ease. You relate everything to yourself, as if you were the God of the earth and as if all else had been created only in order to be sacrificed to you. But, quite on the contrary, God has created you only for your people.

(Fénelon: *Letter to Louis XIV*, written after 1691)

NOTES

1. Sir William Temple affects to trace the progress of arts and science, from east to west.

2. Urged by those who contended for the excellence of modern learning.

SUGGESTIONS FOR
FURTHER READING

I. GENERAL READING

A. General Reference

(The following three volumes are part of a series entitled *The Rise of Modern Europe,* edited by W. L. Langer and published by Harper & Brothers, New York, 1934—. Each volume contains an excellent bibliography for further reading in more specialized fields.)

Friedrich, C. J. *The Age of the Baroque,* 1610–1660 (1952).

Nussbaum, F. L. *The Triumph of Science and Reason,* 1660–1685 (1953).

Wolf, J. B. *The Emergence of the Great Powers,* 1685–1715 (1951).

B. Primarily Historical

Clark, G. N. *The Seventeenth Century.* 2nd ed. New York: Oxford University Press, 1947.

Ogg, David. *Europe in the Seventeenth Century.* 3rd ed. New York: Macmillan, 1938.

Taine, H. A. *The Ancient Regime,* Book III, *The Spirit and the Doctrine.* New York: Henry Holt & Co., 1885.

C. History of Ideas

Bethell, Samuel L. *The Cultural Revolution of the Seventeenth Century.* London: D. Dobson, 1951.

Cragg, G. R. *From Puritanism to the Age of Reason.* Cambridge: Cambridge University Press, 1950.

Guérard, A. L. *Life and Death of an Ideal: France in the Classical Age.* New York: Charles Scribner's Sons, 1928.

Hazard, Paul. *The European Mind, 1680–1715.* New Haven: Yale University Press, 1953. (Also by Penguin Books.)

Highet, Gilbert. *The Classical Tradition.* New York: Oxford University Press, 1949.

Mazzeo, J. A. *Reason and the Imagination: Studies in the History of Ideas, 1600–1800.* New York: Columbia University Press, 1962.

Voltaire. *The Age of Louis XIV.* Everyman's Library.

Willey, Basil. *The Seventeenth-Century Background.* New York: Columbia University Press, 1942. (Also by Anchor Books.)

349

II. PHILOSOPHY

Höffding, Harald. *History of Modern Philosophy.* 2 vols. New York: Dover Publications, 1955.

Lecky, W. E. H. *History of the Rise and Influence of the Spirit of Rationalism in Europe.* 2 vols. Rev. ed. New York: Appleton, 1914.

Randall, J. H. *The Making of the Modern Mind.* Rev. ed. New York: Houghton Mifflin, 1940.

III. SCIENCE

Butterfield, Herbert. *The Origins of Modern Science.* New York: Macmillan, 1951.

White, A. D. *A History of the Warfare of Science with Theology.* 2 vols. New York: George Braziller, 1955.

Wolf, Abraham. *A History of Science, Technology, and Philosophy in the Sixteenth and Seventeenth Centuries.* New York: Macmillan, 1950.

IV. POLITICAL AND SOCIAL THOUGHT

Bury, J. B. *The Idea of Progress.* New ed. New York: Dover Publications, 1955.

Gooch, G. P. *English Democratic Ideas in the Seventeenth Century.* 2nd ed. Cambridge: Cambridge University Press, 1927.

Hearnshaw, F. J. C. *Social and Political Ideas of Some Great Thinkers of the Sixteenth and Seventeenth Centuries.* London: G. G. Harrap, 1926.

Sabine, G. H. *A History of Political Theory.* Rev. ed. New York: Henry Holt & Co., 1950.

V. THE ARTS

Bousquet, Jacques. *Mannerism.* New York: George Braziller, 1964.

DuPont, Jacques. *The Seventeenth Century; the New Developments in Art from Caravaggio to Vermeer.* Geneva, N. Y.: Skira, 1951.

Leichtentritt, Hugo. *Music, History, and Ideas.* Cambridge: Harvard University Press, 1938.

Rolland, Romain. *Some Musicians of Former Days.* New York: Henry Holt & Co., 1915.

Sypher, Wylie. *Four Stages of Renaissance Style: Transformations in Art and Literature, 1400–1700.* New York: Doubleday & Co., 1955. (An Anchor Book.)

VI. HISTORY OF LITERATURE

Bush, Douglas. *English Literature in the Earlier Seventeenth Century, 1600–1660.* New York: Oxford University Press, 1948.

Caudwell, H. *Introduction to French Classicism.* London: Macmillan, 1942.

Francke, Kuno. *History of German Literature as Determined by Social Forces.* 12th impression. New York: Henry Holt & Co., 1927.

Grierson, H. J. C. *Cross-Currents in English Literature of the Seventeenth Century.* London: Chatto & Windus, 1929.

Northup, G. T. *An Introduction to Spanish Literature*. Chicago: Chicago University Press, 1960.

Wilkins, E. H. *A History of Italian Literature*. Cambridge: Cambridge University Press, 1954.

VII. THEATER

Bentley, Eric, ed. *The Classic Theatre*, Vol. III, *Six Spanish Plays*. New York: Doubleday & Co., 1959. (An Anchor Book.)

———. *The Classic Theatre*, Vol. IV, *Six French Plays*. New York: Doubleday & Co., 1961. (An Anchor Book.)

Molière. *Eight Plays*. Translated by Morris Bishop. Modern Library.

Restoration Plays. Everyman's Library.

Six Plays by Corneille and Racine. Modern Library.

VIII. POETRY

Brereton, G., ed. *The Penguin Book of French Verse*, Book 2, *Sixteenth to Eighteenth Centuries*. Penguin Books, 1958.

Flores, A., ed. *An Anthology of Spanish Poetry*. New York: Doubleday & Co., 1961. (An Anchor Book.)

Forster, L., ed. *The Penguin Book of German Verse*. Rev. ed. Penguin Books, 1959.

Kay, George, ed. *The Penguin Book of Italian Verse*. Penguin Books, 1960.

Martz, Louis L., ed. *The Meditative Poem: An Anthology of Seventeenth-Century Verse*. New York: Doubleday & Co., 1963. (An Anchor Book.)

Mourgues, O. de. *Metaphysical, Baroque, and* Précieux *Poetry*. New York: Oxford University Press, 1953.